COSSACK

Warrior Riders of the Steppes

A battle between Tsarist forces and Circassians in 1841, by G.G. Gagarin. Cossacks were in the forefront of Russia's drive to annex more and more of the Caucasus, begun under Catherine the Great, but only fully completed in 1878. Prolonged contact between Cossacks and the Caucasian peoples profoundly influenced many aspects of the Cossack way of life – among them dress, food and horsemanship.

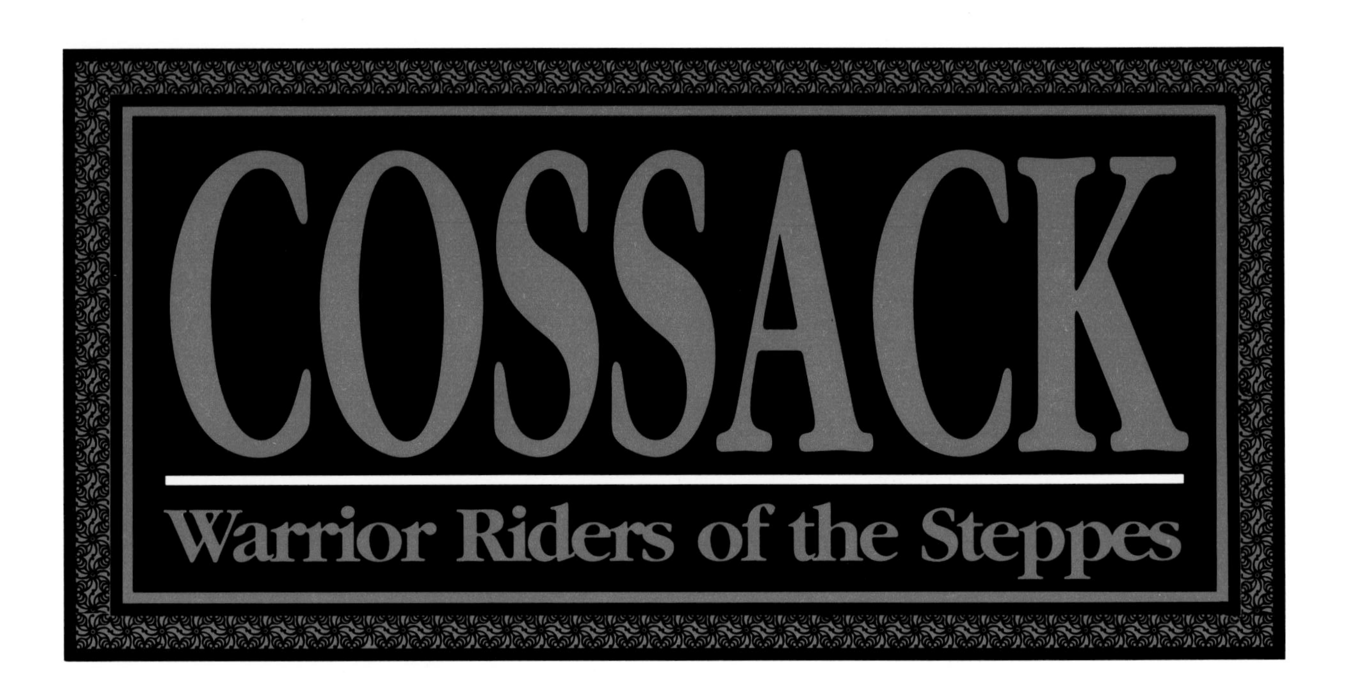

by
M.A. Groushko

Sterling Publishing Co., Inc. New York

To my family and to Cossack believers in freedom and democracy everywhere.

Library of Congress Cataloging-in-Publication Data
Available

This book was edited, designed and produced by
Morgan Samuel Editions
11 Uxbridge Street, London W8 7TQ

2 4 6 8 10 9 7 5 3 1

Published 1992 by Sterling Publishing Company, Inc.
387 Park Avenue South, New York, N.Y. 10016
Originally published in Great Britain by Cassell PLC
Villiers House, 41/47 Strand, London WC2N 5JE,
England

Distributed in Canada by Sterling Publishing
c/o Canadian Manda Group, P.O. Box 920, Station U
Toronto, Ontario, Canada M8Z 5P9
Typesetting by Sprint Reproductions Ltd, London
Film separations, printing and binding by
Toppan Printing (HK) Ltd, Hong Kong

Sterling ISBN 0-8069-8703-0

Contents

INTRODUCTION 6

CHAPTER 1:
Horsemen of the Steppes 8

CHAPTER 2:
Cossack Dawn 28

CHAPTER 3:
Revenge and Rebellion 48

CHAPTER 4:
Clipping the Eagles' Wings 72

CHAPTER 5:
On the World Stage 92

CHAPTER 6:
Revolution and Civil War 112

CHAPTER 7:
A Flickering Candle 128

GLOSSARY AND
BIBLIOGRAPHY 140

INDEX 141

ACKNOWLEDGEMENTS 144

Right: 19th century painting of a Zaporozhian Cossack.

Introduction

Everyone has an image of Cossacks – colourfully clad, warlike semi-barbarians galloping in search of glory and plunder, or carousing wildly under the stars. Poets and painters, composers and film-makers have all fostered it. So have the owners of circuses and cabarets, where a 'Cossack troupe' on the bill holds promise of exotic, exciting entertainment.

It is, of course, a stereotype and, like all stereotypes, it is accurate up to a point. But the true Cossack story is far more complex and fascinating than such one-dimensional imagery can convey. This book attempts to show how and why.

Those who thrill to Cossack blood and thunder should not be disappointed. There is plenty in the following pages. But it is set in a broader context of the influences – geographical, historical, political, religious – that drove and shaped Cossack men, women and children over the past 500 years, and the influence the Cossacks in their turn exerted on those around them.

In that respect, 'Cossack' differs from most conventional histories of Russia, the Ukraine and Poland. On their pages, Cossacks flit in and out like the contrivances of ancient drama – the deus ex machina that makes and unmakes rulers, or the Greek chorus that gives voice (and, in the Cossack case, often violent expression) to the hopes and fears of the large mass of ordinary people. With a few exceptions such as Philip Longworth's excellent study of 1969 (see Bibliography), there is little about who they actually were, or how they lived their lives.

That may be due in part to the nature of Cossackry itself. It evolved first as a movement, of the oppressed and adventurous to lands where they could live free. It developed, gradually and with

regional variations, into a collection of communities whose members sought to make their own rules and to remain beholden to none. Then, in Russian areas of influence, it became a military or quasi-military caste, used to fight Russia's wars and push out the borders of the largest contiguous empire the modern world has seen.

But Cossacks are not a distinct ethnic group and they were never, in any meaningful sense, inhabitants of a coherent nation-state of their own. As most history tends to be written in terms of either race or nation, the Cossacks – who in any case were not great keepers of written records – have had to resign themselves to being represented, more often than not, as merely incidental characters in the stories of others.

That explains, among other things, why historians' depictions of Cossacks vary so wildly. They are either 'gallant knights' or 'devils on horseback', depending on who is writing and when. Rarely are they anything between.

Napoleon himself put the black-or-white case when he predicted Europe would eventually be 'either Cossack or republican'. Perhaps he had a point; one of the more tragic modern Cossack leaders, Kaledin of the Don, tried in 1917-18 to be both – and was driven to suicide.

So, with the few exceptions noted, the most rounded descriptions of the Cossack way of life come not from historians, but from fiction-writers of genius – particularly Tolstoy in 'The Cossacks', but also Pushkin, Gogol and Sholokhov in his early books. Their steppe-horsemen and families are not black or white caricatures. They are real living, breathing human beings, with the capacity for most gradations of good and evil. For that reason, relevant works by all four authors are cited extensively in this celebration of the many facets of a unique and proud people.

Below: M.G. Dereguss's painting of the Cossack dance (Kazachok), an illustration for the novel 'Taras Bulba'.

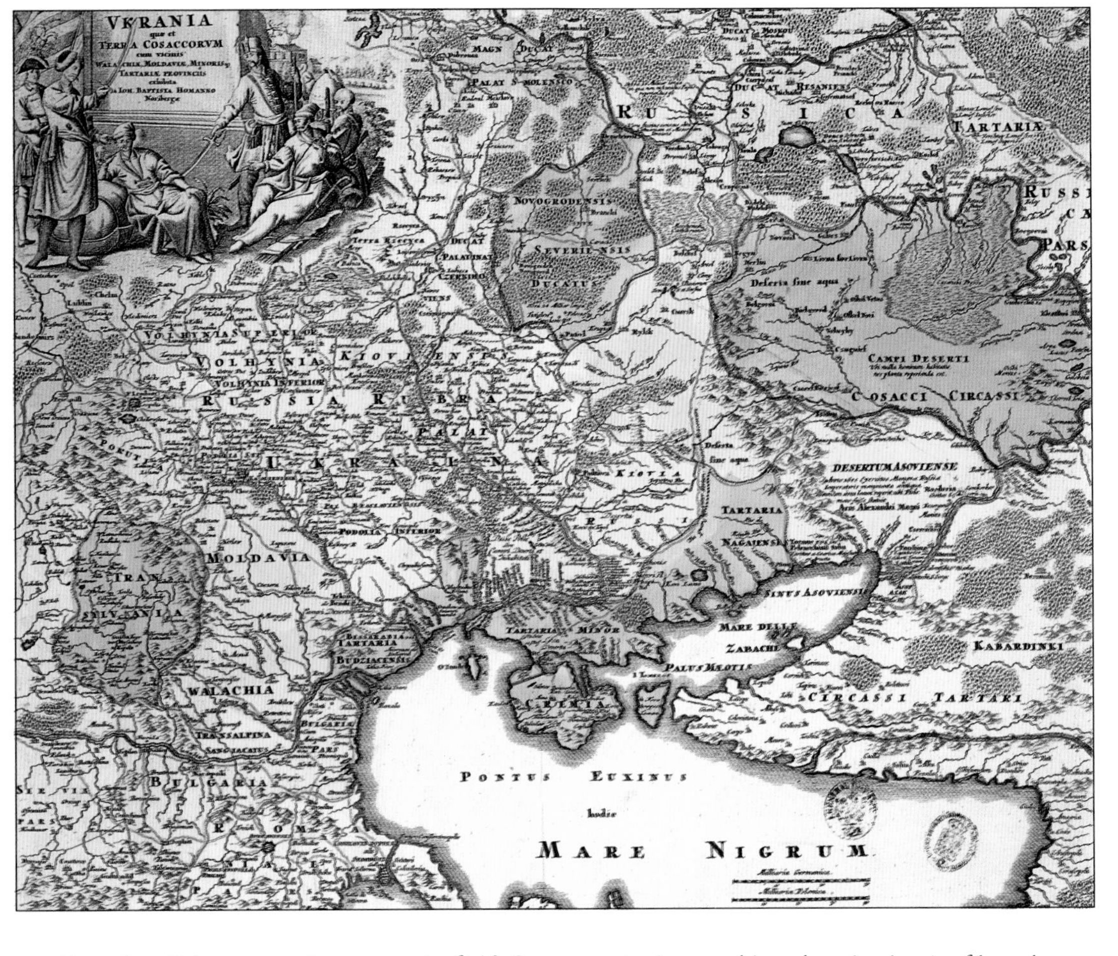

Left: 'The Ukraine and Lands of the Cossacks.' This German map of the region dates from 1710.

Cossack politics, even today, are a minefield. So are those in the former Soviet Union. It was not my intention in writing this book to offend the sensibilities of anyone entitled to have them. If I have done so, I apologise unreservedly.

I also apologise to anyone upset by some of the spellings or terms used. They were chosen for simplicity or familiarity, not to meet ultimately non-existent academic standards. They are most certainly not intended to bear any political significance whatsoever.

Finally, this book's timing is largely coincidence, since no one could have fully foreseen the momentous events of 1991 in the former USSR. But it is fortuitous, as the Cossacks there are seemingly now able to breathe the air of long-lost freedom. May they flourish in peace and prosperity.

Mike Groushko
London 1992

Author's royalties from this book are donated to projects assisting the peoples of Russia and the Ukraine.

The author would like to thank Kate Ray and Dr Laurie Harwood for their specialist assistance. Any errors are entirely his own.

Below, left: A Cossack worker from Kiev.

Below: Present day Cossacks gather at the monument to Ivan Sirko, a 17th century ataman of the Zaporozhian host.

Horsemen of the Steppes

Eurasia's Prairies

From Manchuria in the east to Hungary in the west, the steppe region rolls across the heart of Asia and into Europe, a vast river of grassland up to 960 km (600 miles) wide and 8,000 km (5,000 miles) long – further than the distance from Moscow to New York. Like the prairies of North America, it is a land of sharply alternating hot and cold seasons with low rainfall. At its eastern end, behind the Altai Mountains where Mongolia, China and the former Soviet Union meet, it has one of the bleakest climates in the world. In winter, the average temperature there plunges to -34°C (-29°F) or below. Rain is scarce and the vegetation is poor.

West from the Altai, conditions gradually improve. The climate becomes milder, there is more rain and the natural plant life is richer, until, having entered Europe below the Ural Mountains, the steppe grows positively hospitable. It is watered by mighty south-flowing rivers, such as the Volga, the Don and the Dnieper, and, in its primeval state, provided bountiful pastureland for horses and cattle. This area, much of which lies in the modern-day Ukraine, was the heart of Cossack country for more than four centuries.

Another transformation affects the steppe in this region, too. For most of its sprawling journey across Eurasia, it is hemmed in to the north by the taiga – the tangled, insect-ridden, near-impenetrable coniferous forests of Siberia and eastern Russia. To the south lies an arid barrier of deserts such as the Gobi and the Kara Kum. But as the steppe nears its western end, the taiga gives way to deciduous woodland and the desert expires by the shores of the Caspian Sea. Freed from both these constraints, the steppe debouches towards central Europe like a river reaching its estuary.

The comparison is not fanciful. For more than 3,000 years, nomadic tribes originating from the harsh terrain around the Altai drifted westwards along the steppe in search of pasture for their animals. Wave upon wave of these invader-settlers rested for a time – sometimes two or three centuries – on the grasslands between the Volga and the Caucasus, until the pressure of new arrivals from the

Below: From the bleak lands of central Asia, generations of nomadic horsemen drifted west across the steppes towards Europe.

WILDLIFE OF THE STEPPE

Until man took a hand, the steppe – a word derived from the Russian for lowland – was typically an endless-seeming tract of feather and other grasses and wild cereals, punctuated here and there by clumps of shrubs such as trefoil, acacia, blackthorn and steppe cherry. Briefly, in early summer, areas became bright with colour as flowers including tulips and irises bloomed. But they soon shrivelled for lack of rain.

Trees were rare except in river valleys and hollows, and along the northern fringes where the steppe gradually merged into forest or taiga. Birches and conifers were prevalent along much of this border strip, but oak and ash appeared at its European end. On the most southerly desert fringes, the only vegetation was scrub.

Large mammals, including wild horses, were once abundant. Now, the main survivor west of the Altai Mountains is the strange-looking saiga antelope. Small mammals still thrive – wolves, foxes, hares, marmots, voles, hamsters and the like. Ground squirrels called susliks live in large colonies, throwing up earth mounds that can cover thousands of square miles.

The hazel-grouse (ryabchik) is among the most renowned of the steppe birds; it is found in many other parts of the Soviet Union, too, and has been prized eating for centuries. Other game includes quails and partridges. Song birds such as white-winged and black larks are traditionally also hunted for food. Birds of prey include indigenous species of eagles and hawks.

There are many reptiles, among them the steppe viper, the yellow-bellied snake and various lizards. Tortoises live in large numbers on the desert edges. Even today, the steppe has an enormous insect population, ranging from destructive locusts to beautiful and unique butterflies; stinging and biting insects have always been an irritating summer plague on the grasslands.

Below: Present-day survivors of the once-teeming fauna of the grasslands include (from left) the saiga antelope, the ryabchik and the suslik.

east moved them on again. From the Volga-Caucasus region, they poured north and west into Europe or southwards towards the Middle East and India.

This human traffic shaped the civilisations and history of Eurasia. It eventually helped to bring the Cossacks into being and influenced their way of life – in particular, their disdain for farming and their near-mystical relationship with the horse. Ironically, it was largely the Cossacks who stemmed the westward flow, and then reversed it.

Right: Moonlight glistens on the Dnieper, one of the huge rivers that traverse the western steppes, in this painting by the Russian artist Arkhip Kuindzhi (1842-1910).

Day of the Chariots

Even today, when much of the steppe west of the Altai Mountains has been tamed and transformed by farmers, a few wild ponies are said to survive on its fringes. In prehistoric times, their forebears roamed in huge numbers. Sometime before the third millenium BC, the steppe-dwellers of central Asia began to herd them, as they were already herding sheep, goats and cattle for their milk and flesh, skins and bones. The development radically altered steppe society – and most of Eurasia – for ever.

Horses need more and better pasture than sheep or goats do, so their owners were forced to move further afield to find it. Family groups of horse-herders, probably numbering 50-100 people, ranged anywhere between 150 and 800 km (100-500 miles) in this search each year, accelerating their westward nomadic drift towards Europe.

In the process, they discovered that their horses could be used to pull burdens behind them, initially on a form of sled, but later on wheeled carts. At roughly the same time, somewhere on the western steppe, the nomads learnt how to make weapons and other items in bronze, possibly acquiring the technique from Mediterranean traders.

These two skills came together, to devastating effect, from shortly after 2000BC, when the steppe of the Volga-Caucasus region could no longer support all the nomads seeking to live there. Bands of fighting men burst out of the grasslands to find new territories. Some surged westward again, into central Europe, where they subjugated farmers still living in the Stone Age. Others headed south across the deserts and mountains to Asia Minor, Arabia and India, overthrowing or taking control of established civilisations.

These invaders from the east are known to us as Aryans or Indo-Europeans. The languages they spoke were akin to ancient Sanskrit, and the forerunners of many modern European tongues.

The Indo-Europeans were well-armed, with distinctive battle-axes, bows and arrows and bronze daggers or swords. But what made them so successful in their urge for conquest was their realisation that the homely horse-drawn carts of the grasslands could be adapted into formidable war-chariots, capable of carrying one or two archers in addition to a driver.

Chariots revolutionised early warfare, providing the Indo-European bands with speed and mobility in deploying for battle, and the equine strength to force through and scatter groups of enemy foot-soldiers ahead of their own infantry. The chariot-led invaders gave the rest of Eurasia its first bloody experience of the horsemen of the steppes. It was far from being the last.

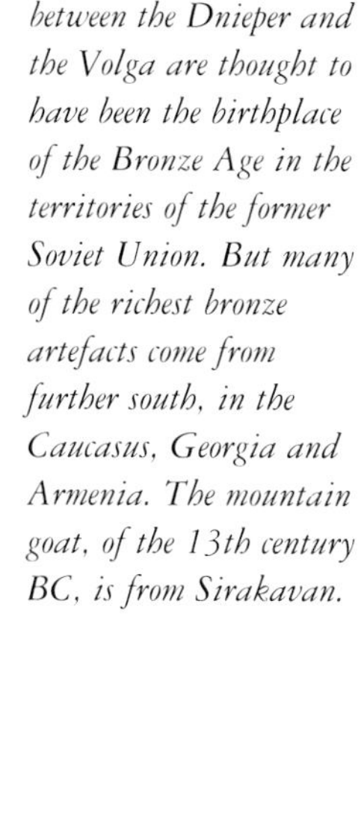

Top right: The steppes between the Dnieper and the Volga are thought to have been the birthplace of the Bronze Age in the territories of the former Soviet Union. But many of the richest bronze artefacts come from further south, in the Caucasus, Georgia and Armenia. The mountain goat, of the 13th century BC, is from Sirakavan.

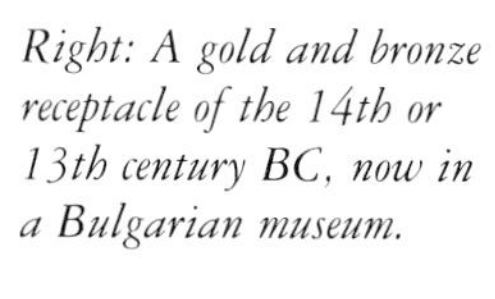

Right: A gold and bronze receptacle of the 14th or 13th century BC, now in a Bulgarian museum.

Left: Chariots such as those of the Assyrians revolutionised warfare from the second millennium BC. Experts believe horses were not ridden into battle until about 900BC. But new discoveries from Dereivka on the Ukrainian steppes suggest men developed the mouth-bit, and so were able to ride, far earlier than previously thought – some 6,000 years ago. Below: A Bronze Age ornamental head-dress in the Hermitage Museum, St Petersburg.

Early riders

Wild and semi-wild horses – even the small shaggy ponies of the Eurasian steppe – can be terrifying creatures when first roped. They buck, twist and kick, snort and bite, threatening the lives and limbs of their captors. To tame them to draw carts and war-chariots required courage, skill and patience. To mount and try to ride them needed even greater nerve. Instinct tells an unbroken horse that anything leaping on to its back is a predator seeking to kill it. It goes into a frenzy in an effort to shake the aggressor off.

No one knows for sure when or where horses were first trained for riding. But it was somewhere on the steppe, among the horse-herding nomads, before 2000BC and possibly before 4000BC. There is no archaeological evidence that horses were actually ridden into battle until about 900BC – that is, eight centuries or so after the steppe tribes had shattered previous concepts of warfare, and their enemies, with their chariots.

The long interval most archaeologists place between the two events may have been due in part to the difficulties of schooling horses to carry fighting men. In particular, the mount needed to be controllable with only knee-pressure from the rider, so that in battle he could drop the reins and have both his hands free to use a bow and arrows. That was an art the steppe warriors perfected between 900 and 700BC.

In any case, however, the chariot served its military purpose well enough on flattish terrain, such as the steppes themselves or the dry plains of the Middle East, as its survival into Roman times indicates. It was only gradually that the steppe tribes, and some of their kinsmen elsewhere in Eurasia, came to realise that forces using individual mounts were cheaper, more manoeuvrable and better-suited to rough ground than chariots, and the concept of cavalry was born. Its first flower bloomed on the steppe among one of the most bloodthirsty and mysterious of ancient races – the Scythians.

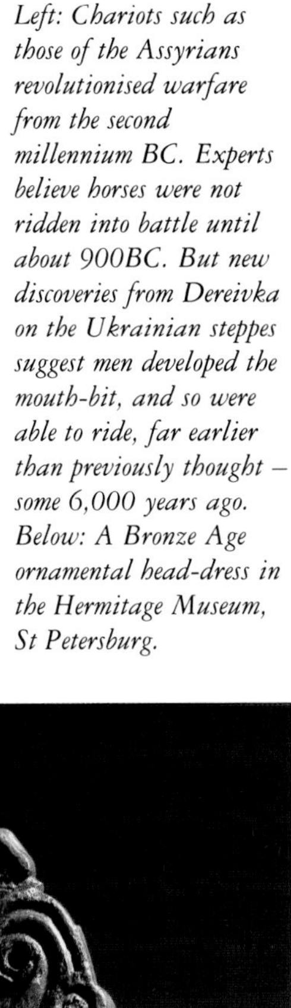

Battle Triumphs of the Scythians

With the gory scalps of fallen enemies tied to their belts, Scythian warriors controlled the steppe around the Black Sea for five centuries through their devastating skills as mounted archers. Their presence blocked the expansion of some of the ancient world's mightiest empires, and they periodically broke out of their homelands to wreak havoc from Poland to Persia. When not actually at war, some Scythians may have sold their fighting services to other rulers, starting a tradition of mercenary cavalrymen the Cossacks would eventually follow.

According to Herodotus, the Greek 'Father of History' writing about 200 years after the event, the Scythians first appeared on the south-western grasslands early in the 7th century BC, having migrated west from the Altai Mountains like so many tribes before them. They displaced another warrior people whom Herodotus calls Cimmerians. The fate of the Cimmerians is not known. However, as the Scythians practised both human sacrifice and slavery, it would have been brutal.

The Scythians were not entirely warlike. They traded apparently peacefully with the Greek colonies along the Black Sea shore, established settlements to exploit iron ore deposits around the lower Dnieper River, and farmed grain and cattle from earthwork strongholds. At their capital of Neapol-Skifskii in the Crimea they developed a rich urban culture akin to that of the Greeks.

They also refined the art of selective horse-breeding. Small, shaggy ponies like those of the wild steppe remained the general mount for ordinary Scythians at work, play or war. But in later centuries, when some Scythian warriors wore heavy plate-armour into battle, bigger, heavier horses were bred to carry their weight. A third, tiny type of horse may have been raised solely as food.

Nevertheless, it is as cruel and cunning fighters that the Scythians are chiefly remembered. One of the favoured battle tactics of their horsemen in the face of strong enemies with or without horses of their own was to retreat. As the enemy followed, his soldiers became increasingly disorganised, and the Scythians would add to the disarray by twisting on their mounts to loose arrows at the pursuers. Then, depending on circumstances, the Scythians would turn to fight on ground of their own choosing and begin harrying the enemy mercilessly back. Alternatively, the horse-archers would simply gallop to vanish in the endless steppe.

This form of fighting defeated King Darius of Persia when he attempted to conquer the Scythians with an army of hundreds of thousands of men just before 500BC. Used by the Parthians, a tribe descended from the Scythians, it halted the Roman army at the River Euphrates some 400 years later. It also gave us the expression 'Parthian shot' for a

Right: A gold plaque worn as a dress ornament shows a Scythian horseman armed with a javelin, in pursuit of a hare. It dates from the 5th century BC.

STAYING IN THE SADDLE

The Scythians in their heyday could put thousands of warrior-riders into battle against their enemies. But their historical reputation as the founding fathers of cavalry would not have been earned by numbers alone. Their horsemen were both disciplined and adept at manoeuvring – attributes that required them to have total control of their mounts. They exercised it with just their hands, knees and thighs, and the near-minimum of harnessry.

The basic harness used by the Scythians seems to have evolved many hundred years before their era. It consisted of a halter of rope or leather straps around the horse's head, connected to a one-piece or jointed metal bar passing through the animal's mouth – the snaffle-bit. A single rein was connected to either end of the bit. By pulling on the rein, the rider pressed the bit uncomfortably into the horse's gums, encouraging it to do his bidding.

However, earlier horse-warriors are thought to have ridden bare-back, greatly increasing the risk of slipping in the twists and turns of combat or the hunt. The Scythians are credited with inventing the first saddle. It consisted of two flattish cushions or pads, lying either side of the horse's backbone and joined by straps or wooden crosspieces. An arrangement of more straps around the horse's chest, belly and rump held the saddle firm.

Unlike later saddles used, for example, by the Celts and Romans, the Scythian version was not shaped back and front. Nor, it is believed, did the Scythians ride with stirrups, which the steppe tribes are known to have developed only after the 1st century AD. Both stirrups and a high back to the saddle are said to be essential to get the maximum leverage from the rider's body when making a sword or spear thrust or hurling a javelin from a horse. Yet the Scythians were pastmasters at such warrior arts.

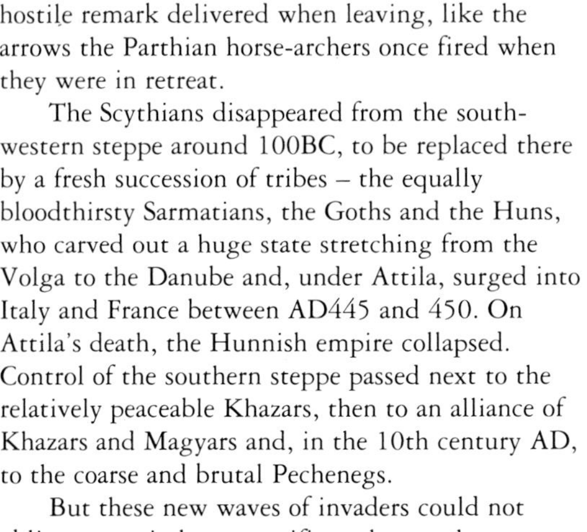

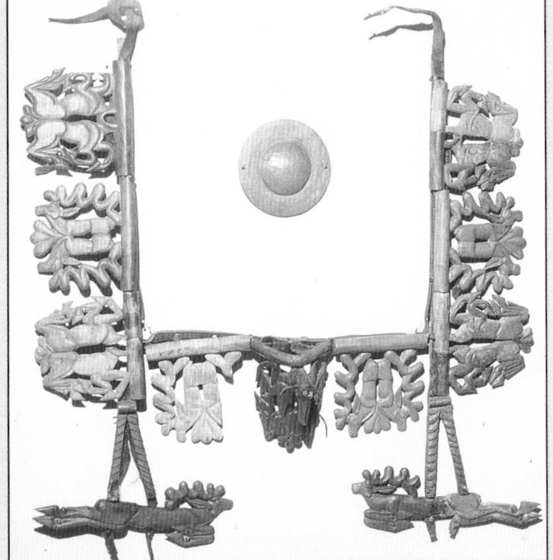

Left: A saddle and two sets of horse-head trappings used by nomadic horsemen on the Siberian steppe around 400BC.

hostile remark delivered when leaving, like the arrows the Parthian horse-archers once fired when they were in retreat.

The Scythians disappeared from the south-western steppe around 100BC, to be replaced there by a fresh succession of tribes – the equally bloodthirsty Sarmatians, the Goths and the Huns, who carved out a huge state stretching from the Volga to the Danube and, under Attila, surged into Italy and France between AD445 and 450. On Attila's death, the Hunnish empire collapsed. Control of the southern steppe passed next to the relatively peaceable Khazars, then to an alliance of Khazars and Magyars and, in the 10th century AD, to the coarse and brutal Pechenegs.

But these new waves of invaders could not obliterate entirely a magnificent legacy the Scythians had left hidden under their burial mounds on the grasslands.

Left: Women in long dresses dance together on this gold plaque found at the burial-ground of Kul-Oba, source of many splendid Scythian artefacts.

TOMBS OF THE STEPPE RIDERS

The scalpings, human sacrifices and other grisly battle rites of the Scythians and Sarmatians were matched by equally bloody ceremonies when one of their own chiefs died. Slaves and horses were slaughtered to accompany the leader to his grave on the open steppe, in which he was laid with all the rich trappings of his earthly life. A large earth-mound or barrow called a kurgan was raised over the tomb, and more men and horses were killed. Their bodies were positioned around the site like cavalry on guard.

These macabre sentinels failed to deter grave-robbers, and over the centuries most of the kurgans were plundered. Only a few survived more or less intact. The artefacts recovered from them show that, for all their bloodthirstiness, the steppe riders appreciated craftsmanship and even beauty.

From the Greeks to whom they sold grain, fish and amber, the Scythians bought wine, oil, textiles – and luxury items such as an exquisite gold comb found in a kurgan at Solokha. On its spine are depicted a horseman and foot-soldiers in battle.

Clockwise from above: Buried treasure of the Scythians. A plaque of blood-brothers drinking from Kul-Oba, a decorated comb from Solokha and an electrum vase, also from Kul-Oba.

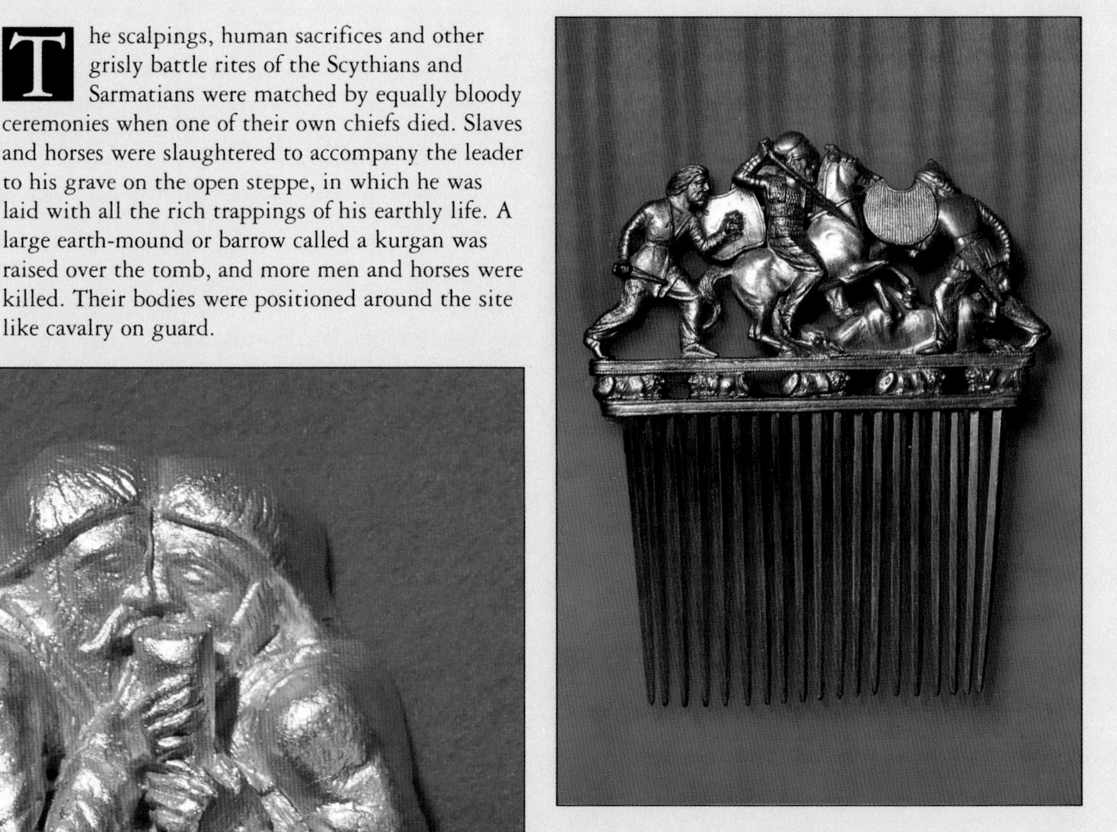

Scythian craftsmen working in gold or electrum, a natural alloy of gold and silver, produced items of equivalent splendour. Often, they were embellishments for weaponry, armour or horse-trappings, the everyday tools of the trade for most on the steppe.

Even purely decorative or domestic articles continue the warlike themes. A gold plaque from a kurgan at Kul Oba in the Crimea shows two Scythian warriors sharing a drinking horn in a ritual of blood brotherhood. An electrum vase from the

same region has portraits of warriors resting, spears to hand. A Sarmatian brooch depicts a warrior flourishing his enemy's severed head, perhaps prior to preparing the skull as a drinking cup – common practice among these tribes.

Animals, often highly stylised, feature prominently in Scythian art. Gold carvings of stags found in the Kuban, southern Russia, and elsewhere are typical, with swerving, curling antlers the length of their backs. Some examples have both real and mythical creatures on their flanks.

From the well-preserved bodies of several horsemen and their mounts found in graves on the Siberian steppe in the Altai region in the 1920s, we know that some tribesmen of the Scythian era were extensively tattooed with similar animal designs, which also appeared on brightly coloured rugs and wall hangings. The graves contained examples of the early saddles that the Scythians introduced to the west. The mummified head of one of the horsemen, possibly a chief, had been damaged by a blow from a battleaxe.

Above: A saddle-cloth decorated with felt figures of a mountain goat and a griffin, from a grave in the Altai region of Siberia.

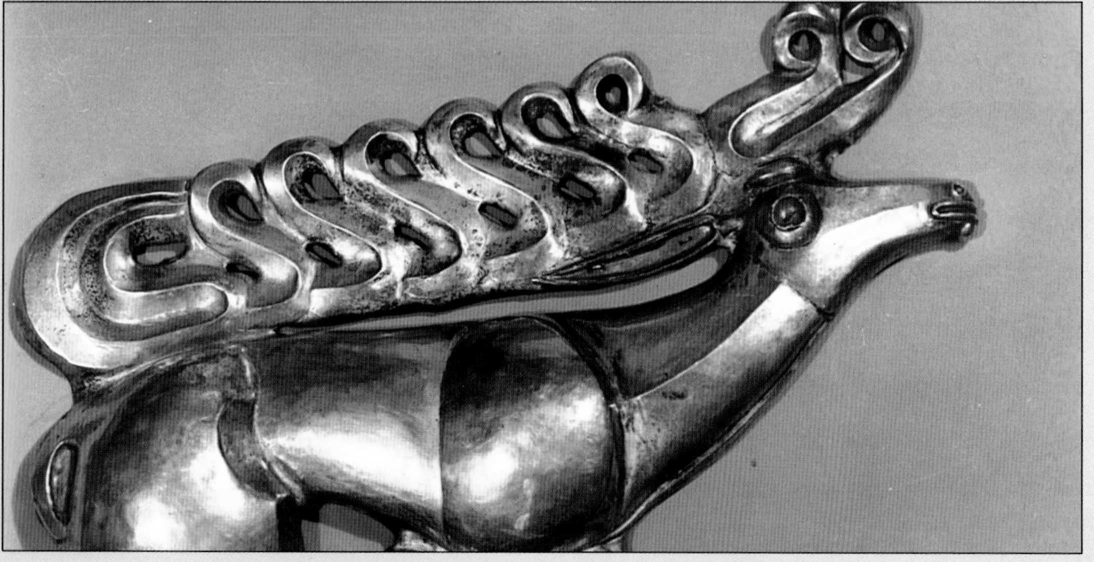

Left: Gold carving of a stag, from a kurgan at Kostromskoi.

The Rise of Rus

Top right: From the 5th century AD, groups of Slavs migrated from the steppe to woodland and forest further north.

Bottom right: The Varangian (Viking) Prince Rurik founded Russia's first ruling dynasty in AD 862.

Below: Oleg the Seer attacked Constantinople in AD 907, forcing its powerful rulers to sue for peace and conclude a trade treaty. To mark his triumph, he nailed his shield to the city wall.

Lands around the Carpathian Mountains at the westernmost end of the Eurasian steppe were inhabited in the 5th century AD by people of Asiatic origin whom contemporary writers called Slavs. As Attila the Hun's empire disintegrated after his death in 453, groups of Slavs started migrating. Some moved north and eastwards, deep into the forest zone usually shunned by the steppe nomads. There, they laid the earliest foundations of what was to become Russia – and a new thread begins to weave into the Cossack story.

The Slavs established settlements along river banks. Like the Lithuanian and Finnish forest tribes they gradually displaced, they at first practised a primitive form of farming in areas they had cleared of trees.

But the territory they came to occupy encompassed the headwaters of two sets of river networks – the south-flowing systems of the Dnieper and the Volga, which spill out from the forest across the steppe, and the north-flowing systems of the Western Dvina and the Neva, which empty into the Baltic Sea. That geographical fact transformed the Slavs' existence over a period of three or four centuries.

At several points in the forest zone, a north-flowing river and a south-flowing one were close enough together for voyagers to make a portage, carrying boats and their contents across the land in between. With sufficient organisation, just the cargo could be hefted from a boat on one river and transferred to a vessel waiting on the other. Using a short land-bridge, it was relatively easy to travel and move cargo from the Baltic via the Dnieper to the Black Sea and Constantinople beyond, and by way of the Volga into the Caspian Sea towards Baghdad.

Intrepid Viking seafarers from Scandinavia seem to have been the first people to fully appreciate the vast potential for trade and booty of these north-south water highways. Around the beginning of the 9th century, they began to explore them in their longboats, and to appear in large numbers in the land of the Slavs.

Rurik the Varangian

The Scandinavian incomers were known as Varangians by the Greek-speakers of Constantinople. The Slavs called them 'Rusi', a term whose meaning is uncertain, but from which the name Russia is derived.

Scholars disagree about the early relationship between the Varangians and the Slavs. In some places, the Varangians may have subjugated the local population and exacted tribute from it. In others, the two groups seem to have coexisted as equals. But in any case, where they encountered each other, they mingled freely.

The presence of the Varangians coincided with the first surge in water-borne trade from north-eastern Europe down the Volga to Baghdad. Early in the 9th century, merchants described as 'Slavic' by an Arab writer were in Baghdad, offering for sale slaves, salt, Baltic amber, honey and furs. As this traffic expanded, some Slav/Varangian settlements became important staging posts and centres – among them Kiev on the River Dnieper, where forest and steppe meet. A small upper class of merchants and warriors began to emerge.

But changes were taking place yet again on the turbulent steppe, around the lower reaches of the Volga in lands then controlled by the Khazars. By the standards of Asiatic nomads, the Khazars were peaceful; many of their leaders had converted to Judaism, and they allowed the river trade to develop. However, around 860 they were over-run by the Pechenegs, new and much more warlike arrivals from the east, who not only threatened commerce on the Volga, but looked likely to attack the emergent Slav/Varangian townships.

According to legend, the Slavs formally implored the Varangians in Scandinavia itself to protect and rule them. In 862, the Scandinavians obliged, sending chief (or prince) Rurik to accept the fealty of Slavs and Varangian settlers alike. He established himself in the northern centre of Novgorod near Lake Ilmen, as the founder of Russia's first ruling dynasty.

Above and left: Novgorod 'The Great', beside the Volkhov River near Lake Ilmen, built on its role as Rurik's capital to become a fiercely independent feudal city-state.

On Rurik's death in 879, his brother-in-law Oleg, nicknamed 'the Seer', assumed power. With an army, he secured the whole of territory south of Novgorod to Kiev, made Kiev his capital and began building fortified outposts on the edges of the steppe to keep back the nomad tribes. Oleg recognised that, with the Volga trade route to Baghdad now menaced by the Pechenegs, the Dnieper – and the market-place of Constantinople – had become vital.

In 907, he attacked Constantinople, forcing its Byzantine rulers to conclude a trade treaty. This treaty was the first of several; relations between Constantinople and Kiev were often stormy because of territorial disputes and Varangian/Slav piracy. But in periods of peace between the two cities, princes of Kiev made a point each spring of travelling down the Dnieper with the season's first cargo of slaves and furs, supervising its portage around the rapids in the river's lower reaches, and accompanying it across the Black Sea to Constantinople. Eventually, the same route brought Christianity back to Kiev.

ST VLADIMIR AND HOLY KIEV

Right: Vladimir's monument in the city he brought to Christianity.

Vladimir I, great-grandson of Rurik and ruler of Kiev from 980 to 1015, was an unlikely candidate for sainthood. His contemporaries knew him as an 'immense fornicator', with several wives, 800 concubines and an appetite for deflowering virgins. He was also a man who would stop at nothing, including fratricide, to win and hold on to power.

Even his adoption of Christianity in 988 was a dubious affair. Typically, Vladimir followed his own conversion by compelling his subjects to be baptised in droves. For bringing Christianity to the Russian people, he eventually became revered in the Orthodox Church as a saint and near- apostle.

There are many conflicting stories about how Vladimir came to the Byzantine version of the Christian faith. According to one, he determined as a matter of policy that he and his people should abandon paganism, but he could not decide what should replace it. So he invited representatives of various religions and churches to put their respective cases.

Islam was rejected because of its ban on alcohol, so alien to the Slav temperament. Judaism was turned down because the Jews were scattered so widely, and Vladimir wanted a religion that would be a centralising, unifying force in his territory.

Below: Boris and Gleb, two of Vladimir's many sons, were murdered on the orders of their brother Svyatopolk during the struggles for power in Kiev from 1015 to 1025. Svyatopolk was eventually overthrown by another brother, Yaroslav. But the fraternal feuds went on until Yaroslav reunited Vladimir's succession in 1035.

The Church of Rome offended Vladimir by sending a representative arrayed in splendour outshining his own. Only the Byzantine Church in Constantinople, which had not then completed the split with Rome that eventually separated Christianity into Roman Catholic and Orthodox branches, did not seem anxious to argue or impress. Vladimir was so taken by this diffidence that he ordered Byzantine priests to attend him immediately, or he would sack Constantinople.

The probable truth is more prosaic, though cynical. After one of the periodic skirmishes between Kiev and Constantinople over territories and trade, Vladimir and the Byzantine co-emperors Basil and Constantine were ready to negotiate terms. As part of those, Vladimir was to relinquish the captured Byzantine city of Gherson in the Crimea. In return and to cement the bargain, 'the immense fornicator' wanted to marry the emperors' sister Anna. Before agreeing to that, the emperors insisted Vladimir should become a Christian and give up his former licentiousness.

During his lifetime, Vladimir established by politics and force the basis for a unified Russian state centred on Kiev – Kievan Rus. It stretched roughly from the Carpathians in the west to present-day St Petersburg in the east. From north to south, it encompassed much of the forest and some of the western steppe, though not the Black Sea shore, nor the Baltic coast apart from a stretch on the Gulf of Finland.

Above: *St Sophia's Cathedral in Kiev was dedicated in 1037 by Prince Yaroslav, to celebrate his victory over Pecheneg steppe-tribes.*

After Vladimir's death, the fortunes and boundaries of Kievan Rus fluctuated, with brief periods of unity separated by long spells of feuding over who should rule where. Between 1015 and 1025, for example, 12 sons of Vladimir contested the succession in bloody quarrels.

That period of fratricidal strife ended with the division of Kievan territories between Prince Yaroslav, known as the Wise, and Prince Mstislav. The lands were reunited under Yaroslav when Mstislav died in 1035. But on Yaroslav's death in 1054, his sons started feuds of their own.

Nevertheless, Kievan Rus contrived to become a civilised and powerful state, comparable with most others of its time in Europe. Kiev itself – 'The Holy Mother of Russian Towns' – developed into a magnificent city. Thanks to Vladimir's legacy, it soon became the primary centre of the Orthodox Church in Russia, a position emphasised by its great Cathedral of St Sophia, started in 1037, and its Monastery of the Caves.

But in the 12th century, amid more squabbles among the Russian princes and new threats from Asiatic hordes on the steppe, Kiev's political significance declined and it lost its former place as the foremost Russian principality. The power centres shifted north and east, to Novgorod, Rurik's old capital, and to the principality of Rostov-Suzdal, whose ambitious ruler Yuri Dolgoruki or 'Long Arms' was founding a string of new settlements and fortresses – among them Moscow.

Left: An 11th-century mosaic of the Virgin Mary in St Sophia's.

Left: Tomb of Prince Yaroslav the Wise, St Sophia's.

'Emanations of the Devil'

Nothing in Europe's long history of invasions from the Asiatic steppe compares with the onslaught launched by the Mongols in 1236-37. In four years, their horse-soldiers smashed their way to the Danube, routing all who tried to stop them. At the gates of Vienna, undefeated in battle and for reasons no one can fully explain, they chose to withdraw and consolidate the western frontier of their steppe empire behind the Carpathians. With their local capital at Sarai on the River Volga, they sat on Russia's southern doorstep for 250 years.

The Mongols were no ordinary steppe nomads with a penchant for fighting. In Mongolia, their supreme leader Genghis Khan (c.1162-1227) had welded their able-bodied males into a superb cavalry force estimated by some to be 800,000 strong. Its units were tightly organised in multiples of 10, with the 'tumen' or division of 10,000 men as the major fighting formation. That in itself was not an innovation, but Genghis used it in both military and civil administration to break up tribal loyalties and instil an iron discipline of his own.

Most of the horsemen were archers, armed with bows capable of killing a man at 200 metres, and an axe or sword for close-quarter work. Some, armoured with iron or leather, were lancers. The Mongols' success in open warfare rested on their ability to move swiftly in small groups, coalesce into larger ones to confront the enemy, and when necessary to divide again to draw opponents and encircle them. These complex manoeuvres were thoroughly rehearsed, and signals for them were given with flags and drums.

Originally, Mongol soldiers were not only unpaid for fighting (a task they seem to have regarded as sport rather than work), but they were required to contribute goods to a central fund for the privilege. So they lived on booty, shared among them according to strict rules.

By the time the Mongols invaded Europe, they had made themselves masters of northern China and much of central Asia. In the course of these previous conquests, they had developed methods for capturing walled cities and fortresses, usually a weakness with cavalry.

In part, those relied on the skills of captured Chinese siege engineers to make massive, but portable, wall-breaching catapults and siege towers. However, the Mongols had other ploys at their command. They would lay waste surrounding areas before the siege started, forcing civilians into the fortress in order to spread panic and to increase the strain on food and water supplies.

Once one fortress was taken, the Mongols might drive some of the defenders before them to the next, to act as a human shield or to be slaughtered in front of its walls. But above all, they let it be known that they would be merciful if the fortress surrendered – and merciless when they captured one that resisted. Generally, they kept the bargain.

Far right: Genghis Khan, supreme ruler of the Mongols from 1206 to 1227, built his vast empire with the help of a formidable cavalry force raised and trained on the steppes.

Right: In the time of the fifth Great Khan, Kublai (reigned 1260-94), the centre of Mongol power shifted from the steppes to China. As a result, the Golden Horde, far away on the fringes of Kublai's territories, increasingly became an independent entity.

RULERS OF THE WORLD

The man who unleashed the Mongols on Europe and Asia was named Temuchin by his father, a minor tribal chieftain on the central Asian steppes. Genghis Khan – 'Emperor within the Seas' or 'World Ruler' – is a title, taken when Temuchin, at around 50, had forcibly unified the Mongol tribes and become their overlord.

At his birth, the tiny Temuchin is said to have been clutching in his hand a clot of blood, a portent of his future. Certainly his outlook was bloody enough; 'The greatest joy a man can know is to conquer his enemies ... ride their horses ... plunder their goods ... see their dear ones' faces wet with tears ... embrace their womenfolk', he is supposed to have declared as an adult.

Genghis built one of the greatest empires in history, stretching from the Pacific to the Black Sea and the Persian Gulf. It passed in 1260 to his grandson, Kublai Khan, who became emperor of China and first of the Yuan dynasty.

Sheer size eventually broke up the Mongol empire. Between 1370 and 1405, another warlike leader, Timur or Tamerlane, tried with considerable success to revitalise it. Timur, a Turkish-speaking Muslim of Mongol descent who was lame in both his right arm and his right leg, made Samarkand the centre of his state. In his campaigns, he attacked both the Golden Horde and its Russian tributaries – making little distinction between them.

Left: The forces of Timur or Tamerlane rampaged over the steppes between the Volga and the Ural from 1391 to 1396, as he sought to bring his fellow-Mongols of the Golden Horde into his new empire. Unlike Genghis Khan, whom he resembled in his greed for territory, Timur had a reputation for wanton cruelty. His head was reconstructed on the skull in the 1940s, when Russian scientists investigated his tomb at Samarkand.

Rus at bay

Before their organised attack on Europe, the Mongols had made a foray towards it along the steppe in 1223-24. In that incursion, they defeated a mixed army of Russians and steppe tribesmen at the Battle of Kalka near the Sea of Azov, after which the Mongols held a victory banquet on boards laid over the living bodies of captured Russian princes. At that time, a Russian chronicler described them as 'emanations of the Devil' and referred to them as Tartars – a name actually used only by one of many steppe tribes, but which is appropriately close to a Greek word for 'hell'.

By the second invasion, Genghis Khan was dead, succeeded as supreme ruler by one of his sons, Ogedei. Under the complicated inheritance system of the Mongols, Ogedei's nephew Batu had been promised unallocated territory on the steppe 'as far west as a Mongol pony's hoof has trod'. So the arrival of Batu's hordes in Europe was partly to secure a bequest.

They stormed across the Volga and, unlike most previous invaders, moved off the steppe, to attack the Russian strongholds. The Russian leaders were in the middle of one of their endless internecine squabbles, so there was no coordinated resistance.

Riazan and Moscow fell. The cities of Vladimir and Suzdal were sacked. Novgorod held out only because the spring thaw made its approaches too marshy for the Mongols to cross. Kiev was temporarily spared, but in the year 1240 Batu's hordes reduced the proud Mother of Russian Towns to ruins.

Altogether, nine principalities of Russia fell under the 'Tartar yoke', subject to Batu's rule from his capital of Sarai. True to nomad traditions, Sarai was predominantly a city of tents, of which Batu, as leader, had the most splendid – possibly of gold cloth. At any rate, the Russians came to name their local Mongol oppressors 'The Golden Horde'.

Below: When the Mongols besieged Kiev in 1240, the noise made by their carts, horses and camels prevented the defenders from hearing each other speak. The city fell on St Nicholas's Day, December 6.

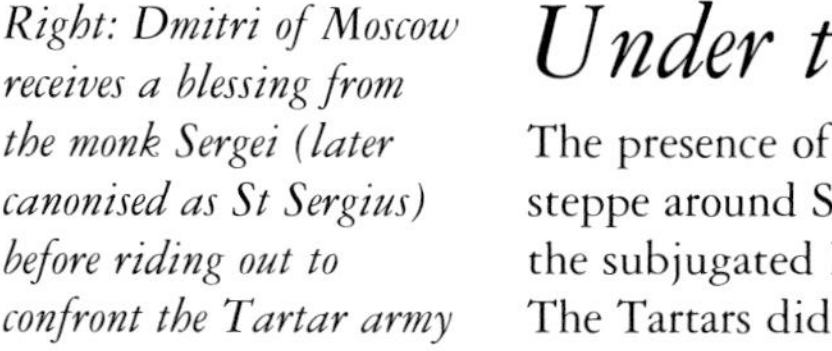

Right: Dmitri of Moscow receives a blessing from the monk Sergei (later canonised as St Sergius) before riding out to confront the Tartar army in 1380.

Under the Yoke

The presence of the Tartar Golden Horde on the steppe around Sarai was like an iron blanket over the subjugated Russian principalities to the north. The Tartars did not need to garrison Russia; they simply moved swiftly and cruelly to stamp out any sign of resistance to their suzerainty or to the crushing taxes they imposed. Even Novgorod, which they had not captured, deemed it wise to pay tribute to them.

To some extent, therefore, the Russians were left to their own affairs and customs. The Tartars did not generally interfere so long as their wishes were obeyed and the taxes and tributes kept pouring in. They allowed the Russians to rebuild the cities that had been destroyed, and even placed the Orthodox Church under their specific protection.

However, there were two important exceptions to this general policy of non-interference. The Tartars seized the right to confirm in office the rulers of the Russian principalities. And, after a while, they made these same rulers responsible for tax collection.

Given the perennial jealousies and rivalries between the Russian princes, this situation was custom-built for intrigue and treachery. Shamelessly, noble after Russian noble turned up in the Golden Horde's capital of Sarai, seeking Tartar support for his ambitions to rule a principality, to expand its territory, or to thwart a rival. Lavish extra tributes, exacted by threat or force from an already heavily burdened population, were the quickest way to secure Tartar help. Marriage to a Tartar princess was one way to sustain it.

Below: The victory at Kulikovo is regarded by Russians as a turning-point in their history. When the battle was over, the field was 'planted with Tartar bones and drenched with their blood'.

Some of the most renowned names in Russian history played this game ruthlessly. One was Alexander, ruler of the independent-minded city of Novgorod. He protected its territory from the rapacious attentions of its northern neighbours with his victories over Sweden at the Battle of the Neva in 1240 and over the Teuton Knights of the Sword at the Battle of the Ice on frozen Lake Peipus in 1242. As a result of these victories, he was later canonised as St Alexander Nevsky by the Orthodox Church. Yet, despite his reputation as a saint, in 1252 he summoned a Tartar army to defeat his own brother Andrei in a territorial dispute.

Another was Ivan I of Moscow, nicknamed Kalita or 'Moneybags' and a great-grandson of Alexander Nevsky. In 1328, by lavish gifts to the Khan of the Golden Horde, he secured for himself and his descendants as Grand Dukes of Moscow the sole right and duty to collect taxes and tributes on the Khan's behalf from the whole of Russia. In doing so, he could exercise the Khan's unlimited power over all Russians – the root of later autocracy.

Ivan Kalita's ploy consolidated Moscow's emerging position as the new centre of Russia. He further enhanced it by making the city the seat of the Metropolitan, head of the Orthodox Church in Russia. That honour had once belonged to Kiev,

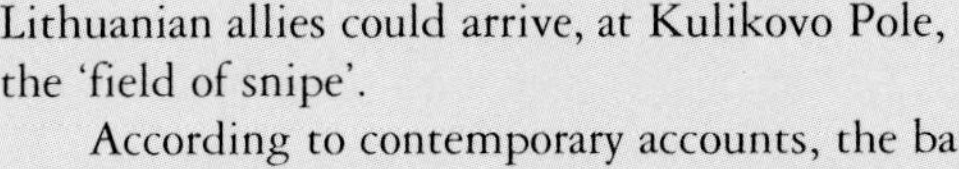

DMITRI OF THE DON

In the summer of 1380, Khan Mamai of the Golden Horde decided that his Russian vassals, and in particular Grand Prince Dmitri of Moscow, should be taught a sharp lesson. Nine years earlier, Mamai had reduced the tributes collected on his behalf by Dmitri. But since 1376 they had not been paid at all and a Tartar force sent to collect them had been turned back in a skirmish on the River Vozh.

Now Mamai was taking no chances. He concluded an alliance with the Lithuanians on the Russians' western flank and pushed a large Tartar army across the Volga. Then he sent a message to Dmitri. Effectively, it said: 'Pay up in full at the old, higher tribute rate...or else'.

Dmitri and his advisers, including the monk Sergei of Radonezh, were not cowed. Despite the lack of support from Novgorod and some other principalities, the Grand Prince of Moscow led a Russian force south. It crossed the River Don and, on September 8, engaged the Tartars before their Lithuanian allies could arrive, at Kulikovo Pole, the 'field of snipe'.

According to contemporary accounts, the battle was extraordinarily violent. Corpses from both sides were piled high like corn-stooks and the River Don ran red with blood for three days. But in the end Mamai and his hordes were routed, leaving treasure, spare horses and camels in their flight.

The defeat was the first of major proportions inflicted on the Tartars, and news of it spread all over Europe. The Russians, who had not expected to win, were jubilant, but nervous. They anticipated retribution and it duly came. In 1382, under the new Khan Tokhtamysh, the Tartars captured and plundered Moscow and other cities. One by one, Dmitri and his fellow-princes were forced to renew their pledges of fealty.

But the victory at Kulikovo had shown both the Tartars themselves and their enemies that the Golden Horde was not invincible. It earned for Dmitri the soubriquet Donskoi: 'Lord of the Don'.

Below: Dmitri of the Don, like other rulers of Moscow in the 14th century, took the title Grand Prince, reflecting the city's growing importance in the eyes of its Tartar overlords.

Left: The original Kremlin in Moscow was a rough-timber fort built about 1186. Some 200 years later, during Dmitri's reign, the wooden enclosing wall was replaced by ramparts of white stone, set with nine watch-towers.

which, like several other ancient western Russian regions, had been swallowed up by the expansion of Lithuania from 1307.

In the years following Ivan Kalita's death in 1340, the previously monolithic Golden Horde began to show signs of internal divisions. By then, it had officially converted to Islam from the shamanism or spirit-worship practised by most Mongols. However, the disagreements seem to have had more to do with territorial and leadership disputes than with religion. Briefly, from 1376, the Horde reunited under Tokhtamysh, a protege of Timur, who was then striving to revitalise the declining Mongol empire. Timur himself ousted Tokhtamysh in 1395. Before that, though, the Russians had taken their first positive steps towards throwing off the Tartar yoke and lifting the long years of oppression.

Century of Upheaval

The 100 years or so following Dmitri Donskoi's victory at Kulikovo saw huge upheavals and shifts in the balance of power in the lands around the western steppe. At the start of the 15th century, the Russian principalities came more tightly under the Tartar yoke than at any time since the fall of Kiev in 1240 – the price they paid for Dmitri's gallant, if ultimately futile, defiance of the Golden Horde. As the century progressed, more and more Tartars of all social levels came to settle in Russian lands, many of them marrying the local inhabitants and adopting a Russian way of life.

To the west, Lithuania and Poland had united and were pressing claims on large tracts of what had once been the territory of Kievan Rus, in regions that came to be known as Belorussia (White Russia) and the Ukraine ('The Marches', or Little Russia). The dispute between Poles and Russians over the western Ukraine has flared periodically ever since. From the beginning it had a religious dimension; after the 11th-century schism in the Christian church and the failure to repair it at the Council of Florence in 1439, the Poles were Roman Catholics and the Russians were Orthodox.

Further south, the old order was changing. The Ottoman Turkish empire based in Asia Minor revived after setbacks at the hands of Timur. Its leader, Sultan Mehmet I, declared a holy war on behalf of Islam against the Orthodox Christians of Constantinople and in 1453, after a long siege, the city fell, marking the end of the Byzantine empire. In Europe, the Turks came to control the Balkans, Transylvania and Hungary.

Changes were taking place among the Tartars, too, as their internal divisions grew worse. In 1438, the Golden Horde was officially split into two – the Great Horde and the Khanate of Kazan, around the middle reaches of the River Volga. In 1441, two more separate Tartar Khanates were created, at Astrakhan by the Caspian Sea and on the Crimean pensinsula separating the Sea of Azov from the Black Sea. About 1475, the Crimean Tartar leader Mengli Girai accepted the rule of the Ottoman Turks, and in 1502 in their name he attacked and destroyed the Great Horde, thereby weakening the Tartars irreparably.

Ivan the Great of Muscovy

The problems of the Golden Horde created opportunities a ruthless and cunning man could exploit. In 1462, such a man inherited the Grand Duchy of Moscow – the devastatingly handsome Ivan III.

Ivan's father Basil II had already begun the process of subjugating the other Russian principalities to Moscow, with a combination of force and diplomacy. Ivan continued it by the same means, eventually bringing even the mighty Novgorod and its dependencies to heel. He welded the principalities into a centralised northern state governed from Moscow and larger than any other in Europe – Muscovy.

In the 11th year of his reign, Ivan married Sophia Palaeologus, heir of the last ruler of the Byzantine Empire. It was hardly a love-match. Ivan's good looks and the power he wielded could have given him the pick of almost any woman inside or outside his realm, while Sophia was plain

Below left: The fall of Constantinople to the Ottoman Turks in 1453 enabled Moscow to claim its place as the spiritual centre of Orthodox Christianity.

Below right: The plain and hefty Sophia, heir to the last Christian ruler of Byzantium, as seen through the eyes of the painter Ilya Repin 400 years later.

and so fat that the bed collapsed under her on their wedding night. But in effect it made Muscovy the successor-state to the Byzantine Empire, and Moscow the spiritual successor to Constantinople, now in the hands of the Turks, as a hub of the Christian Church – the 'Third Rome'.

From Sophia's emperor-uncle, Ivan received as a wedding present a magnificent ivory throne bearing the Byzantine insignia of a double-headed eagle, symbolising Constantinople looking east and west. Ivan promptly adopted that as the emblem of Muscovy, displacing the old standard of St George and the dragon. He surrounded himself with imperial pomp and splendour, and imported Italian and Byzantine architects to make Moscow into a capital worthy of an empire.

With the Russian principalities under his thumb, Ivan set about building one. He waged territorial wars against the Baltic states and in the region around the ancient Russian capital of Kiev, now in Lithuanian-Polish hands, though without marked success. And he flouted the once-iron authority of the Golden Horde.

In 1473, Ivan refused to pay tribute to emissaries of the Tartar Khan, reputedly trampling the Khan's portrait under foot to show his contempt. Long negotiations followed without the tribute being resumed, and in 1480 Khan Akhmad, like Mamai before him, struck an alliance with the Russians' Lithuanian-Polish enemies. Akhmad marched with a Tartar army to the River Ugra, on the boundary between Lithuania and Muscovy, where his allies were to join him; Basil and the Russians soon arrived at the same spot.

But this was no bloody Kulikovo. All through the summer of 1480, Tartars and Russians watched each other across the river – Akhmad waiting for the Lithuanians, who did not arrive, and Ivan just waiting. Then in November, the Tartars withdrew for unexplained reasons. Possibly, Akhmad had learnt of new conflicts among the Tartars left at home; he was assassinated by a rival Khan on his return. At any rate, the Russians had won without a clash of arms, and historians generally regard 1480 as the final lifting of the Tartar yoke – though there were more battles to come before the Tartars were thoroughly vanquished.

Ivan's legacy

Ivan ruled for 43 years, until 1505. His achievements in the 'gathering of the lands', as the subjugation of the principalities to Moscow is called, in outfacing the Tartars and in recodifying Russian law earned him the name Ivan the Great.

But the means by which he achieved his ends disaffected many people. They included the petty rulers and landowners, whose powers and freedoms he drastically reduced, and the citizens of Novgorod and other principalities, whom he slaughtered or deported in large numbers.

This disaffection came to a head in Muscovy during the reign of his grandson Ivan IV, with terrible results. It also stimulated the flow of Russians to the steppe lands around the Black Sea where the writ of Muscovy did not run and Tartar power was waning – Cossack country.

Above: The marriage of Ivan III to Sophia Palaeologus in 1472 was a dynastic match to further Ivan's boundless ambitions.

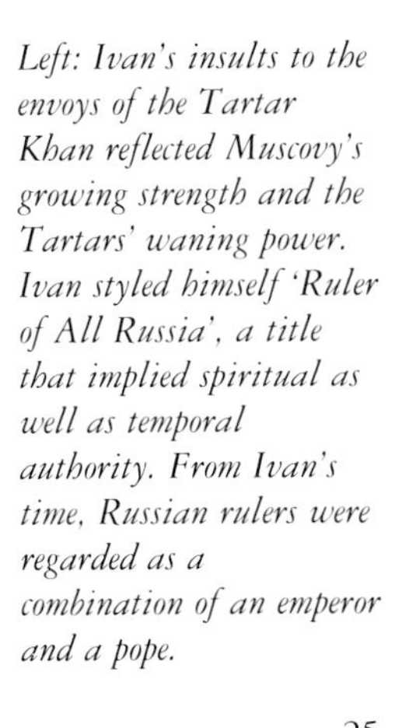

Left: Ivan's insults to the envoys of the Tartar Khan reflected Muscovy's growing strength and the Tartars' waning power. Ivan styled himself 'Ruler of All Russia', a title that implied spiritual as well as temporal authority. From Ivan's time, Russian rulers were regarded as a combination of an emperor and a pope.

The First Cossacks

In the early 14th century, Byzantine Greek traders around the Black Sea reported the presence of Tartar bands looting and plundering merchants' caravans and staging-posts on their own account, without orders or permission from the rulers of the Golden Horde. These freebooting outlaws were referred to as Kazaks, a term that may originally have been Arabic. Adopted into Turkish, Tartar and eventually Russian and Polish, it acquired layer after layer of meaning. All carry the same underlying message: the Kazak, or Cossack, was his own man.

Little is known about the first Tartar Cossacks, though much can be surmised. The rigid discipline instilled by Genghis Khan in his Mongol horsemen a century or so earlier may have been breaking down with the dissensions inside the Golden Horde, but the penalty for disobedience remained torture and death. So whatever the reasons for some Tartars to turn renegade, those who did so must have been fearless or desperate, or both.

They would have taken with them into outlawry the fighting and survival skills imbued in all Tartar horse-soldiers – the ability to move fast, strike quickly with bow, sword or axe, and live off the land. Probably, they would have copied Mongol systems of organisation, based on fighting groups of ten men. Certainly, they would have known that their horses were the key to their survival in the vastness of the steppe, and would have cherished them accordingly.

In the turbulent first half of the 15th century, the ranks of the Tartar Cossacks grew rapidly. Their numbers emboldened them to the point where they not only preyed on caravans and isolated villages in lightning hit-and-run attacks, but were prepared to risk encounters with the organised forces of the Russian principalities, Lithuania-Poland and the Tartars themselves. They were also willing to sell their services as mercenaries.

In 1443, for example, a Tartar Cossack band launched a foray into the south-eastern Russian principality of Riazan in search of plunder. Their ferocity and numbers seem to have cowed the Grand

Right: A Mongol horse-archer, forerunner of the first Cossacks. Both dress and riding style were emulated by Europeans who drifted to the steppes.

KUMISS AND MEAD

To Cossacks, getting drunk was a religion, according to the great Russian novelist Leo Tolstoy, who lived among them in the 19th century. If so, it was one shared by both the Tartars and the Slavs in their family tree.

The Tartars' favourite alcoholic tipple was kumiss, made from the fermented milk of mares. It could be extremely potent, to judge from the number of Mongol leaders whose death is attributed to drink. The nominal conversion of the Golden Horde to Islam, with its ban on alcohol, appears to have made no difference to many of the Tartars' drinking habits.

The early Slavs made mead from honey and fermented various grains to produce a sweetish beer called kvas. In later times, distillation of the grain yielded vodka ('little water'), at its best a pure drink. Similar highly alcoholic spirits were distilled, under rough conditions, from any available fruit or berries, sometimes with fatal results. Tolstoy reported that in his day all Cossack villagers made their own alcohol.

Wine-drinking was not really part of either Russian or Tartar culture. But both groups had a long history of contact with wine-producing regions – and wine was highly prized plunder in Cossack raids from the earliest days. Tales abound of Cossacks breaking into wine-stores during their forays, drinking themselves into stupors and remaining there to be captured or slaughtered by their foes.

Left: Heavy consumption of alcohol was common among Tartars and Slavs alike. In the 13th-14th centuries, groups of up to 50 Slav men and women formed drinking clubs to buy mead, racing through huge quantities of it in all-day sessions called stravitsi. Some even sold their children into slavery to pay for their appetites, according to the Venetian traveller Marco Polo.

Duke of Riazan. Rather than oppose them, he made a deal granting them a winter base on his territory. By the following year, as 'Riazan Cossacks', they were fighting alongside Russian forces in order to protect their adopted allies against other Tartar would-be raiders.

At roughly the same time, Basil II of Moscow, who underwent many vicissitudes in his struggle for power and had been blinded at the hands of his rivals, reached a mysterious agreement with a breakaway group of Tartars led by Khan Kasim. Under this pact, Kasim and his followers were granted lands between Moscow and the Khanate of Kazan, in return for serving Moscow as 'Kasimov Cossacks' against Tartars and other Russian principalities alike.

But the Tartar Cossacks were not only for sale to the Russians. About 1445, some enlisted as irregulars for Lithuania-Poland – the beginning of a division in allegiances that was to prove enduring and bitter.

The Wild Land

As empires crumbled and reformed around the western steppe, it became a frontier no man's land where groups of Tartar Cossacks roamed free, living by hunting and fishing when they were not plundering or fighting as mercenaries.

Their way of life proved alluring to many besides Tartars. From the Russian principalities, Lithuania, Poland and even Scandinavia, Europeans drifted to the grasslands to emulate it – criminals, adventurers, the poor, starving or dispossessed.

At first, these refugees may have operated separately from the Tartar Cossacks, and fought them. But from about 1470 the two groups began to mingle, and by the 1550s the process of integration was well under way.

Tartar steppe-craft and a rough-hewn Slavonic culture were combining to produce a distinctive Cossack society, last heir to the traditions of steppe horsemen that stretched back to the Scythians some 2,000 years earlier.

Cossack Dawn

To Dnieper and Don

The European runaways who teemed to the western steppe to practise the Cossack way of life were summer migrants at first. As winter approached, they suspended their brigandry, hunting and fishing, drifting back to the frontier towns and villages of Poland-Lithuania and Muscovy until the weather improved.

Their lawless presence disturbed the Polish-Lithuanian and the Muscovite authorities. Both sought to bring the Cossacks to heel by enrolling some of them for military duty or as border guards. In return, such 'registered' or 'service' Cossacks, as they came to be known, received wages, and sometimes land grants and other privileges. By 1620, the number of registered Cossacks in Polish border service had reached 6,000.

Thousands of other Cossacks were not so lucky. If they ventured close to the frontiers, they were simply seized by the Poles or Russians and reduced in effect to serfdom, a condition from which many had only recently escaped. So they were forced to make a year-round home of the steppe, drifting south and east, deeper into no man's land, closer to Tartar and Turk. They called themselves 'free' Cossacks, to distinguish themselves from their registered, more respectable cousins.

The earliest permanent villages, or stanitsi, of the free Cossacks were little more than fortified camps. Copying their Tartar counterparts, the Cossacks used any timber they could find for the frames of their dwellings, and then covered them with animal hides. When the camps were being built, they were sometimes ringed with carts as a defence, like the protective circles formed by Wild West wagon-trains. Later, they were enclosed by deep ditches and earth mounds.

By about 1550, two groups of these encampments had grown into quite large settlements, almost capitals of free Cossackry. One was on the River Don, well to the south of the Muscovite border, but near the Tartar stronghold of Azov. The other was at the western edge of no man's land, on islands by the rapids in the River Dnieper. It was named the Zaporozhskaya Sich

Below: Map engraved in 1562 showing Russia, Muscovy and Tartary. The pictures are based on Marco Polo's account of his travels.

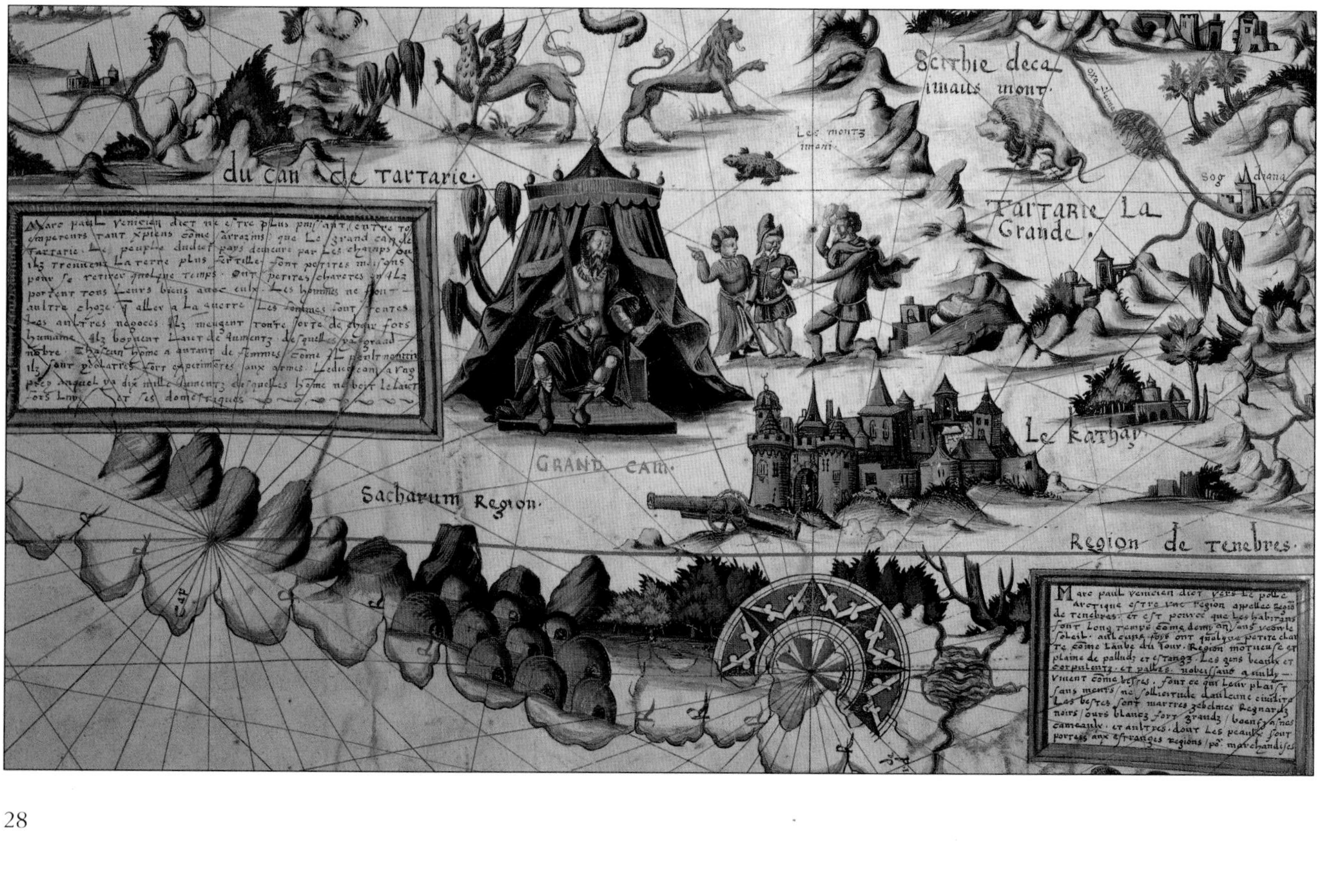

(the clearing below the cataracts). For two hundred years, the Dnieper Cossacks – Zaporozhians or Zaporozhi – were the fiercest, most proud of the guardians of Cossack liberty.

Life in the Sich

From an early stage, free Cossack communities, or 'hosts', were run on a peculiar mixture of democratic and military lines. Each year, an assembly of all adult Cossack males elected a leader, called an ataman, and a council of elders to run the community's affairs. The ataman's powers were absolute when the Cossacks were actually fighting or raiding, and nearly so the rest of the time.

Sometimes, however, an ataman might convene the general assembly to consider particularly important matters, such as whether to conduct a certain raid. The assembly took its decisions by popular acclaim, in which the faction making the most noise carried the day. Occasionally, these turbulent shouting-matches turned into violent and bloody fights.

Women had no direct say in the running of the Cossack hosts. The first Cossacks had few women in their numbers, and they relied for female companionship on captives taken in raids on the Tartars and other steppe tribes. Later, as the communities grew and became more settled, many of the runaways joining them brought wives or daughters along. In the Zaporozhskaya Sich, bachelor Cossacks lived in fortified barracks from which women were excluded, while their married counterparts had homesteads outside. Other Cossack hosts – on the Don and, by 1600, the Rivers Yaik (Ural) and Terek – do not seem to have segregated single males.

Religion and raids

The Cossacks' way of life did not lend itself to religion. On their raids by land and by water, they plundered Catholic and Orthodox Christians, Jews and Muslims without distinction. Conversely, they were prepared to welcome to their ranks anyone who could fight, irrespective of creed.

Even in relatively peaceful activities, they offended the teachings of most churches with their habitual drunkenness, their proclivity for rape and theft and their general view that might was right, though they did have a rough-and-ready morality within their own ranks. A male Cossack, for example, who murdered another might be sentenced by the elders to be tossed into the river bound to the body of his victim, or buried alive.

But in general, religion or moral teaching in any form was long regarded as a sapping influence. Priests were specifically barred from the Zaporozhskaya Sich, and for a century or so from 1550 there was no church among the Cossacks of Dnieper and Don.

It was only as a result of later religious upheavals in Poland and Russia that Cossackry came to be associated with Russian Orthodox Christianity in various of its forms.

So when the Cossacks made their first significant appearance in a Russian military campaign, against the remnants of the Tartar hordes, it was not a crusade. They were fighting, as always, for money and booty, at the behest of a Muscovite ruler whose reputation for cruelty matches their own.

Right: Morning on the River Dnieper.

Below: As the Cossacks grew and spread, they began to build permanent homes and forts.

Far right: Two artistic views of Ivan the Terrible (reigned 1533-84) – sculptured in brooding old age, and shown in his prime.

Ivan the Terrible

The gathering of the Russian lands begun by Ivan the Great was continued enthusiastically and ruthlessly by his son Basil III. But when Basil died in 1533, his own heir – also baptised Ivan – was only three years old. With an infant on the Moscow throne, the greedy and ambitious Russian nobles felt free to resume their characteristically murderous squabbling and plotting.

They seem to have left young Ivan largely alone, in the company of a half-witted brother and a monk called Sylvester. Occasionally, though, Ivan was dragged out, dressed in Grand Ducal finery, to receive the obeisance of the nobles in ceremonies that may have had a mocking edge. Certainly in adult life he maintained a deep and violent hatred of the old nobility.

Some say Ivan was a relatively normal child, though others claim he amused himself by various sadistic means, such as dropping pet dogs from the towers of his palace or riding pell-mell through Moscow with a band of cronies, whipping anyone in his path. In any case, at 14 he decided he had come of age, and for the first time during his reign he summoned the nobles on his own initiative. When they were assembled, he ordered the arrest as a traitor of their leader, Prince Andrei Shuisky. The astounded Shuisky fled, only to be captured by rivals anxious to ingratiate themselves with Ivan, and executed. The event set a pattern for Ivan's career, which was to bring him the nickname grozni – literally, 'formidable' or 'dread', but usually in English 'the terrible'.

Right: The face of the man – or the monster. Ivan's head has been reconstructed from the skull this century.

The first Tsar

By 1547, at the age of 17, Ivan had married Anastasia Romanov, the daughter of a minor noble, and secured his coronation, in a lavish ceremony, as Ivan IV, Tsar (Caesar) of All the Russias. He was the first ruler officially to adopt that title, and to support it he drew up a fanciful genealogy claiming to prove his descent from the Caesars of Rome. He refined the theory, too, that he ruled by the divine will of God, and therefore stood above both the Church and all institutions of state.

THE BLACK INQUISITION

Dressed entirely in black, riding black horses with dogs' heads and brooms attached to their saddles, the oprichniki were Ivan the Terrible's far-from-secret police. Their official task was to administer the Russian territories that Ivan had extorted or seized as his personal fief, the oprichnina. As part of this role, they were supposed to sniff out traitors to the Tsar, regarded solely as treacherous curs to be decapitated, swept away and quickly forgotten.

But the oprichniki's real purpose was far wider. Ivan had created them in 1564 to crush the power of the old, independent minded Russian aristocracy – the ruling families of the principalities and the boyars, who for centuries had accumulated wealth and influence as advisers to the throne.

Many of the oprichniki were aristocrats themselves. They went along with Ivan's black game for self-preservation at a period when an accusation, true or false, of treason led to torture, death and forfeiture of lands.

Ivan and his henchmen set up headquarters at Alexanderskaya Sloboda, a fortified parody of a monastery where they indulged in pseudo-religious ceremonies and orgies when they were not tormenting and murdering their victims in the vilest ways they could devise. No one knows exactly how many people died at the hands of the oprichniki. But the tally runs into thousands, and the land confiscations brought half of Muscovy into the Tsar's personal control. The victims' kin and retinues were also slaughtered or evicted.

By the end of Ivan's reign, the boyars and princely families who survived were vassals of the throne, mostly impoverished. Large sections of their estates had been dismantled and handed over, under the oprichnina system, to a growing middle class of gentry and functionaries who held their land as hereditary tenants in return for military service to the Tsar. In towns, merchants and artisans were also drawn into a system of military obligation.

At the bottom of this social pyramid were the so-called free peasants and the remnants of a slave class which had existed since Varangian times. In practice, under Ivan's bloody reorganisations, there was not much difference between the two groups. Need and hunger kept most of the free peasants where they were, sinking into a dependence on the tenanted gentry which came closer and closer to bondage. In 1550, their legal right to move from one village to another was severely restricted and in the 1580s it was curtailed again – steps towards the official imposition of serfdom, which came in 1649. In such circumstances, those peasants and slaves with the nerve and spirit fled Muscovy altogether, to join the Cossacks outside the feudal system and live in freedom, if not luxury, on the steppes. So Cossack numbers grew.

Below: Violence was never far away in Ivan the Terrible's Muscovy. A fist-fight was one of the milder forms it took.

From this early age, Ivan's behaviour was bizarre and cruel even by the standards of time and place. A delegation from the city of Pskov presented him in 1547 with a petition that for some reason offended him. Ivan poured boiling wine on the delegates, set fire to their hair and beards and ordered them to lie naked on the floor. As he was preparing to have them executed, a church bell somewhere in Moscow crashed down from its tower, distracting Ivan's attention and so saving their lives.

But he also instigated major reforms in the legal code and local government between 1550 and 1560, encouraged steps to reduce corruption in the Church, and set about creating a mighty, modern Muscovite army. One of its first tests came against the old foe – the Tartars.

Mother of All Russia

The mighty River Volga, rising in the Valdai Hills west of Moscow, flows 3,690km (2,293 miles) to the Caspian Sea. In the age of the Varangians, as part of one of the two great water highways linking the Baltic to the trade centres of Asia, it had played a central role in the development of the rudimentary Russian states – contributing to the reverence in which it is still held as the 'Mother of All Russia'. The invasion of the Mongols and the creation of the Tartar Golden Horde cut off its lower reaches, making it highly dangerous to the Russians as a communications route.

When Ivan the Terrible had himself crowned as Tsar in 1547, much of the power of the Golden Horde had already been broken. But the Tartars were still encamped on Muscovy's doorstep, in the fastness of the Crimea and at two centres on the Volga itself – Kazan, due east of Moscow, and Astrakhan, on the shores of the Caspian.

Undoubtedly, there were at that time free Cossack settlements on the Volga, as there were on the Dnieper and the Don. However, little is known about them, because Ivan determined in his first external military campaign to bring the whole of the Volga under Muscovite control. His eventual success made the region too uncomfortable for free Cossacks to stay there in large numbers.

In 1552, Ivan assembled a powerful army under the command of Prince Andrei Kurbsky and others, cajoled and bribed some bands of Cossacks to join it, and laid siege to Kazan. Amid fire and slaughter, the stronghold fell – the first major Russian armed victory over the Tartars since Kulikovo 170 years previously, and the first Russian military engagement in which Cossacks played a significant part. To mark this achievement, Ivan commissioned the building of the Cathedral of the Intercession (St Basil's Cathedral), the domed and spired masterpiece which dominates Moscow's Red Square. He also ordered his 'Kazan hat', a new crown in gold filigree, trimmed with sable and studded with precious stones.

The fate of the craftsmen who made the Kazan hat is not recorded. But legend says one of the architects responsible for St Basil's fell victim to a typical piece of Ivan's cruelty. The Tsar was delighted with his creation of swirled domes, all different in shape and colour to represent various fruits. To ensure that such splendour could not be emulated elsewhere, he ordered the architect's eyes put out.

While similar tales are told about other rulers in other places, no one doubts Ivan could and would have done such a thing had he wished.

Right: Russian craftsmen made Ivan's magnificent sable-trimmed gold crown to mark his victory over the Tartars at Kazan.

Below: St Basil's Cathedral in Moscow was begun in 1554 to commemorate the taking of Kazan. Each of its eight chapels represents one of Ivan's battle triumphs.

On to Astrakhan

With Kazan taken, the Muscovite army rampaged through the surrounding Tartar lands and south down the Volga. As it drove the enemy before it, more Cossacks joined its ranks. Among them may have been one Yermak, descendant of a peasant from Suzdal who had fled to the Volga sometime around 1500. Kurbsky was still among the commanders, collecting so many wounds that he was later to write, in a letter to the Tsar: 'My entire body is one mass of scars'.

Four years after the Battle of Kazan, Muscovites and Cossacks took Astrakhan, and the 'Mother of All Russia' was free from source to sea. There remained pockets of Tartar resistance to mop up along its eastern banks, a process that took several

Ivan's Army

Ivan the Terrible is credited, among the positive achievements partly offsetting the cruelties he perpetrated, with the creation of Russia's first standing army. It seems to have grown out of his Volga campaign, and to have been refined in wars against Poland-Lithuania and Sweden.

Its two main components came to be cavalry regiments drawn from the registered Cossacks settled along the Muscovite frontiers, and fusiliers known as streltsi, the 'ones who shoot', mostly from the poorer artisan classes. They were armed with halberds, as well as with muskets.

Neither group was under arms the whole time. Between campaigns, they could go back to farming. But, like modern-day reserves, they had to present themselves from time to time for manoeuvres, and received payment for their services.

In war, their numbers were swollen by militia from all classes, under the concept of universal military obligation which Ivan the Terrible did so much to propagate. Free Cossacks joined them from time to time, depending on their whim, and so did foreign mercenaries.

Militia officers were largely drawn from the landed classes. Free Cossacks took commands from their ataman and his lieutenants, as they always did. Only the regular regiments had what might be termed professional officers – initially these were Russians, but in due course mercenaries were also hired from Germany, Sweden, Poland, Scotland and elsewhere, hired by the Muscovite authorities. The French were not considered suitable; their Roman Catholicism might have tainted the Orthodox Christians under them.

Below: Ivan the Terrible and his army set out from the Moscow Kremlin on one of his military campaigns.

years. The Tartars of the Crimea, with the backing of the Turks, were also still a powerful threat – and one that was certainly capable of bursting through the chain of Muscovite frontier posts built to contain them and threatening Moscow itself, as they did in 1571.

But the last vestiges of the Tartar Yoke had been thrown off, and Muscovy was free to look eastwards for expansion, to the vast forests and steppe of Siberia, the 'sleeping land' Yermak and his fellow-Cossacks were about to shake awake at Ivan the Terrible's suggestion.

Their pioneering exploits rivalled any in the opening-up of the American West, and eventually brought untold wealth, as well as an immense amount of territory, to the Russian throne. But it was an expansion that suffered many setbacks before it was complete.

Years of Madness

Right: Breastplates or chainmail were commonplace among the mounted warriors of Ivan's time. But the Cossacks mostly came to scorn such protection, both because of its weight and because it made stealth impossible.

The death of his first wife Anastasia in 1560 seems to have pushed Ivan the Terrible over the thread-thin border between autocratic brutality and insanity. He believed she had been poisoned at the instigation of the old nobility, and unleashed against them the wave of terror that found its organised expression with the black horsemen of the oprichniki. In 1564, Ivan's feelings of betrayal were heightened by the defection of his military commander Prince Andrei Kurbsky to Muscovite Russia's arch-enemy Lithuania.

Perhaps encouraged by his successes against the Tartars of the Volga, Ivan had begun a territorial war against his western neighbours in 1558. It lasted on and off for 25 years and saw Russia fighting Poland-Lithuania and Sweden, while having to repel several massive Crimean Tartar attacks from the south. After some successes, the Muscovites suffered a series of defeats at the hands of the Polish-Lithuanian King Stephen Batory. When peace was finally concluded, Muscovite Russia ceded land on its northern fringes and remained, as it had started, cut off from most of western Europe.

The exception was England, whose merchant-adventurers under Sir Richard Chancellor had opened a summer trade route via Muscovy's White Sea coast. The hard-pressed Ivan vainly proposed an English-Muscovite alliance, and marriage to Elizabeth I or one of her court ladies. Annoyed by the Virgin Queen's coolness to these plans, Ivan later addressed her in a letter as a 'common tart'.

Cossacks divided

In Ivan's 25-year western campaign, Cossacks fought on both sides and began to build a reputation in the rest of Europe as roving mercenaries with little fear and an eye for booty. The divisions that became apparent in Cossackry between 1558 and 1583 shaped its future history, and that of eastern Europe to the present day.

Both Muscovy and Poland-Lithuania had their settled, registered Cossacks whose services they expected to rely on in time of war. From the beginning, the Poles enlisted their Cossacks individually, and in the 1570s they started welding them into Cossack regiments with Polish officers appointed by the crown. The Muscovites eventually copied this approach with their registered Cossacks, but at first Ivan seems to have taken them on as groups with their own commanders.

A problem was posed for both sides by the free Cossacks, on the Ukrainian marches between Poland-Lithuania and Muscovy and in their strongholds on the Dnieper, the Don and elsewhere.

Below: Ivan the Terrible shows some of his regal treasures to the English ambassador Sir Jerome Horsey. Ivan hoped for an alliance with England, but it did not materialise.

A Murderous Rage

The fits of blind rage to which Ivan the Terrible was prone grew worse as he became older and more paranoiacally suspicious of all around. On one occasion, he had an elephant hacked to pieces because it would not bow to him. More often, the victims were human – sent for torture and death by the oprichniki, or struck down by Ivan himself with the iron-tipped stave he habitually carried.

In 1581, during one temperamental storm, he killed his son and heir Ivan Ivanovich with the stave. Supposedly, the younger Ivan had been trying to protect his pregnant wife from the Tsar. As a result of this horrendous experience the hopeless woman miscarried.

Full of mixed remorse and anger, Ivan became even worse in his behaviour. His officials, fearful at all times for their lives, studiously avoided him. Legend says his aged nurse was the only person who dared approach him in the final years leading up to his death in 1584.

Much-married Ivan's murder of his rightful heir left the throne to his second son, Feodor, weak in body and feeble of mind. It paved the way for the darkest period in Russian history, the Time of Troubles, when the Cossacks became kingmakers.

Below: Ivan cradles the heir he has murdered, in a painting by one of Russia's most eminent artists, the prolific Ilya Repin (1844-1930).

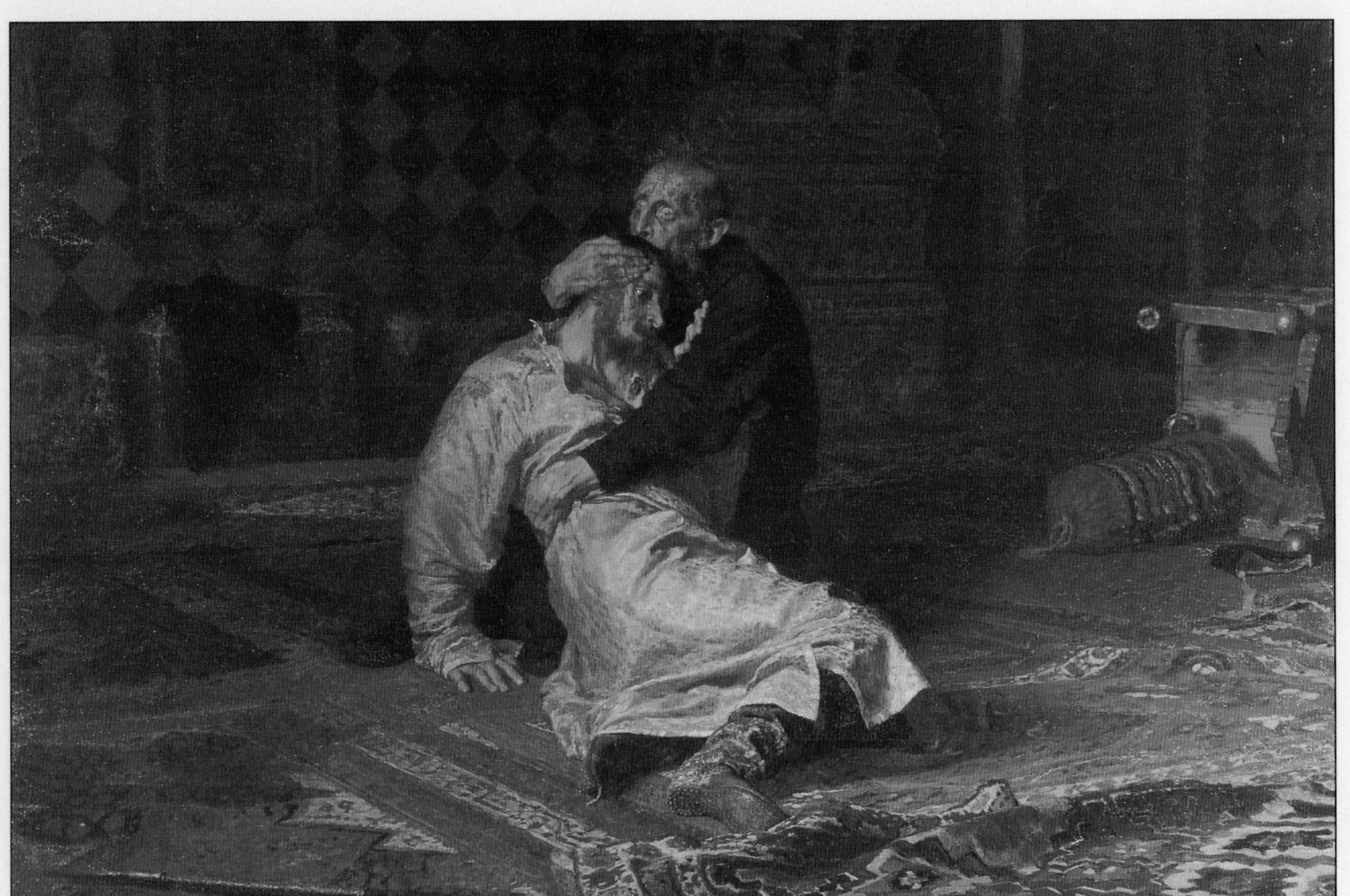

War and repression were swelling their numbers, and as renegades they had no loyalty to any state.

When the Poles started to impress free Cossacks from the border-zone of the Ukraine in the war against Muscovy, they again dealt with them as individuals, absorbing them into their military structure and persuading as many as possible to take registered status by a combination of bribes and threats. Those who resented this treatment and could evade it skulked seething in the Ukraine, joined the Muscovites or fled south to the Zaporozhskaya Sich. By contrast, the Muscovites recruited their free Cossacks en bloc, negotiating terms of service with the ataman and leaving Cossack command structures intact. There is evidence that Ivan the Terrible did not like the practice; in fact, he wrote a stinging denunciation of free Cossacks, contemptuously describing them as runaways, and in about 1578 tried to seal his borders to prevent more joining them. But he was forced to accept the situation, and the lack of control it implied.

It paid him some dividends in the west. Free Cossacks in Russian service helped to thwart Stephen Batory's army with its registered Cossacks at the siege of Pskov in 1581. However, it also stored up endless trouble for later rulers of Russia.

THE SLEEPING LAND

While many leading families lost lands and wealth in Ivan the Terrible's Muscovy, other clans seized the opportunity presented by the upheavals and the defeat of the Kazan and Astrakhan Tartars to take their place. None flourished more than the Stroganovs, who amassed by far the biggest single fortune in Russia at the time.

As the Stroganovs were not warrior nobles, they were not an immediate target for Ivan's paranoid suspicions and hideous extirpation. They were merchants and businessmen, whose early success had been built on the supply of salt, always needed as a food preservative in Muscovy, and of furs, the state's main export.

In 1558, Ivan granted them a charter to develop and exploit the newly acquired lands around Perm, between Kazan and the Ural Mountains. The arrangement was not without self-interest on the Tsar's part. The presence of the Stroganovs created a buffer between Moscow and the Tartar Khanate of Sibir or Siberia (a name that means 'sleeping land'), in the taiga immediately east of the Urals.

After the fall of Kazan, the Siberian Tartars had initially treated Ivan with respect, sending an annual tribute to him of 1,000 sable pelts and 1,000 squirrel skins. But in 1562 a new ruler, Kuchum Khan, had seized the Siberian Tartar leadership. He stopped the tribute, and began sending raiding parties of Tartars and other tribesmen over the Ural mountains, into Stroganov territories. Ivan, though he was later to take a sour view of the Cossacks, still held them in esteem as a result of the Volga campaign. In 1572, he advised the Stroganovs to recruit a band of the free steppe horsemen as protection.

The move worked well enough for a while. But if they were to be really effective, the Cossacks had to be able to chase the raiders into Siberia itself – something even the powerful Stroganovs did not dare allow without Ivan's express permission. In 1575, they got it, and much more, too. In another gesture of magnanimity mixed with canniness, Ivan granted the Cossacks a deed that gave them the right to exploit the whole of western Siberia, if they conquered it at their own expense.

Right: Cossacks proved as adept at survival in the coniferous forest of the Siberian taiga as they did on the grassland of the steppes.

Left: A 19th-century sculpture of Yermak, mysterious leader of Siberia's earliest Cossack pioneers.

Wealth of the east

To the Stroganovs, it was a further glorious opportunity. They knew the Siberian taiga from the Urals to the River Ob was a treasure-store of timber and furs, and that there was rich farming and grazing land in the river valleys and on the steppe. They hoped, rightly, that the land was also rich in minerals, tin and copper, zinc and lead.

By 1581, they had assembled a private expeditionary force of 840 men. Its leader was Yermak Timofeyevich, the Cossack who may have played a part in the Volga campaign. He brought with him some 500 freebooters from the Volga-Don region, while the Stroganovs supplied the rest from among their own employees. Though Cossacks predominated, the band included Muscovites, Lithuanians and Germans. The men were well-armed with flint rifles and halberds, swords and daggers. The Stroganovs had supplied them generously with salt meat and grain.

Yermak's force set out for Siberia along the River Kama, in shallow-drafted Cossack boats, which could either be rowed or sailed, depending on conditions, or manhandled overland. As necessary, they built other boats and rafts from the plentiful forest timber.

During 1582, Yermak and his men moved steadily east. There were occasional skirmishes with Kuchum's bands, but their bows and arrows were a poor match for the invaders' firearms. Then, in a pitched battle near the River Tobol, the Tartars and their tribal subjects were defeated.

The victory was a turning point. Yermak had lost 100 or so men, and the survivors were exhausted and near starvation. But the tribal levies had deserted their Tartar masters, and the Tartars themselves were forced to abandon their fortified capital on the River Irtysh. Yermak and his followers occupied it on October 26, 1582, and passed the long Siberian winter there, receiving tributes from the local tribes.

From this base, he sent a messenger back to Muscovy, bearing gifts of furs for Ivan the Terrible and the news that Siberia had been conquered. The unpredictable Ivan was overjoyed, rewarding Yermak with a gold breast-plate and free pardons for those of his band who were outlaws. The Tsar formally incorporated the captured territory into Muscovy and sent 500 of his regular soldiers to assist Yermak.

All this was premature. In 1583, Yermak resumed his exploration and conquest. But the Tartars had reconsidered their tactics. In hit-and-run raids, they picked off the invaders in twos and threes. Ivan's reinforcements arrived in the autumn, too late to tip the balance. Finally, on a stormy night in August 1584, Kuchum's men surprised the remnants of Yermak's followers, killing the wily Yermak himself.

The survivors fled back behind the Ural mountains. Briefly, Siberia was under Tartar control again. In 1586, the Russians returned in numbers, to find the native tribes willing to join with them against the forces of their Tartar overlords. In that year, the Russians built their first Siberian fort, or ostrog, at what is now the city of Tyumen. By 1604, they were established at the site of present-day Tomsk, deep in the Siberian heartlands, and much of the 'sleeping land' had been permanently won for the Tsar.

Left: Rivers were the highways along which Yermak and his successors opened up Russia's 'wild east'.

The Conqueror Of Siberia

Far right: Cossacks under Yermak force a river crossing during their defeat of the Siberian Tartars in 1582.

Right: Yermak's exploits are commemorated by a bust at Irkutsk, long the capital of eastern Siberia.

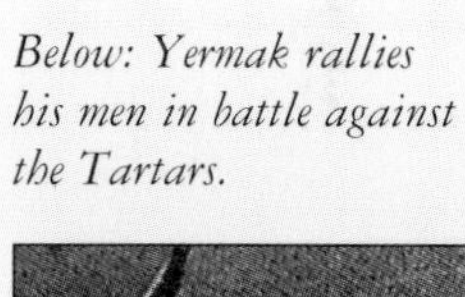

Yermak Timofeyevich's death in battle with the Siberian Tartars in 1584 is said to have been by drowning. In trying to get to safety across the River Irtysh, he was dragged down by the gold breastplate sent to him by Ivan the Terrible. According to Siberian legend, his body was found many weeks later, uncorrupted and with fresh blood running from the nose, by a fisherman who pulled it from the Irtysh waters.

Fearing the tall, bushy-bearded Cossack leader was still alive, the tribesmen summoned to inspect Yermak fired arrows by the score into his remains. From each wound, more fresh blood ran. So they left the corpse in the open, for the foxes to eat. After days, it was untouched, and the Siberians were forced to give it a respectful burial.

Like all such legends, this one hides a truth. For in the campaign that won him the nickname 'Conqueror of Siberia', Yermak made and kept a rule saintly enough by Cossack standards to preserve his corpse undecayed: Siberian tribespeople and even Tartars who fell into Russian hands were to be treated well.

Below: Yermak rallies his men in battle against the Tartars.

There were practical reasons. With a force of fewer than 900 men, Yermak could not afford to make more enemies than necessary. Nevertheless, his generosity bore its own reward. The speed with which his successors penetrated Siberia was achieved partly because many of the tribes, remembering Yermak, welcomed the Russians as kindly liberators from the oppressive Tartars.

Nothing else in the little known about Yermak suggests he had a kindly streak. He is thought to have been born about 1540, a third-generation Cossack whose surname was Alenin. He could have been among the Volga Cossacks uprooted as a result of Ivan the Terrible's conquests. Many of those fled to join the Cossacks of the Don, and most historians describe him both as a Don Cossack and as a former pirate on the Volga.

If that is true, he may have joined the Muscovite army as an irregular when it was fighting its way to Astrakhan – he boasted of having been in 40 battles – and turned to piracy later, as trade on the Volga increased. When Ivan sent his streltsi to clear out the Volga pirates, hanging those captured on floating gallows, the opportunity to work for the Stroganovs would have been attractive.

The Cossacks Yermak and his second-in-command Astashka Lavryentevich assembled for the Siberian expedition included many notorious desperadoes, used to getting their own way. To bring them into line, Yermak had any of his followers who questioned his orders bound in weighted sacks and dropped in a river – this was a traditional Cossack form of execution as well as an eery foreshadowing of his own legendary manner of death. Among the many folk songs and stories celebrating Yermak and his deeds, one has him confronting Ivan the Terrible with the captured Siberian Khan, Kuchum, and seeking the royal pardon for his past crimes. Neither the capture nor the meeting with Ivan actually took place, but the implicit equation of Siberia with expiation endured for centuries after Yermak's day.

Below: Tobolsk was founded in 1587 as a fort, near to both the old Siberian Tartar capital and the spot where Yermak reputedly drowned in 1584.

Right: Boris Godunov (reigned 1598-1605) found the Cossacks ranged against him.

The Time of Troubles

Simple-minded Feodor I, cast by a temper tantrum as Ivan the Terrible's successor, occupied the Muscovite throne for 14 years. When he died in 1598, he left no direct heir, and his only distinguishing mark on history is as the final Russian ruler from the Rurik dynasty.

It could have been otherwise. By the last of his seven wives, Ivan the Terrible had another son, Dmitri, whose claim to the Tsardom was not absolute by the complex rules of church and state, but who would have been the leading contender had he survived Feodor's death.

He did not. Dmitri perished in 1591, possibly by cutting his own throat during an epileptic fit. The path to the throne was clear for one of Ivan the Terrible's cronies, and the real ruler of Muscovy during Feodor's reign – Boris Godunov. After an initial show of reluctance, Boris accepted the Tsardom offered to him by a people's assembly.

As a ruler, Boris was in the late Ivan's mould, though he hid the fact for a long while under a cloak of seeming amiability. Once Tsar, he adopted Ivan's policy of harassing the nobles through banishments, executions and land seizures.

The lower classes of near-serf peasants and slaves were equally oppressed at first. Yet more restrictions were put on their movements, while the removal or impoverishment of many landholders meant those depending on them no longer had means of support. Then, in 1601-03, famine struck.

To his credit, Boris seems to have tried to alleviate its effects, among other things by easing restrictions on peasant movement. At the same time, however, the Muscovite borders were sealed more tightly than they had ever been, both to stop emigration to the free Cossacks and to prevent Cossacks from entering Muscovy. The result was to set huge bands of destitute, peasants and slaves roaming within the state, and to add the Cossacks to the list of people with a grievance against Boris.

Below: Hero at the Crossroads – a painting by Victor Vasnetsov (1848-1926) evokes death and doubt. Both characterise Russia's Time of Troubles.

Below right: Boris's presumed murder of the real Dmitri and the emergence of a pretender drive the plot of Alexander Pushkin's play 'Boris Godunov', on which Modest Mussorgsky's powerful opera is based.

The False Dmitri

According to Boris Godunov's supporters, the Dmitri who seized the Tsardom in 1605 was Grigori Otrepev, simultaneously an unfrocked monk and a runaway peasant who practised black magic, sodomy and the rape of nuns. Basil Shuisky, the noble who eventually killed him, at various times declared him to be an impostor and Ivan the Terrible's true son.

From the little really known about Dmitri, he seems to have been an educated Russian with some knowledge of Latin, whom the Polish nobility found congenial. He was also an excellent swordsman and horseman, qualities that would have gained him a welcome from the Zaporozhian Cossacks, among whom he is said to have lived for a while. The Zaporozhi were the first Cossacks to support his ambitious claims.

He was also almost suicidally independent minded. Once installed in Moscow, he alienated the Poles by declining to impose Roman Catholicism on the Muscovites, and the Russians by marrying his Polish sweetheart Marina and filling his court with foreigners. That brought his death in a nobles' plot led by Shuisky in 1606. His corpse was blown to pieces by a cannon, but the myth of a living Dmitri found new personifications.

Below: Swept briefly to power with the help of Zaporozhian Cossacks, False Dmitri gives an audience in the Moscow Kremlin.

The Pretender

Rumours that Boris ordered Dmitri's murder had flowed and ebbed since 1591. In Moscow, by 1600, a new version had developed – that Dmitri was not dead, but was preparing to emerge from hiding, evict Boris and take his rightful throne.

Within a couple of years, someone claiming to be Dmitri had appeared in Poland and won recognition of his identity from the Polish government. To consolidate his unofficial support from the Poles, he embraced Roman Catholicism and announced his betrothal to Marina Mniszek, daughter of a Polish noble who assisted him.

False Dmitri, as he is known, assembled an army of about 4,000 Polish adventurers, Muscovite malcontents, and Zaporozhi Cossacks, and in October 1604 he crossed the River Dnieper to march on Moscow, calling on the Cossacks of the Don to join him. That they did in their thousands, spurning a similar plea from Tsar Boris Godunov. Roaming bands of peasants and slaves, motivated by the Cossack ideal of land and freedom as well as by hunger, rallied to the cause, too.

The ragtag army suffered setbacks and defeats. But there was a seemingly endless supply of free Cossack horsemen to stiffen its sinews. Gradually, Dmitri forced his way nearer to Moscow. Then, in Holy Week 1605, Boris died suddenly after a meal, and resistance to Dmitri dissolved. On June 20, he entered the Muscovite capital to a general welcome. It was the Cossacks' first taste of kingmaking, but they achieved it only with the aid of nobles and landholders whose interests were not the Cossacks' own. In a year, they were ready to try again.

Right: *A monument to Minin and Pozharsky, who led Russian resistance against the occupying Poles in the early 17th century, now stands in a small garden by Moscow's Red Square.*

The Darkest Hour

When Basil Shuisky murdered the False Dmitri and proclaimed himself Tsar Basil IV, he cast Muscovy into a turmoil of plot and counter-plot almost beggaring description. The free Cossacks were clear from start that the control Shuisky and his clique of fellow-nobles sought to impose threatened them with serfdom. By the summer of 1606, within a few weeks of Dmitri's death and a year after they had helped put him in Moscow, the Cossacks were in revolt again, egged on by the disaffected noble Grigori Shakhovskoi.

Their leader was a runaway slave, Ivan Bolotnikov, who had fled to the Ukrainian steppe as a boy and had spent some years as a prisoner of the Tartars. His campaign against Shuisky was given a gloss of spurious legitimacy by various claims that it was to restore Dmitri or his heirs. In fact, Bolotnikov preached out-and-out revolution – death to the landholders and the rich, with the distribution of their estates, wealth and womenfolk to the poor. It proved to be an effective message with which to rally once more the Cossacks of Dnieper and Don, as well as the roving peasant masses of Muscovy.

In December 1606, within sight of Moscow, Bolotnikov's revolutionaries were defeated by Shuisky's forces. For the next year, they were hounded down. Many, like Bolotnikov himself, were executed, often by slow drowning, or enslaved. Most were just driven back to the no man's land of the steppe – readymade followers for the next revolutionary leader to emerge.

There was no shortage of those. In 1607-08, dozens of self-styled heirs to the throne appeared and disappeared. Among them was a second False Dmitri, about whom even less is known than the first. Like his predecessor, he won the support of the Poles, assembled an army which included Zaporozhian and Don Cossacks and marched to the outskirts of Moscow, where Marina Mniszek threw herself into his arms.

Enter the Poles

With the Cossack rebels outside the city gates, Shuisky resorted to desperate measures, accepting long-proffered assistance from Sweden. That enabled him to drive off the besiegers, but gave Poland an excuse for an official invasion of Muscovy. By 1610, Shuisky had been deposed by his fellow-nobles and forced to take monastic vows, and the Poles were in Moscow with Cossack supporters of their own from the Ukraine and the Dnieper. A prolonged wrangle developed over the Tsardom, which eventually fell to the King of Poland's son, Vladislav. The second False Dmitri, favoured by the rebellious Cossacks and peasants, was conveniently killed in a brawl.

Then the Polish faction sought both to unite the Polish and Muscovite thrones and to impose Roman Catholicism on Muscovy. Its Muscovite support dwindled, making the anarchy absolute. The Cossacks were in the thick of it – some still with the Poles, more with the rebel army of the late second False Dmitri, and others simply freebooting, seizing control of cities and towns as they could. In 1612, on the Volga, another uprising began.

Below, left: *Minin and Pozharsky's forces, Don Cossacks among them, drive the starving Poles out of the Moscow Kremlin in autumn 1612.*

Below, right: *A 16th-century woodcut showing typical Muscovite warriors.*

MARINA AND IVAN ZARUTSKY

Marina Mniszek, the Polish noblewoman whose marriage to the first False Dmitri briefly made her the wife of a Tsar, had driving ambition and nerves to match. After Dmitri's murder in the Moscow Kremlin, she somehow escaped the accompanying slaughter of Poles and Lithuanians, emerging to be banished to the Russian town of Yaroslavl. Freed later by Cossack rebels and brought to the headquarters of the second False Dmitri, she eagerly acknowledged him as her 'husband', living with him on his campaign until he too was killed.

Next she took as a lover the most powerful man to hand – Ivan Zarutsky, an ataman of the Don Cossacks who supported the second False Dmitri and who continued to press his rebellion. At around this time Marina gave birth to a son, Ivan nicknamed Vorenok ('little rebel'), whom she and Zarutsky shamelessly proclaimed the legitimate heir to Muscovy. Even in the 'Time of Troubles', the lie must have been apparent to many who heard it, but it suited them to believe.

Zarutsky himself was a complex character. In the chaos of shifting alliances, he and his Don Cossacks twice came close to seizing permanent power – once alongside a landholders' militia led by Prokopy Liapunov, whom the Cossacks murdered, and later with the militia of Minin and Pozharsky, which many Don Cossacks joined, but Zarutsky's immediate followers did not.

What Marina, set on regaining a place of eminence in Moscow, thought of this is not known. Zarutsky himself apparently hated the landholders more than he wanted Marina's son on the throne – and Marina went where Zarutsky went.

After the break with the other rebels, that was south to Kolomna, to Riazan and finally to

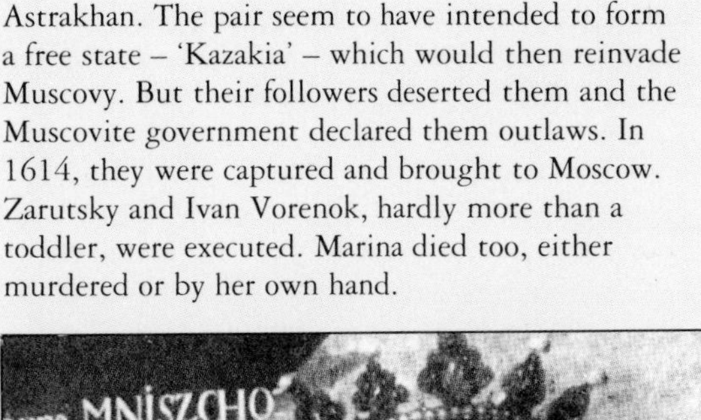

Astrakhan. The pair seem to have intended to form a free state – 'Kazakia' – which would then reinvade Muscovy. But their followers deserted them and the Muscovite government declared them outlaws. In 1614, they were captured and brought to Moscow. Zarutsky and Ivan Vorenok, hardly more than a toddler, were executed. Marina died too, either murdered or by her own hand.

Below: Marina Mniszek, wife of the first False Dmitri. Her designs on the Russian throne ultimately cost her her life.

This time its instigators were not Cossacks and peasants, but the middle classes in the persons of a butcher, Kuzma Minin, and a soldier and landholder, Dmitri Pozharsky. Their programme was simple: first, the Cossacks had to be tamed, and then the Poles had to be evicted. After that, a new Russian-born Tsar would be elected and order – that is, from their viewpoint, the rights of the middle classes – restored.

Against all the odds, Minin and Pozharsky succeeded, raising a people's militia backed by landholders which cleared the freebooting Cossacks from Muscovy's northern provinces. Next, Minin and Pozharsky contrived to divide the Cossack followers of the second False Dmitri, persuading some to join them in besieging the Poles in Moscow while the rest drifted away. After a long siege, during which the defenders ate human corpses to survive, the Poles were driven from Moscow on October 26, 1612. The stage was set for the election of a new Tsar.

Left: A Russian horse-soldier of the 16th century.

Right: Michael (reigned 1613-45), first of Russia's Romanov rulers.

Cossacks' Tsar

At the age of 16, Michael Romanov was an unprepossessing young man – sickly, shy and hardly educated. But he was distantly related to Ivan the Terrible through the family of Ivan's first wife, and both his parents were strong-willed power lovers forced into the Church for their parts in plots against Boris Godunov. When an elective assembly met in Moscow on February 21, 1613, to find a new Tsar of All the Russias in the hope of ending more than a decade of anarchy, the adolescent Michael was its unanimous choice.

The details of this election are disputed. However, the Don Cossacks who had helped Minin and Pozharsky's militia drive out the Poles clearly played a major role. Thousands of Cossacks from the Don and elsewhere were in Moscow, armed to the teeth, drunken and ever-bloodthirsty. Some, such as the Ataman Mezhakov, were members of the assembly itself.

According to one version of events, the Cossacks had decided well in advance that Michael Romanov was their man, though the reasons are obscure. Before the Mass with which the assembly was to open, a group of Don Cossacks visited the celebrant, the Abbot of Sergievo. As a result of this encounter, the Abbot preached a thundering sermon. 'You are here to choose a Tsar', it concluded. 'The Tsar is father of Russia; Moscow is mother of Russia. You cannot choose your father or mother, who are given to you by God'. From the congregation, voices cried out: 'Who then has God sent us as Tsar?' Back came the Abbot's answer: 'Michael Romanov'.

If anyone had lingering doubts about the candidate, they were dispelled by the sight of Ataman Mezhakov and the Cossack delegates rushing to be first to vote for Michael, and then glaring fiercely around as if challenging the rest of the assembly to disagree with them. The Cossack kingmakers had achieved their most notable success.

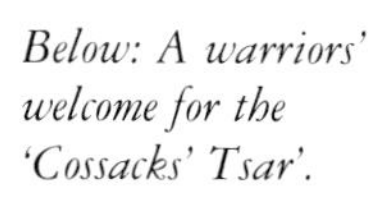

Below: A warriors' welcome for the 'Cossacks' Tsar'.

START OF A DYNASTY

Michael Romanov's father Feodor was renowned as the biggest dandy in Moscow when, in 1601, Boris Godunov forced him to take religious vows and incarcerated him in a monastery, for alleged treason and sorcery. Feodor's wife, Michael's mother, paid the same penalty, adopting the name Sister Martha in her nunnery.

Martha exerted considerable influence over Michael when he first came to the throne. But Feodor, who had risen steadily in the Orthodox Church hierarchy under the name Filaret, was by then a prisoner of the Poles. It took six years for Tsar Michael to secure his release. When that was achieved in 1619, Feodor/Filaret was promptly raised to the rank of Patriarch, head of the Russian Orthodox Church.

As both Patriarch and father of the Tsar, Filaret was the power behind Michael's throne, playing a role comparable to that of Cardinal Wolsey in England or Cardinal Richelieu in France. He demanded to be called 'Majesty', and was officially recognised as co-ruler until his death in 1633. Under Filaret's tutelage, Michael gradually restored a precarious stability in Russia. He governed with the assistance of a representative assembly, a contrast with the absolutism of Tsars both before and after. But despite this, and his generally good treatment of the free Cossacks, Michael passed laws bringing the peasantry even closer to serfdom.

The Romanov dynasty which started with Michael was to last until the Russian Revolution of 1917. Michael died in 1645, and was succeeded by his son Alexis.

Far left: Patriarch Filaret; Tsar's father, church leader and power behind the throne.

Left: Young Michael Romanov enters Moscow in 1613, the year of his election to the Tsardom.

Repaying a debt

Michael's realm was devastated and bankrupt when he came to the throne. Wars and famine had reduced the population by one-third, to fewer than 9 million. Hordes of Cossacks and landless peasants still roamed the countryside, supporting an increasingly bizarre collection of self-styled heirs to the throne. The Poles, Swedes and Crimean Tartars were still menacing. Guided at first by his mother and a national assembly, and later by his father, Michael took years to restore any semblance of order to his realm.

The 'Cossacks' Tsar' was quick, however, to reward those who had helped put him where he was. He chose, or was advised, to do so through their leaders and their free communities on the rivers of no man's land. One result was gradually to draw the roving bands out of Russia and to the south and south-west.

The Don Cossacks were the first favoured. By the end of 1615, Michael had concluded arrangements to send them regular sums of money, grain and ammunition. They were allowed to move freely in and out of his Tsardom, and to trade there without paying tax. In return, he expected their loyalty as 'protectors of Russia'.

Using the Don Cossacks as emissaries, Michael eventually struck similar bargains with other free Cossack hosts on the River Yaik (Ural) and on the Dnieper – the unruly Zaporozhi. Settlements depleted in the Time of Troubles grew again.

Michael's dealings with the Cossacks were born out of desperation, more on his side than on theirs. Although he exacted a degree of loyalty from them, he also left them a great deal of freedom in their affairs. They went eagerly back to their old occupations of brigandry and piracy, though the Tsar's realm was in theory out of bounds. They also largely decided for themselves who, when and where to fight. This freedom created endless opportunities for embarrassing and angering the Moscow authorities, as the Cossacks frequently did.

THE COSSACKS AT HOME

With Russian government money and grain assured and permission to trade, the free Cossack communities of the Lower Dnieper and Don, the Yaik and the Terek began to prosper and grow in the 17th century. Their rivers were full of fish, the steppe was full of game – and what they lacked could be acquired by raids on the affluent Turkish empire to the south.

Cossack life changed to reflect this new prosperity. Their settlements became more permanent affairs of wooden huts rather than improvised hovels. But the Cossacks continued to spurn farming, other than the seasonal haymaking from the steppe grass that was necessary to provide winter fodder for their horses. Long absences fighting did not sit well with agriculture.

The fierce egalitarianism of the earliest, wildest days in theory remained. But the annually elected ataman was no longer a scruffy first among equals. He became an imposing figure amid his horsetail standards – the symbol of authority copied from the Tartars – and rich banners such as one presented to the Don Cossacks by Tsar Michael Romanov. With his lieutenants, the ataman took most decisions for the community. Full assemblies of all Cossack males, when summoned, were mostly to confirm plans already made, though what was lost in power was gained in pomp.

Their kingmaking activities, and the flattery they received from Tsar Michael or others seeking their fighting services, increased the Cossacks' self-esteem. The bachelor warriors of the Zaporozhi styled themselves ritsari (knights) and Michael referred to the 'Knights of the Don'.

Chivalry, however, was never part of any free Cossack code. Women were a pastime like drinking and killing – and seemed to accept that. Their numbers grew as the Cossack way of life became relatively settled, and marriage was common, though usually unblessed by clergy. But the womenfolk were as free as the men to change partners, and participated as freely in Cossack orgies of drink and sex, so eye-witnesses say. They also fought alongside their men when necessary.

Below: From the 16th century, famines, poverty and social upheavals drove thousands of Russian peasants to the steppes, to swell the free Cossack communities.

Left: The royal stamp of Tsar Michael, who granted extensive privileges to free Cossacks on the borders of his territory.

Below: Peter Sahaidachny was leader of the free Zaporozhian Cossacks when they launched a massive raid against the Crimean Tartars in 1617. Later, he entered Polish service, commanding a Ukrainian Cossack force to victory over the Turks. The feat brought the Cossacks little reward, and that nurtured their mounting list of grievances against Poland.

The hosts mingle

By using the Don Cossacks as his emissaries in no man's land, Michael increased the contacts between the free Cossack hosts. Although each had its roughly defined territory, all shared the twin ideals of land and freedom that had driven Cossack rebels such as Ivan Zarutsky during the Time of Troubles. There was plenty of both commodities on the south-western steppe in the first half of the 17th century, despite the return of surviving Cossacks who had gone campaigning with Zarutsky and his like, and the continued influx of Russian peasants and serfs.

The Zaporozhi and Don Cossacks, oldest and biggest of the hosts, frequently cooperated in raids on the Crimean Tartars and Turks. In the 1620s, for example, hundreds of Zaporozhi warriors were living semi-permanently on the Don, so that massive joint attacks could be quickly mounted. The Yaik (Ural) Cossacks from east of the Volga often joined in, too. Those from the Terek, between the Caucasus Mountains and the Caspian Sea, were partly cut off from the rest by hostile steppe tribes in between. But there were regular contacts, in particular, between the Terek and the Don.

To the north and west, in the Ukraine, was by far the largest Cossack group of all, numbering anything up to 500,000 against the few thousands of Dnieper and Don. But the Ukrainian Cossacks were not free hosts under generous Russian patronage. They were held down by Polish and Lithuanian governors who used the individual registration system as whip and spur. While the free Cossacks thought of plunder and, occasionally, the Tsar, their counterparts in the Polish Ukraine thought of revolt.

Revenge and Rebellion

Turbulent Marches

When Tsar Michael I was elected to the Russian throne in 1613, much of the Ukrainian border region between Russia and Poland had been brought under Polish control, first by creeping settlement and then by formal annexation. But the Cossacks who had originally come to the Ukraine in the quest for land and freedom passionately resented Polish authority, which sought to limit both.

The main focus of their anger was the Polish registration system, which recognised a few thousand individual Ukrainian Cossacks as privileged free men in return for military service, while leaving the rest as tied peasants or serfs.

Below: Polish fighting men of the 17th century.

In itself, the division between the registered few and the unregistered many was an affront to Cossack ideals of liberty and equality. The Poles made matters worse by using the system cynically. When they needed Cossacks to fight for them, they sometimes promised to enlarge the register. Once the need seemed to have disappeared, they either completely ignored the pledge, or immediately set about undermining it. So Cossacks who had spilt blood for Poland often found themselves rewarded only with a return to oppression. Notably, that was the case for most of the men enlisted by Peter Sahaidachny in 1620, for Poland's war against Turkey. Though the Cossacks delivered victory, they received little.

The Poles frowned, too, on the Cossack tradition of freebooting. As early as 1584, for example, they had three dozen Cossacks tortured to death in front of the Turkish ambassador for unauthorised raids on the Crimean Tartars, whom Poland at that moment did not want to offend.

As discontent grew, Cossack uprisings in the Ukraine became more and more frequent. Generally, these involved unregistered Cossacks, often provided with assistance by the free Zaporozhi of the lower Dnieper River. But registered Cossacks took part, too.

The Poles responded by tightening the screw. In 1596, they declared lands held by unregistered Cossacks to be forfeit. A few years later, they tried to abolish the Ukrainian Cossacks' own system of self-government, by making them subject to the authority of local landowners or the Polish crown. Eventually, they decreed that Cossacks could live only on crown estates, thereby forcing many from their homes.

From time to time, the Cossacks managed to secure an increase in the numbers on the register. In 1630, Ukrainian rebels and Zaporozhi Cossacks defeated a Polish army, and the Poles bought them off by enlarging the register from 6,000 to 8,000 names. In 1632-33, the Cossacks refused to fight for Poland against Russia until the register was extended again. Even after they had got their way, there were perhaps ten unregistered adult male Ukrainians claiming to be Cossacks for every one who was registered.

These Cossack successes, few and small though they were, proved counter-productive. The Poles determined to stamp out Cossack rebellion at what they considered to be its source – by removing the influence of the free Zaporozhi.

CHAMPIONS OF THE ORTHODOX FAITH

Jesuit missionaries of the Roman Catholic Church, who appeared in their scores in eastern Europe from about 1570, lit religious fires that are still burning. In a way they could never have foreseen, they also raised religious awareness among the Cossacks.

Officially, the Jesuits' purpose was to counteract a growing wave of Protestantism. But on Poland's eastern marches they found an older and equally despised rival – Orthodox Christianity, which had parted company with Rome five centuries earlier. Ukrainian Orthodoxy, in particular, was in disarray, with leaders said to be as greedy and corrupt as the worst of the Cossacks.

The zealous and aggressive Jesuits set about bringing the followers of Orthodoxy to Rome. Orthodox landowners, who ultimately relied on the favours of Roman Catholic Poland to prosper, were cajoled and pressured into Catholicism. Their tenants and serfs were then converted by force.

One large faction of the Orthodox hierarchy made a special deal. Its leaders submitted to the authority of the Roman Catholic Pope, but were allowed to keep an Orthodox form of religious ceremony. These were the Uniates, and their form of Christianity survives, despite vicissitudes, in the present-day western Ukraine.

The Uniates seized control of many Orthodox churches, including those in Kiev, cradle of the Christian faith in Russia. Non-Uniate priests were driven away or killed. Any of their followers who did not accept Uniatism were denounced as heretics and traitors. Even Orthodox graves were despoiled as part of a purge instigated by the Uniate Archbishop Joasaphat of Tobolsk.

The doctrinal aspects of these sometimes violent religious disputes were of little interest to most Cossacks, whose previous attitude towards all religion had been apathetic when it was not hostile. But Roman Catholicism and Uniatism came to be seen as instruments of Polish repression, and the persecuted Orthodox cause became a standard the Cossacks could raise to rally support.

In 1620, as part of complicated negotiations over the assembly of a force to help fight the Turks, the Cossack leader Peter Konashevich Sahaidachny persuaded Poland to accept the restoration of an Orthodox hierarchy in Kiev. That concession was the first obtained by the Cossacks in their unlikely new role as champions of Orthodoxy.

Roman Catholicism and Uniatism were not the only creeds the Cossacks came to oppose in the name of Orthodoxy. Poles who had taken over land on the steppe often installed Jews to manage estates or run stores on their behalf, and so Judaism, too, became associated with Polish domination. Many historians believe that contributed to the anti-semitism which disfigures the Cossack story from the 17th century.

Below: Palm Sunday in a 17th-century Russian settlement. Such moments of peace were rare for the Orthodox inhabitants of the troubled Ukraine.

A UKRAINIAN HERO

Right: Bogdan Khmelnitsky (1595-1657), Cossack leader of the Ukraine.

For the mass of Ukrainian Cossacks – the golota, or 'have-nots' – life under Polish domination around the start of the 17th century was a harsh struggle for survival. But for those securely placed on the all-important Polish Cossack register, matters were very different. Loyal military service could bring its rewards in the shape of an income, a small estate and the chance to live as a country gentlemen in between spells of duty.

That was the enviable situation of Michael Khmelnitsky in 1595, when his wife gave birth to a son. Perhaps in recognition of such good fortune amid the deprivation of his fellow-Cossacks, Michael named the boy Bogdan – 'God's Gift'.

The young Bogdan Khmelnitsky proved himself both bright and brave. After being educated by the Jesuits, he went to learn the arts of war Cossack-style from the bachelor 'knights' of the Zaporozhskaya Sich, joining them in various raids aganist the Turks and Tartars. Then, in his mid-twenties, he came back to inherit the family estate and settle down.

For fifteen years or so, Bogdan flourished, marrying, raising a family and obtaining the important post of adjutant to the registered Cossack host. In 1637-38, things started to go wrong, disrupting the settled existence Bogdan had chosen.

Below: Painting of a Ukrainian landscape in the evening, by the 19th-century artist Kuindzhi.

Fed up with constant Cossack rebellions, the Polish authorities had begun their toughest campaign against them. They built a fort on the River Dnieper above the Zaporozhskaya Sich to prevent the Zaporozhi from entering Polish territory and to stop Ukrainian Cossacks from fleeing south to join them. They inflicted defeats on a succession of rebel Cossack forces. And they set about reforming the Cossack register. The number of registered Cossacks was cut from 10,000 to 6,000, and those excised from the list were deprived of their estates. The last vestiges of registered Cossack autonomy – including a say in the selection of their officers – were removed.

It is not clear what part Bogdan Khmelnitsky played in these events. By the end of them he had lost his adjutancy and was demoted to a mere company commander. His lands were not forfeit, but in 1647 he was driven from them by a terror campaign organised by local Polish officials, during which one of Bogdan's sons was killed.

Khmelnitsky's revolt

With his own life under threat and little faith in Polish justice, Bogdan fled like so many before him to the Zaporozhskaya Sich where he had served as young man. There, he succeeded in persuading the free Cossacks to mount yet another onslaught on the Poles. Deviously, he also managed to obtain backing from the Tartars of the Crimea, by convincing them that they were about to be attacked by Poland.

Early in 1648, the Zaporozhi stormed the Polish fort on the Dnieper. They sacked it, and the registered Cossacks in the garrison joined them. Then, at the head of a Cossack force 8,000 strong and with several thousand Tartars in support, Bogdan marched north. In two pitched battles within two weeks, he defeated the cream of the Polish army, luring many more registered Cossacks to his ranks and capturing dozens of Polish nobles for later ransom.

It was a signal for all the oppressed masses of the Ukraine to rise in revolt against their Polish masters – and anyone else who had offended them. For the Cossacks and the Ukrainian peasants, that included the Jews. Hundreds of Jewish men, women and children were tortured and slaughtered, and their synagogues desecrated. Only those few who would accept Orthodox Christianity, or those lucky enough to be taken by Tartars, were spared.

In 1649, after another heavy defeat, the Poles negotiated peace with Bogdan. Cossack self-government was restored and the register was expanded to 40,000 names. The Ukraine east of Kiev was to become effectively a Cossack state from which Jews and Jesuits were barred, and in which Roman Catholics were forbidden to own land. Bogdan was to rule over it as hetman (the Polish version of the Cossack title ataman), answerable only to the Polish king.

The agreement lasted hardly a year. The Poles succeeded in subverting Bogdan's Tartar allies, and he faced dissent among sections of his followers. In an attempt to buy peace, Bogdan allowed Poland to reduce the list of concessions it had granted him earlier, but his supporters would not approve the changes. That meant another war with the Poles, this time without Tartar help. In desperation, Bogdan sought to put the Ukrainian Cossacks under the protection of the Russian Tsar, Michael Romanov's son Alexis.

The Russians, who for some time had been supplying the Ukrainian Cossacks with weapons, were not keen on a closer association. They dithered for three years while bloody skirmishes brought the Cossacks nearer to total defeat and devastated the Ukraine. Finally, Moscow agreed. In January 1654, Bogdan's Cossacks took their oath of loyalty to the Tsar. In return, the Cossacks secured an enlargement of the register to 60,000 names, the right to self-government, and freedom to conduct diplomatic relations with all states apart from Poland and Turkey. It was, in one view of events, the crowning achievement of Bogdan Khmelnitsky's up-and-down career.

Above: Bogdan's monument near the Cathedral of St Sophia in Kiev.

Divided by the Dnieper

If the Cossacks and peasants of the Ukraine burned with hatred of Polish rule and religion, so did many Russians when they remembered Poland's attempts to seize the Russian throne during their own Time of Troubles. An armistice of 1618 brought those hostilities to a close, but to conclude it Russia had been forced to cede a large slice of its westernmost territories. The switch in allegiance of Bogdan Khmelnitsky's Ukraine from Polish King to Russian Tsar made it certain that Poland would declare war again. The Russians, with a new Cossack host at their disposal, struck first.

In 1654-56, Ukrainian Cossacks and Russian troops together thrust north and westward, regaining the old Russian city of Smolensk and capturing the ancient Lithuanian capital of Vilna. Then Sweden joined in by invading Poland. Russia promptly attacked the Swedes.

His Cossack eye, as ever, on the main chance, Bogdan Khmelnitsky used the confusion to approach the Swedish King Charles X with a scheme to turn the Ukraine into an autonomous state under Charles's protection. In Russian eyes, it was a staggering act of treachery by a man who, only a couple of years earlier, had struck a similar bargain with the Tsar. As a result, Moscow never fully trusted the Ukrainian Cossacks again.

The plan came to nothing, and for Bogdan it hardly mattered. Broken by years of campaigning, plotting and hard drinking, he died of a stroke in 1657, at the age of 62. With his death, the last hopes of Ukrainian autonomy vanished. The Cossacks promptly fell into disarray. Ivan Vygovsky, Bogdan's adjutant, seized the leadership and took the Cossacks over to the Polish side. Then he made the fatal mistake of using Tartar mercenaries to suppress discontent among his poorer followers. Yuri Khmelnitsky, a son of Bogdan, was swept to power in Ivan's place. Briefly, Yuri honoured his father's pact with the Tsar, before he, too, switched allegiance to Poland.

But not all the Ukrainian Cossacks followed him. Those in the eastern Ukraine, furthest from Poland, elected a new leader, Ivan Briukhovetsky, and kept faith with Russia.

When Russia and Poland, worn out by their struggles, signed the 13-year Peace of Andrusovo in 1667, this division between east and west was formalised, with the River Dnieper as the frontier. Russia kept control of the eastern Ukraine – the left bank of the Dnieper – and the city of Kiev, while Poland's territory ended at the right bank. The Cossacks either side of the river were divided, too, between Briukhovetsky's 'Russian' host and the 'Polish' host under a new leader, Peter Doroshenko.

Buying loyalty

The Polish registration system which enabled some Ukrainian Cossacks to become landed gentry did not always secure total loyalty, as Khmelnitsky's career showed. That did not prevent the Russians from copying it once their influence expanded in the Ukraine. Ivan Briukhovetsky, ataman of the Left Bank Cossacks, was rewarded for his support for Moscow with estates, the noble rank of boyar and the hand of a noblewoman in marriage. Not only did he accept these bribes, but he revelled in them, becoming an owner of serfs.

Right: Cossacks at rest. Taras Bulba and his sons lie sleeping, in an illustration from Gogol's novel.

TARAS BULBA

The real-life Bogdan Khmelnitsky probably helped to inspire the character of one of Russia's best-known fictional Cossacks, Taras Bulba, hero of Nikolai Gogol's 1835 novel of that name. Like Bogdan, Taras was a 17th-century Ukrainian Cossack leader who spent years struggling against the Poles.

In the novel, Taras's son Andrei falls in love with a Polish girl and deserts the Cossacks for her. The pair are inside a Polish fortress which the Cossacks besiege. When Andrei takes part in a sally, he encounters his father Taras, who kills him as a traitor. Taras's other son, Ostap, is meanwhile captured, tortured and killed by the Poles. Taras is depicted as a pipe-smoking, moustachioed man of action, both endearing and cruel. The combination very much reflects a Russian view of the Cossacks at the time Gogol was writing, after the Napoleonic Wars in which they had played a crucial role. Gogol's forebears were gentry with Cossack connections, from the eastern Ukraine. One of his ancestors reputedly sided with the Poles in the 17th-century Ukrainian conflicts.

The novel 'Taras Bulba' is not only rich in descriptions of Cossacks and Poles in battle, but evocative, too, of the Ukrainian countryside.

Below: Taras Bulba, with splendid drooping moustache in the Ukrainian and 'Zaporozhian Cossack style... and his less-flamboyantly moustached creator, Nikolai Gogol (1809-52).

Nothing could have been better calculated to inflame the masses. Doroshenko's Right Bank Cossacks stormed across the Dnieper, overthrew and murdered the 'corrupt' Briukhovetsky and briefly reunited the Ukraine. Then Doroshenko decided to cut all links with both Poland and Moscow, seeking protection from the Turkish sultan. His action unleashed a triangular struggle between Poles, Russians and Turks over possession of the Ukraine, with the Cossacks caught in the middle, shifting allegiances as circumstances dictated.

It lasted two decades, a period of Ukrainian history called The Ruin. At the end of it, about 1689, Russia controlled both banks of the Dnieper, but the southern Ukraine was still a no man's land at the mercy of the Crimean Tartars and Turkey. The Ukrainian Cossacks were largely under Moscow's thumb and fast losing their separate identity. Continuing the process begun by Poland, the Russians bolstered the position of a few landed Cossacks, who became largely indistinguishable in behaviour and attitudes from landowners in Russia itself. The vast mass of Cossacks came to be treated, both by their immediate overlords and by the Russians, as ordinary peasants or serfs. Ultimately, all trace of their Cossackry was to disappear.

But on the lower Dnieper the free-spirited Zaporozhi kept the Cossack flame burning brightly. Wisely, they had rejected Bogdan Khmelnitsky's advice to join his original alliance of the Ukraine with Russia, and the Russians had failed to secure control of the fastness of the Zaporozhskaya Sich. That particular lack of success was to goad Moscow for years to come.

LAND WARRIORS OF RENOWN

Spectacular victories against the might of Poland in Bogdan Khmelnitsky's campaign of 1648-49 confirmed the growing international reputation of the Cossacks as doughty land warriors. Swedes, Turks, Austrians, even the English writer and clergyman Samuel Purchas all spoke respectfully of their courage, fierceness, endurance – and their aptitude for surprise attacks. Any army that could afford to buy their loyalty was glad to have them on its side.

Bogdan's host of 4,000-8,000 Zaporozhi and Ukrainian Cossacks was heavily influenced by Polish military traditions and so not altogether typical of Cossack fighting groups of the time. When it set out to confront the Poles in the spring of 1648, it had, for example, the luxury of several cannons under a specialist commander of ordnance. Among the Zaporozhi, foot-soldiers outnumbered horsemen, and in several of Bogdan's encounters his Tartar allies played the sort of role Cossack horse-warriors soon came to make their own. In other respects, though, all Cossack fighters had much in common with each other.

Like the Mongols before them, they were theoretically and loosely organised into platoons of ten and companies of one hundred. Uniforms were largely non-existent, a characteristic that lasted among the free Cossacks until the 19th century; however, kaftans and baggy trousers tucked into boots or Turkish-style slippers were common wear. The Cossacks scorned armour. What they lost in protection they gained in the ability to move quickly and silently, whether on horseback, foot, or in a boat.

A curved sabre, daggers and a musket (later, a carbine) were their chief weapons, to which they added a pike or lance and pistols as occasion or opportunity arose.

Below: A.M. Gerrassimov's painting of Taras Bulba, the fictional archetype of Cossack warriors.

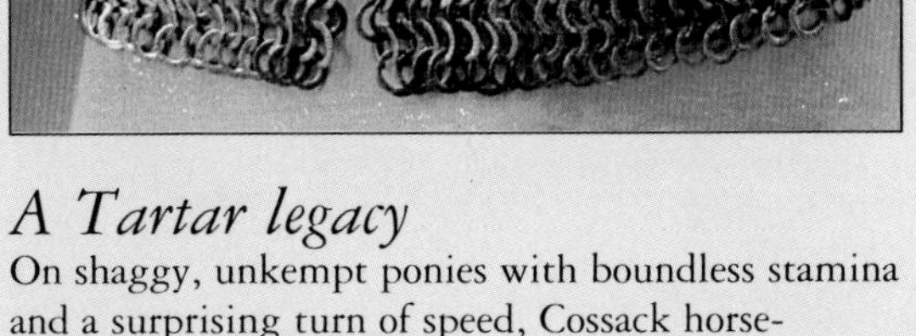

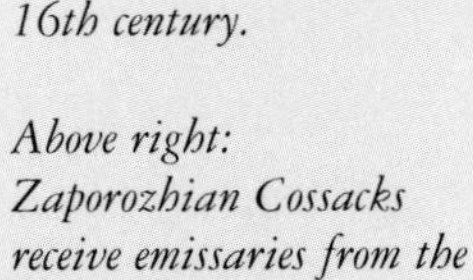

A Tartar legacy

On shaggy, unkempt ponies with boundless stamina and a surprising turn of speed, Cossack horse-warriors were the direct heirs of the Mongol and Tartar invaders of the steppe and enjoyed a heritage of formidable military skills. From the Tartars, they learnt how they and their mounts could live more or less permanently off the land when campaigning, even when forage was thin. They learnt, too, the Tartar arts of horsemanship – amazing feats of daredevilry in which, for example, a rider could pick objects from the ground or stand on his feet or his head in the saddle, all at full gallop.

The control needed for these and other skills was the more impressive because the Cossacks rode their horses lightly. Mostly, they did not wear spurs, though all carried a whip. Their bridlery was knotted together, with at most one or two metal buckles or rings, and throughout their history the Cossacks stuck to a single rein with a simple snaffle-bit, rather than the complex, four-reined snaffle-and-curb arrangements that more orthodox cavalry came to prefer. Again, the absence of metal helped Cossack horse-patrols to move quietly; the slightest clink of weaponry or accoutrements was a heinous crime when Cossacks were scouting or laying ambush.

Cossack – style riding was not just a series of party tricks. The horsemanship it honed came to formidable practical use in fighting – notably in the way the Cossacks, like the Mongols, often approached an engagement in dispersed groups, coalescing only at the last moment. In one version of the Cossack charge, horsemen would spread wide in three or four lines abreast stretching beyond the enemy's flanks, galloping in that formation to engage until a weak spot revealed itself. Then they would come together with uncanny precision to over-run it. In another version, the horsemen would gallop towards the enemy, each riding in an individual, disconcerting, corkscrew pattern until the last moment. Such bewildering formations made it much more difficult for their opponents to pinpoint exactly where the full impact of the charge would come.

The same swift precision could be used defensively. Large groups of Cossacks on the march with supply waggons could, if attacked, form a tabor – akin to US Wild West waggon circles – to shelter men and horses in a matter of minutes. From those, they were hard to dislodge, even when heavily outnumbered.

But the Cossacks' chief value to orthodox army commanders, as it came to evolve from the 17th century, was as scouts, organisers of ambushes and harriers in front of and behind the lines. In all of those roles, their steppecraft made them unequalled. From Bogdan's campaigns onwards, mounted Cossacks had another special and terrible function – to pursue and ride down a retreating enemy. It was one they continued to perform without mercy for more than 200 years.

Above left: Russian chain-mail armour of the 16th century.

Above right: Zaporozhian Cossacks receive emissaries from the Tsar. Relations between the Dnieper and Moscow were always stormy.

Tartar and Turk

Right: The Ottoman Turks forcibly converted suitable male Christian prisoners-of-war to Islam and made them serve as infantrymen in the Sultan's personal guard. They were called janissaries, from Turkish words meaning 'new soldiers'. After about 1600, ordinary Muslims were also allowed to join the janissaries, who acquired a reputation as a 'death or glory' elite. The Corps of Janissaries was disbanded in 1826.

While bloody and complex struggles for power racked the Ukraine during most of the 17th century, other conflicts were taking place in the no man's land of the steppe to the south and east. At their centre were the Crimean Tartars, the last vestige of the Golden Horde and now under the suzerainty of the Ottoman Turkish empire.

The Tartars exploited Russia's weakness during the early years of Michael Romanov's Tsardom and the subsequent Ukrainian troubles, to continue their centuries-old practice of preying on their Slav neighbours. Mostly, that involved raids in search of booty and slaves. But occasionally the Tartars were drawn by the old lure of territory and tribute, when either Poland or Russia seemed off its guard.

Bogdan Khmelnitsky's Zhaporozhi and Ukrainian Cossacks showed they could accept the Tartars as colleagues if expedient; the rest of the time they and their Turkish masters were fair game for Zhaporozhi brigandry and piracy. The Don Cossacks looked on Tartars and Turks as hereditary enemies, and were almost permanently in arms against them. In part, that was why Michael Romanov supplied the Don with foodstuffs and weaponry. However, Michael was anxious not to offend Turkey, so he tried to keep a brake on what could be seen as Cossack provocation.

In the 1620s, Don and Zaporozhi attacks on Turkish shipping started a cycle of reprisal and counter-reprisals with the Tartars, in which both Tartar and Don Cossack villages were burnt and scores on both sides were killed. Fearing Turkey might declare war on Russia as a result, Tsar Michael vented his anger. The Zaporozhi were beyond his reach, but he cut off aid to the Don and threatened its Cossacks with excommunication from the Orthodox Church. A messenger sent from Moscow to ensure the orders against unprovoked aggression were understood was murdered, and the Don Cossacks carried on as before with their bloody private feud.

Below: The strategically sited fort of Azov fell to the Cossacks in 1637, reverted to Turkey, and fell again to Cossack and Russian forces in 1696.

In the 1630s, Tartar forays against Russia's southern flank became more frequent and sustained. Tsar Michael saw no reason to deter the Cossacks from fighting back, and relations between the Don and Moscow improved. As so often, however, there was a basic conflict of aims.

Michael merely wanted the Don Cossacks to protect his frontier. They, though, had been working for years on an altogether grander plan – the capture of the Turkish stronghold of Azov. A host of some 12,000 Don, Zaporozhi and displaced Ukrainian Cossacks set out in spring 1637 to take it, while the Turks were engaged in an Asian war against Persia.

THE IMPORTANCE OF AZOV

Sprawled like a malevolent spider to Cossack eyes, the heavily fortified Turkish port of Azov sat at the mouth of the Don, controlling access from the river out through the Kerch Straits to the Black Sea, with its rich opportunities for piracy. Azov's heart was its citadel, a massive affair of three squat, thick concentric stone ramparts within a deep ditch. Its battlements bristled with cannon, and it was garrisoned by several thousand janissaries, the elite soldier-slaves of the Turkish army.

Don Cossacks could and did work their way around Azov on journeys between their settlements upstream and the Black Sea waters. But to do so was time-consuming, limiting or risky, or a combination of all three. Far better if the port were in Cossack hands.

The Cossack host which streamed down the Don to Azov in 1637 first tried a full-frontal assault. That was easily repulsed, with heavy losses. So the Cossacks invested the citadel for a period of two months, waiting for further reinforcements and consignments of gunpowder. Then they blew a hole in the outer rampart.

Through the gap the Cossacks poured, to take on the janissaries hand-to-hand. The fighting lasted several days, and hundreds died. But finally the janissaries were winkled out. To celebrate their victory, the Cossacks looted vigorously, and began to settle in. Expecting the Turks to mount a counter-attack in due course, they asked the Tsar several times to intervene on their behalf by annexing Azov and sending troops to help in its defence. Cautious Michael declined, though he provided food and ammunition for the defenders.

For four years, the Turks delayed. When they did arrive, in summer 1641, it was in full force – 200 ships with 40,000 men and 100 powerful siege cannon. At an almost leisurely pace, they began reducing Azov's walls, punctuating the bombardment with assaults. Cossack numbers dwindled, food and ammunition ran low and the defenders were near desperation. Suddenly, for no clear reason, the Turks withdrew, and the Cossack survivors were left in peace at last, in sole possession of Azov's ruins.

Again, they asked Michael to annex the port, and again he turned down the offer. In 1642, he ordered the Cossacks to leave. Reluctantly, but recognising that Azov's ruined state made it undefendable, they complied.

By 1660, Azov was back in Turkish hands, refortified and again blocking the Cossacks' route from the Don to the sea. In 1696, in Peter the Great's first military campaign, it fell to a mixed land and sea force of Russians and Cossacks. It was to change hands several times more before it securely became part of Russia.

Below: The Turks as besiegers – attacking a citadel by land and sea in the mid-17th century.

SCOURGE OF THE 'SEAGULLS'

In low, rough-hewn boats called chaiki (seagulls), free Zaporozhi and Don Cossacks continued the marauding Viking tradition of their Varangian forebears on southern Russian rivers and the Black and Caspian Seas throughout the 17th century. A rueful Turkish observer said Cossack pirates were the most skilful and brave seamen of his day.

The Turks and their vassals the Crimean Tartars were the chief targets for Cossack sea-raids. But in their quest for booty Cossacks would attack anyone. Russian, Polish and Persian shipping all suffered at their hands.

Chaiki were simple to make. Some were hardly more than dugout canoes carved from a single tree-trunk. Others were put together from planks, with rope and iron fastenings, upswept at the prow and stern. The biggest were 20 metres (67ft) long and 3-4 metres (10-13ft) wide, with a draught of about 3 metres (10ft) and very little freeboard. In the open sea, they needed bundles of rushes along the gunwales to improve their buoyancy.

The largest chaiki could carry 50-60 Cossacks with their weapons and provisions. Each boat had a single square sail for extra speed in fair weather and a following wind. Usually, though, it was rowed, with two men to an oar when pursuing or pursued, and one per oar at other times. To steer, there was a massive paddle at the stern, and sometimes another at the bow.

Fast and manoeuvrable, the chaiki were more than a match for the cumbersome merchantmen and warships of Turkey and Persia, and for the heavy Russian barges that plied the Volga. Sitting low in the water, they offered very little target for cannons. Their shallow draught enabled them to lurk in creeks where the enemy could not follow. In the last resort, they could be manhandled overland.

Right: A contemporary illustration of Cossack chaiki raiding a fortfied Turkish port in the early 17th century. The small Cossack boats could easily out-maneouvre cumbersome Turkish galleys.

Pirate fleets

Above: Land and water encounter between Turks and Christians, as envisaged by the 16th-century Italian painter Tintoretto.

Below: This 20th-century engraving emphasises the bawdy romanticism associated with Cossack piracy.

To raid merchant shipping, the chaiki generally operated in small groups, slipping out from Cossack river strongholds under cover of darkness. When a likely target vessel appeared, they would shadow it from a distance, and then swarm to attack it out of the sun at dawn or dusk.

But both the Zaporozhi and the Don Cossacks, together and separately, regularly assembled huge fleets of 100 or more chaiki for forays against Turkish settlements around the Black Sea. Even the Turkish capital of Constantinople was not safe from their attacks. In 1615, they set fire to ships in its harbour, and they returned there year after year to wreak havoc.

The Turks were largely powerless to deal with the pirates, though they had some successes. In 1634, for example, they killed or captured 3,000 during a raid on Constantinople. But more often than not, the Cossacks outwitted them, either by using the speed of the chaiki to escape or, in a marine adaptation of their battle-tactics on land, feigning retreat to draw and isolate an enemy before turning on him.

The Turks made attempts to prevent the Zaporozhi Cossacks from getting into the Black Sea by slinging a huge chain across the mouth of the River Dnieper. But in the river network of the southern Ukraine, there were other routes which could be reached by portages – and the Zaporozhi made full use of those. It was only in the 18th century, when the Russians simultaneously developed a navy and brought the southern steppes under firmer control, that Zaporozhian and Don Cossack piracy began to decline.

The Old Believers

The number of fingers a Christian extends when making the sign of the Cross may seem of relatively small importance looked at from a modern, secular viewpoint. In Russia from 1667, it could literally mean the difference between life and death.

That year, a council of the Russian Orthodox Church decided all true believers must use three fingers in crossing themselves, instead of the hitherto traditional two, or five among priests. The aim of the reform, and of many other changes in religious details that went with it, was to bring ritual in Russia back into line with Greek Orthodox practice after several centuries in which they had drifted apart.

The man largely responsible for these developments was Nikon, a half-educated peasant of vast energy who had risen from obscurity to become patriarch or head of the Russian Church. From that position, like Filaret in the reign of Michael Romanov, he operated as the real power behind the throne of Tsar Alexis.

Below: The Holy Trinity, by Russia's greatest icon-painter, Andrei Rublev (c.1360-1430).

Nikon's motives for reforms may have stemmed from a genuine desire to reunite Christianity; he even found some good words to say about the Roman Catholic Pope, a near-blasphemy to the Orthodox. They may have been to strengthen his hold on political power. But he pursued his aims so ruthlessly and with such arrogance that his co-religionists stripped him of the patriarchate and banished him to a monastery.

Nevertheless, the changes went ahead, and the 1667 edict excommunicated as heretics all those who would not accept them. Although only ritual was affected, and not the basic Orthodox system of belief, Russia was torn apart from top to bottom in the ensuing religious conflict. Millions of people – mostly peasants and town-dwellers, but also many clergy and some nobles – refused to recognise the new order, insisting that to do so would deprive them of salvation. They called themselves staroveri (Old Believers). Their opponents called them raskolniki (schismatics or dissenters).

Death at the stake

Church and state persecuted the Old Believers fanatically, killing many who would not change their religious practices. In 1681, the staroveri leader Avvakum was burned at the stake. In 1684, the government decreed that all other Old Believers who refused to recant should be put to death in the same way. The hounding was to last, off and on, for more than 200 years. It was not until the 1860s that Avvakum's writings could be openly published in Russia; in the same epoch, communities of Old Believers migrated to the US and Canada, where they flourish.

Many of the Old Believers themselves were in a frenzy, stimulated by visionaries who claimed Nikon's reforms heralded the approaching end of the world, and that the Tsar was the Anti-Christ. Between 1671 and 1691, thousands died in mass suicides by fire. Thousands more fled to the traditional refuge of Russia's oppressed – the no man's land of the southern steppe where the free Cossacks roamed.

But the Cossacks, whose religious consciousness had been developing since the Time of Troubles, were not immune to the schism. On the Don, Ataman Frol Minayev declared for the new order, and started his own persecution of Old Believers. The Zaporozhi and Ukrainian Cossacks were less concerned, though state oppression of Old Believers was another strand to be woven into general Ukrainian social discontent.

The Cossacks on the Rivers Yaik (Ural) and Terek were shorter on manpower than the other hosts. There, the Old Believers were welcome and settled in large numbers – a factor that came to play a part in later Yaik Cossack revolts.

On the Terek and nearby rivers, Old Believers retained their distinctive rituals and attitudes well into the 19th century. With those went a contempt for Russians practising Nikon's new rites, whom they regarded as apostates.

NIKON THE ICONOCLAST

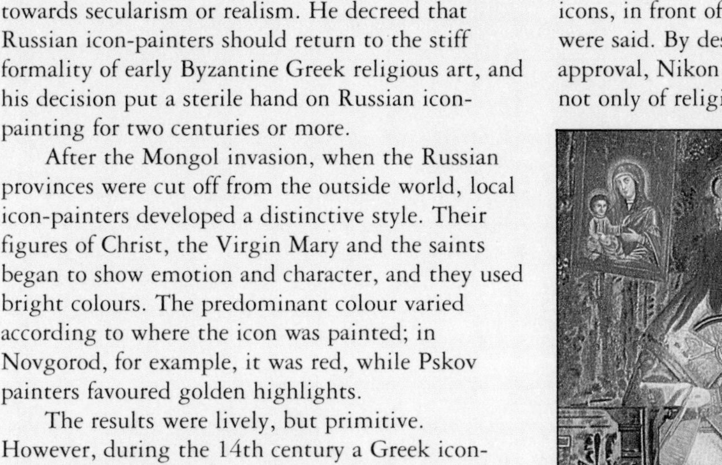

In his zeal to make the Russian Orthodox Church conform with its Greek counterpart, Patriarch Nikon supervised the destruction of thousands of icons in churches and private homes. Nikon disapproved of any holy images displaying western European tendencies towards secularism or realism. He decreed that Russian icon-painters should return to the stiff formality of early Byzantine Greek religious art, and his decision put a sterile hand on Russian icon-painting for two centuries or more.

After the Mongol invasion, when the Russian provinces were cut off from the outside world, local icon-painters developed a distinctive style. Their figures of Christ, the Virgin Mary and the saints began to show emotion and character, and they used bright colours. The predominant colour varied according to where the icon was painted; in Novgorod, for example, it was red, while Pskov painters favoured golden highlights.

The results were lively, but primitive. However, during the 14th century a Greek icon-painter called Theophanes came to work in Novgorod, and succeeded in treating the emergent Russian style with Byzantine technique and discipline. His work began a golden age in which Russia's greatest icon-painter, Andrei Rublev, could flourish. Rublev died in 1430, but others continued to experiment with new ideas. Nikon stopped them in their tracks.

His iconoclasm (literally, image-breaking) was probably more of an affront to the Russians than any of his other church reforms. Although the word icon can be used to describe any picture intended to encourage Orthodox religious devotion, in Russia it chiefly denotes paintings on wooden panels small enough to be hidden from enemies belonging to another faith – a legacy of the Mongol invasion.

Every Orthodox household had its collection of icons, in front of which a candle was lit and prayers were said. By destroying icons that did not meet his approval, Nikon was destroying powerful symbols not only of religion, but of culture and home.

Left: Patriarch Nikon with some of his clergy. Nikon's church reforms drove many 'Old Believers' to flee Russia for the Cossack lands, particularly the Yaik and the Terek.

Far left: 15th-century icon of Our Lady of Tikhvin.

Left: St Ephraim, in a 12th-century icon of the Novgorod School.

The Rise of Razin

In the late summer of 1665, during Russia's campaign against Poland in the Ukraine, a young Don Cossack commander called Ivan Timofeyevich Razin decided he and his men had done more than enough fighting for the Russian cause. It was certainly not a question of cowardice; Ivan had already proved himself to be brave and loyal. He simply wanted to get back to his village of Zimoveiskaya before the winter set in.

As a free Cossack, Ivan regarded himself as answerable to no one outside the Cossack hierarchy. And he was a member of that hierarchy – the equivalent of a senior officer, whose family belonged to the well-to-do inner circles of the Don host. So when the Russians turned down his request for a discharge, he shrugged his shoulders, assembled his men and led them off eastwards anyway. Russian soldiers pursued and finally caught them, hanging the luckless Ivan as a deserter.

Ivan had two younger brothers back on the Don, Stepan (Stenka for short) and Frol. Stenka, in particular, changed character completely after news of Ivan's ignominious death reached him. Until then, he had been a model Cossack, both as a warrior and as a diplomat in the Don's dealings with Moscow. With his privileged background, he seemed destined for the highest honours.

Once Ivan was dead, Stenka rejected all that. The final legal imposition of serfdom in Russia and the troubles of the Ukraine were filling the Don with thousands of refugees it could not feed or accommodate – and in 1667 Stenka appeared at the head of a band of these runaways, several hundred near-starving and desperate men. By open or tacit threats, he persuaded the Cossack elders to equip him with boats and supplies so he could lead his desperadoes away from the Don villages.

Right: Stepan (Stenka) Razin in his prime.

Raids from the rivers

Stenka and his band headed up the Don to the point where it flows closest to the Volga, and dragged their chaiki across the elbow of land between the two rivers. There, with Russian commercial traffic on the Volga before their eyes, they turned to piracy.

Their first major prize was a flotilla carrying goods belonging to the Tsar and private merchants, as well as a convoy of prisoners under escort. The goods were seized, the officers of the escort hanged, and soldiers, boatmen and jailbirds given the choice Stenka was to offer many times in his subsequent career: 'Go if you wish...or come with me to be a free Cossack and smash the rich'. They followed

Below: The mighty Volga, 'Mother of Russian Rivers', was the first hunting-ground for Razin's Cossack pirates.

Above: Opulently dressed and reclining, Stenka is entertained by a musician. Only the setting – a chaika manned by sweating Cossacks – distinguishes him from the potentates he robbed and defied.

Stenka, past the Russian towns of the Volga, out along the Caspian Sea coast and up the River Yaik, where the local Cossacks were ready enough to throw their lot in with him, too.

For by now Stenka had a definite plan – to launch against Persian shipping and settlements around the Caspian the sort of large-scale pirate raids the Zaporozhi and Don Cossacks had conducted so many times against the Turks on the Black Sea. Throughout the winter of 1667 and the spring of 1668 he sent messages to all the Cossack hosts, inviting booty-seekers to join him.

They came in their dozens, from the Dnieper and the Terek as well as from the Don and the Yaik. Soon, Stenka had up to 3,000 Cossacks under his command, with a fleet of captured river and sea vessels, as well as scores of the fast-moving chaiki. He was ready for a full attack on the Persians.

Season of slaughter

The pirates swept through the rich Persian trading-centres around the Caspian coast like a hurricane, slaughtering the inhabitants and seizing anything of value they could carry – gold, silver, gems, jewellery and silks.

First, Derbent fell to them, then Baku, Astara and Rasht, where they set up camp near the city. The Persians were caught by surprise and offered little resistance. But at Rasht, Stenka made an error of judgment by sending emissaries to the Persian Shah in Isfahan to try the Cossack version of the protection racket. The Cossacks would stop their piracy, and guard Persia against other pirates, in return for land and privileges.

The wily Shah played for time, feting the by-now lavishly dressed pirates and seeming to consider Stenka's proposals. Meanwhile, he established that the Tsar was anxious to bring the pirates to book for their activities on the Volga and individual crimes, and laid his plans. Then he struck, ordering Persian troops to attack the Cossacks near Rasht. Many were killed, but the rest hacked their way back to the sea, to resume their murderous raids elsewhere on the coast.

In 1669, the Shah sent a fleet against the pirates. The Cossacks, darting around the lumbering warships in their chaiki, succeeded in defeating it, taking more booty including, it is said, the son and beautiful daughter of the Persian commander. However, they also took heavy losses, and Stenka was forced reluctantly to head home.

Back at Astrakhan at the mouth of the Volga, Stenka found the Russian authorities in ambivalent mood. They wanted the pirates executed. But Stenka's exploits had made him a popular hero, and with a thousand or so men still behind him he was not to be taken lightly. So a deal was struck. Stenka made a show of fealty to the Tsar and the Cossacks agreed to disperse to their rivers – still with their booty, boats and weapons. Stenka and his immediate followers made for the Don, to begin a transformation from pirates to revolutionaries.

Razin's Revolution

The 'quiet Don' of song and story was anything but quiet when Stenka Razin and his pirate band returned there in 1669. The constant stream of runaway serfs and displaced peasants from Russia and the Ukraine was being swollen by a new wave of refugees – Old Believers fleeing from religious persecution in Russia. Cossack elders were at their wits' end trying to cope. Nevertheless, because of their dependence on Moscow for grain and other staples, they had been forced to agree with the authorities that Cossacks would not be allowed to leave the area to wreak havoc elsewhere, as Stenka and others had done.

Aware of the pressures, Stenka's band stayed out of the villages, setting up their own colony on a river island upstream. To survive, they halted passing cargo-boats, enforcing tolls or barter deals for food. That quickly brought Stenka into conflict with the Cossack elders, whose trade suffered, and with Russian authority. At the same time, more and more adventurers were flocking to the island, drawn by hope and Stenka's reputation. By early 1670, the colony had grown to more than 7,000, far too big to support itself. Stenka and his followers had to take to arms again.

Right: The executioner's block in Red Square, Moscow, is preserved as a grisly tourist attraction.

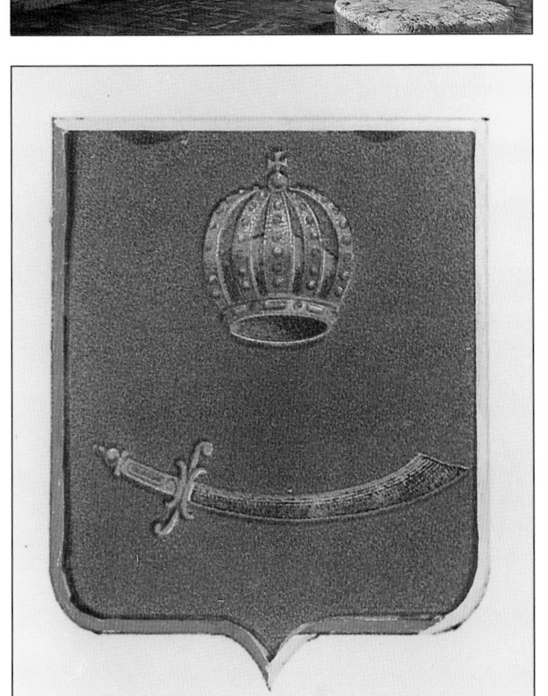

Right: Scimitar and turban were the old emblems of Astrakhan, where Razin reached his brief height of glory.

This time, the targets were the well-defended Russian cities of the Volga. Even the most seasoned of the Cossacks would have difficulty in taking them. Stenka's army needed allies. Peasants and serfs, suffering social and now religious oppression, were available in large numbers. To rouse them, Stenka gave his new campaign a twist. It was not only for booty, but for social justice, he insisted.

To that end, his rabble-rousing slogans were made more specific. The Tsar in Moscow was exempt from criticism, because to attack him even in words would turn Stenka into a traitor rather than a champion to the peasantry, who held the ruler in mystic reverence. But the Tsar's officials, the landowners and churchmen trying to suppress Old Believers were all fair game. So 'Live free and smash the rich!' became 'Stand for the Lord Sovereign (the Tsar)! Kill the landowners! Drive the governors from the towns!'. Demonstrably, there was calculation in the phraseology, for when Stenka saw the opportunity to add discontented Muslim steppe tribesmen to his forces, he devised another rallying-cry: 'For God and the Prophet, Sovereign and (Cossack) Host!'. What the Orthodox faithful thought of that, no one knows.

The Volga ablaze

Tsaritsyn (later Stalingrad, now Volgograd) was the first town to fall to Stenka's Cossacks, in April 1670. The poorer citizens opened the gates to them under cover of darkness. Garrison officers and wealthy merchants were slaughtered, and the luckless governor was hurled into the Volga in the traditional weighted sack. Stenka stocked up on supplies and ammunition, imposed Cossack institutions of self-rule and, with many new recruits, moved on, first upstream to take Kamyshin, then downstream to Cherny Yar.

A Russian army sent from Astrakhan to deal with what was now a fullscale rebellion collapsed without a fight, when its ordinary soldiers killed their officers and deserted to Stenka's side. Astrakhan itself was taken, again with the aid of supporters inside. There, the rebels paused for an orgy of drunken violence and looting. Anyone against whom the Cossacks and their followers bore a grievance had hands and feet hacked off. The luckier ones were then killed outright.

On to Moscow

Stenka sat in the middle of the mayhem like a king, but not for long. Leaving Astrakhan garrisoned by some of his Cossacks, he and the main body of his followers moved up the Volga again, in an entourage now including a spurious Tsarevich Alexis, the heir to the throne; the real Alexis had died a few months previously, but those who knew that did not care. The goal was Moscow itself.

The countryside around the Volga was in open revolt, with thousands of peasants and serfs obeying Stenka's calls to class war. Many came to join the advance, a poorly armed and untrained rabble hemming in the battle-hardened Cossacks.

THE DEATH OF RAZIN

'In our day we commanded thousands...now we must be brave,' Stenka Razin is supposed to have told his brother Frol as the pair were dragged in chains into Moscow in June 1671, to face certain death for an endless list of crimes against the state. Stenka lived up to his own instruction. The crowds of poorer citizens who lined the streets and cheered if they dared saw an upright, handsome, bearded Don Cossack who could still cut a dash in the shadow of the executioner's axe.

For two days, the brothers were subjected to the cruellest agonies Tsar Alexis's experienced torturers could devise. The object was not to extract confessions, which would have been redundant, but to get the pair to beg forgiveness from the Tsar. Frol, a shadowy figure in the Razin history and legend, did so, to earn a quick death. Stenka, who had protested his loyalty to the Tsar personally throughout his career, declined.

He paid the fullest penalty for his fortitude. Led into Moscow's Red Square, packed with soldiers and onlookers, on June 6, 1671, Stepan Timofeyevich Razin was pushed down on to the cobblestones, and quartered alive. As he died, Russia's most romantic legend was born.

Below: Horses pull a serene Stenka Razin to his horrifying death. Frol is chained behind the cart.

Estimates of the numbers range from 20,000 to 200,000.

More Volga cities fell, among them Saratov and Samara. Moscow trembled. But at Simbirsk a small garrison held up the rebels for a month – time enough for Russian regiments under Prince Bariatinsky to reach the scene. Bariatinsky's forces were among the most modern in the Russian army, and the undisciplined peasants not only were easy prey for them, but impeded the Cossack resistance. The engagement turned into a rout of Stenka's men, and he himself was seriously wounded. His Cossacks carried him from the battlefield, on a slow, undignified retreat to the Don. The Volga cities that Stenka had previously captured now protested loyalty to Moscow and refused him shelter. The forces of Russian authority were steadily regaining control, starting a programme of unequalled brutality designed to crush all the remaining rebel bands. Even among his own people, Stenka was not safe. In the spring of 1671, Don Cossacks acting on the orders of their ataman, who in turn had received orders from the Tsar, turned Stenka and his brother Frol over to the harshest forms of punishment that Russian justice could devise. For that, they had to be brought to Moscow.

MYTHS OF STENKA RAZIN

When Stenka Razin's Cossacks abandoned Caspian piracy and returned to Russia, they had in their entourage a captured Persian woman. She may have been the daughter of the Persian naval commander whose fleet Stenka had defeated and pillaged. She may even have been a princess. Certainly, she was a great beauty.

During his stay in Astrakhan, Stenka made her his mistress. An eye-witness account speaks of her appearance at his side, in a striking gold dress and bedecked with gems. Stenka was obviously besotted with her.

But after their brief spell of sumptuous living, the Cossacks were obliged by their truce with the Russian authorities to return to the Don. Stenka could not take his mistress with him because, according to custom, Cossacks were not permitted to bring womenfolk on expeditions, and he may also have had a wife at home.

The Cossack leader resolved the matter decisively. After a last night of feasting and passion on the banks of the Volga, he lifted up the unsuspecting woman, carried her to the water's edge and hurled her in to drown. As he did so, Stenka declared to the Mother of Russian Rivers: 'I have had so much from you and given you nothing; now I offer you the thing dearest to me. Volga-mother, accept my gift!'

The tale, which seems to have some basis in fact, is told in 'The Ballad of Stenka Razin', most famous of the Russian folk songs about Stenka. There are many others, for Stenka alive was a charismatic, if enigmatic, individual. Dead, he swiftly accrued the legends usually associated with similar figures, real or otherwise, in most countries' folklore.

Russian Robin Hood

The most obvious parallel is with England's Robin Hood. Stenka himself declared often enough, in so many words, that he was robbing the rich to help the poor – and his actions, though bloodthirsty, cruel and ultimately tragic, partly support his claim to altruism.

There are similarities, too, with the legends surrounding the British King Arthur. Like Arthur, Stenka is said in some folktales not to be dead, but merely sleeping while awaiting his country's hour of need. However, it is not clear whether he will be needed to save Russia, or to exact retribution.

Other aspects of the Stenka story are typically, though not uniquely, Russian. Immediately after Stenka's brutal death in Red Square, some people claimed that a substitute had been executed in his place, while Stenka lived on in disguise. Russian peasants were willing enough to believe such rumours, and even those who knew better connived at them. The theme runs through Russian history, from the time of the False Dmitris, to Stenka's own 'resuscitation' of the Tsarevich Alexis, to Emilion Pugachov's Cossack rebellion of the 1770s

Below: Maxim Gorki (1868-1936), on the right, created a screenplay for a life of Stenka Razin, but his film was never made. Leo Tolstoy (1828-1910) drew from his experiences in the Caucasus to write 'The Cossacks', considered by many his finest work prior to 'War and Peace'. This photograph of the two Russian authors was taken in 1900.

Above: The exploits of Stenka Razin are flamboyantly celebrated on a lacquerware casket created in 1936. This style of miniature painting on black lacquer comes from Palekh, a small and remote village 150 miles (240km) north of Moscow, and is in the direct tradition of the medieval icon-painters.

(see Chapter 4). There were peasants who thought Pugachov was Razin returned – at an age of well over 100.

A communist dilemma

Stenka's supposed self-discipline – which the episode with the Persian beauty is said to illustrate – and his egalitarianism could have been expected to endear him to Russia's post-1917 communist rulers. But he presented various problems for Marxist-Leninists, with his privileged background, his lack of respect for all delegated authority and his frequent lip-service to the Tsar. 'The Tsar is gracious...not so his kennel-keepers', a Russian proverb often quoted in connection with Razin's rebellion, sat ill with the executioners of Tsar Nicholas II.

A Soviet history of 1962 describes Razin's rebellion as the 'Peasant War of 1667-71', started because 'social differentiations among the Cossacks encouraged the sharpening of class contradictions on the Don', and carried forward by the 'guiding force ... of the Russian peasantry'. Stenka and his Cossacks barely get a mention.

In the 1920s, the novelist Maxim Gorki, who was sympathetic to communism, but not always uncritical of communist policy, wrote a film scenario in which he attempted to draw a parallel between Stenka Razin and Lenin. There were some obvious similarities, beyond their respective revolutionary careers. Lenin came from a relatively well-to-do family and his elder brother, like Ivan Razin, was executed by Tsarist authority. Eerily, Lenin grew up in Simbirsk (later Ulyanov), the Volga town where Stenka's rebellion suffered its fatal setback.

Gorki's scenario was never turned into a script, and the film was never made. The writer had grave problems in equating the hot-blooded, sometimes drunken, womanising Stenka of history and legend with the ascetic, coldly calculating Vladimir Ilyich Lenin, architect of Soviet Russia. In striking contrast with the devil–may–care Razin, Lenin stayed well away from personal danger whenever he could.

At the close of Gorki's scenario, an old man sings of Razin that he 'served God and the people'. Factually, neither is true. Emotionally, Russian folklore accepts both, and the old man's conclusion that 'his grave sins are not for us to judge'. Stenka Razin transcends history, to that realm of myth where he is believed capable of anything, and where even the worst of his trangressions against law or morality probably serve a higher, better end – could lesser men but see it.

The Turks Invade

Bloody government reprisals following Stenka Razin's defeat helped to cow the Don Cossack elders so much that they accepted an indignity they had rejected on many previous occasions – a formal oath of loyalty to the Tsar. In practice, however, it made little difference. Shortly afterwards, in a dispute over the return of criminal fugitives, Don militants declared that they would switch allegiance to the Sultan of Turkey.

The threat came to nothing. But to the west, in the Ukraine, one of the warring Cossack factions had obtained assistance from Turkey's Tartar vassals. That encouraged Turkey itself to renew territorial claims in the region and Sultan Mohammed IV to add 'The Protector of Cossacks' to his long list of titles. In autumn 1672, he ordered a large army into the Ukraine, to secure it as a springboard for a wider invasion of Europe. A subsidiary aim of the Sultan's was to crush the Zaporozhi Cossacks who preyed so devastatingly on his ports and shipping.

Right: Mohammed IV, Sultan of Turkey, added 'Protector of Cossacks' to his grandiose list of titles and sought to claim their lands. The Cossacks were not amused.

Below: Lingelbach's painting of Jan III Sobieski of Poland defeating the Turks before Vienna in 1683. Jan III (reigned 1674-96) ceded large tracts of Cossack country east of the Dnieper to Russia.

In its pursuit of territory, Turkey succeeded to a point, eventually wresting most of the western, right bank of the River Dnieper from Poland, and forcing Russia to pay tribute for the eastern bank. In subduing the wily Zaporozhi of the lower Dnieper, the Turks failed utterly.

According to legend, Tartars under Turkish command were sent by night to make a stealthy attack on the Zaporozhi headquarters, the Zaporozhskaya Sich. They managed to surround it, helped by the fact that the Cossacks were sleeping off a monumental drinking bout. However, a Cossack waking to relieve himself spotted a Tartar, and surreptitiously roused his companions. Despite their hungover state, the Zaporozhi then drove off the invaders amid such carnage that no further attempts were made.

The Russians themselves had been trying to bring the Zaporozhi to heel and, like the Poles before them, had installed a garrison near the Zaporozhskaya Sich. But the Zaporozhi were less dependent than their Don cousins on supplies from Moscow, and so less easy to manipulate. They continued to fight for and against whom they pleased. In 1686, when they were theoretically in loose alliance with Moscow, they nevertheless attacked and drove out the Russian garrison.

Shifting powers

The Turkish invasion of the Ukraine led to lasting changes in the balance of power there. King Jan Sobieski of Poland, in alliance with Austria, halted the Turks' continued westward advance near Vienna in 1683. But Russia's help was needed to push them out of Europe altogether. The price it exacted

Snub To a Sultan

During Turkey's invasion of the Ukraine, soon after Poland and Russia had united in the face of the common enemy, the Turks captured the town of Kamenets. Then they demanded that all of the Ukraine should be handed over to their Sultan, along with the lands on the lower River Dnieper held by the Zaporozhi Cossacks.

The illiterate and free-spirited Zaporozhi, who did not recognise the authority of either Poland or Russia, let alone the Sultan's claim, are said to have found a scribe to write their dictated reply. Supposedly, it opened with an insulting parody of the Sultan's grandiose titles:

'Turkish Devil and Soulmate of Satan! Self-styled Lord of Christendom, who is nothing of the sort! Pot-scraper of Babylon! Ale-vendor of Jerusalem! Goatherd of Alexandria! Swineherd of Upper and Lower Egypt! Sow of Armenia! Brass-necked Infidel! Go to Hell! Cossacks spit on all your present claims and any you dream up later ....'

Ilya Efimovich Repin (1844-1930), one of Russia's most-acclaimed artists, laboured several years to produce his painting of the event, 'Zaporozhi Cossacks Defy the Sultan', completed in 1891. The work, with the story behind it, is said to have been a favourite of Stalin's.

Below: Zaporozhi Cossacks Defy the Sultan – Repin's masterpiece, much admired by the Soviet dictator Joseph Stalin.

was a treaty of 'eternal friendship' with Poland, in which the Poles permanently gave up to Russia the Ukraine east of the Dnieper with the city of Kiev – previously handed over to the Russians only for a limited time under the Peace of Andrusovo.

Cossacks of all persuasions fought for the Holy Alliance, winning praise as the 'best soldiers' that could be sent against the Turks. Gradually, the Sultan's forces were driven out of the Ukraine, so that by 1700 it was free of them.

But campaigns against the Tartar and Turkish strongholds in and around the Crimea were less successful. At Moscow's suggestion, the Zaporozhi conducted a huge raid on the Crimea, a venture for which they needed no second bidding. That was, however, merely an irritant. In 1687, Prince Basil Golitsin, lover of the Russian Regent Sophia, commanded a formal military expedition. It included both Zaporozhi and Don Cossacks, and Left Bank Ukrainian Cossacks under the ataman Ivan Samoilovich. It ended in Russian defeat, for which Samoilovich was blamed. He was stripped of his position and exiled to Siberia, while Golitsin personally chose his replacement – events all indicating how far the Ukrainian Cossacks had passed under Russian control.

The man Golitsin picked as Ukrainian Cossack leader was Ivan Mazepa. A second Crimean expedition, in 1689, fared no better than the first, but Mazepa, unlike Samoilovich, was not made the scapegoat. He was left in his post to become first the friend, then the bitter enemy, of Regent Sophia's half-brother Peter, and to end his days protected by the Turks he had once fought.

TO THE PACIFIC!

'Soft gold' is the name given in Russia to the furs which for centuries have been a major source of her wealth. King of the furs is the dark-brown, luxuriant pelt of the sable, a tree-living animal of the marten family. Yermak's expedition of 1581-84 showed that the virgin northern forests of Siberia teemed with sable, guaranteeing prosperity to those brave and hardy enough to hunt them. In Yermak's footsteps, thousands did.

From the start, the Siberian fur trade was a monopoly of the Tsar. Most of its first trappers were Cossacks like Yermak, reared on the steppe and willing to accept privation and danger for the chance of reward. Others were soldiers, displaced peasants, runaway serfs – and criminals. Pardons were granted to those who would help waken the sleeping Siberian lands for the Tsar.

Small bands of trappers quartered Siberia from 1586, using rudimentary Cossack-style boats and rafts to move up one river and down the next, and building their wooden forts, or ostrogs, at key points to serve as bases and depots. On their heels and with military escorts came government officials, to collect tributes in furs from the Siberian tribes and to supervise the all-important fur traffic.

The whole movement east happened with astonishing speed. Within 60 years of Yermak first crossing the Ural Mountains there were Russian outposts on the Pacific coast 7,000km (4,400 miles) away. Only the opening of the American West two centuries later is a comparable feat – and the Siberian venture was accomplished, according to some estimates, by about 2,000 armed men who did not even have compasses, operating in groups of 30-50 all totally independent of each other, with no central control or strategy.

Before 1630, Cossacks were at Baikal, the huge freshwater lake in the centre of Siberia, where they eventually built an ostrog on the site of present-day Irkutsk. From Lake Baikal, some moved north-east down the Lena River into the vast tribal territory of Yakutia. The Yakuts, like most of the northern Siberian tribes, were not particularly hostile to the Russians. Legends say their chieftain Tigin objected to Cossacks constructing an ostrog on his land, but his people, armed only with bows and arrows, would not go against a foe who had rifles. Tigin then decided to negotiate, and was delighted when the Cossacks told him they only wanted as much ground as could be covered by an ox-hide. He agreed they could have it – only to discover that, by cutting the hide into a thin continuous strip, the Cossacks encircled much more land than he had envisaged. Tigin saw the funny side of the affair and from that point Cossacks and Yakuts were firm friends, according to the story. The reality was less pleasant, as the Cossacks were not above kidnapping Yakuts to sell to other tribes as slaves.

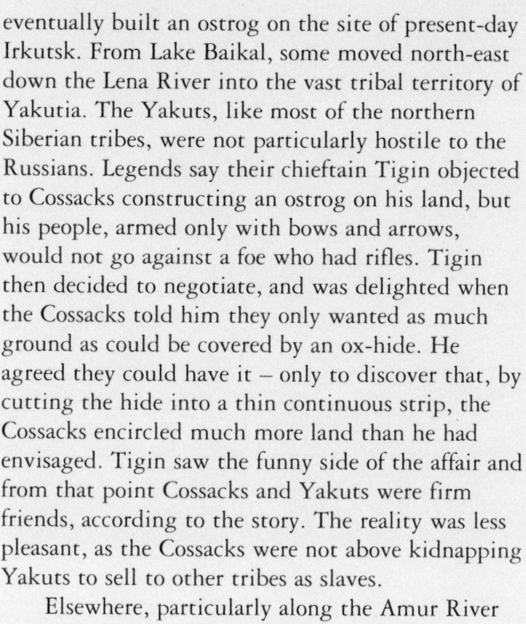

Elsewhere, particularly along the Amur River where the native peoples already paid tribute to the Emperor of China, the Cossacks' penchant for brutality displayed itself in full. In 1650, the merchant Yerofei Khabarov set Cossacks in his hire on a rampage through the Amur villages in which men, women and children alike were slaughtered, some by being burned alive. The Chinese sent soldiers to avenge the deaths, but Khabarov's men defeated them. For 15 years after that, the Cossack ostrog at Albazin was besieged again and again by the Chinese, until the outpost was ceded to them under a treaty of 1667. The defenders, now completely isolated, continued to resist the Chinese until finally forced to surrender, when they were taken as prisoners to Peking. Descendants of the Albazin Cossacks formed an Orthodox Christian community in Peking that survived until the Maoist revolution in the late 1940s.

Above right and below: Sable, principal quarry of the pioneers who opened up Siberia. By the mid-17th century, sable fur had lost some of its popularity in western Europe, but Siberian trappers found many other kinds to supply. By the mid-19th century, the massive slaughter of fur-bearing animals had sent the whole Siberian fur-trade into decline.

COSSACKS OF SIBERIA

All of the vast territory the Siberian pioneers opened up 'belonged' ultimately to the Russian Tsars. There were no private land-owners in Siberia, only land-holders, and serfdom was never legally enforced.

Russia needed to populate her newly won eastern frontier to secure it, and did so in several ways. From the middle of the 17th century, exile to Siberia became both a punishment in its own right – the Ukrainian Cossack leaders Demian Mnogogreshny and Ivan Samoilovich were among those sent there in 1672-88, for suspected treason – and an alternative to execution or imprisonment. Other migrants were encouraged to move there of their own free will, among other things by a policy of not inquiring too closely into their past, social status and motives. Eventually, enforced migration came to play a part.

Many of the early Cossack pioneers made an independent living by hunting and trapping – or by robbing hunters and trappers. Others entered state service as tribute collectors or military guards. These Cossacks were from the beginning hired as individuals, not collectively through a leader as had been Russian practice elsewhere. That arrangement, and the scattered nature of the Siberian Cossack population, prevented Siberian hosts from developing in the same way as they had done on the Dnieper and Don.

Below: Shooting the Shamanskoi rapids in 17th-century Siberia.

The northern passage

Among the rich and fashion-conscious of Europe, the urge to wear sable gave way in the mid-17th century to a fad for otter skin. Northern otters were added to the list of pelts Siberian trappers and hunters were expected to procure for the Tsar. The quest led them north of the Siberian forests to the bleak treeless wastes of the tundra, where the soil is permanently frozen just below its surface.

In 1647, Cossacks based near Okhotsk, on the Siberian fringe of the Pacific, set out under their leader Semyon Dezhnev on an otter-hunt. Their perilous journey first took them inland to the waters of the River Kolyma, and then down the Kolyma in makeshift boats to the icy waters of the Arctic Ocean.

From the mouth of the Kolyma, Dezhnev's band worked their way eastwards along the coast of the Chukchi peninsula. Otters were plentiful and the expedition was going well until the tiny fleet of five or six boats was swamped by heavy seas. Dozens of Cossacks drowned.

The rest, including Dezhnev himself, struggled ashore with the weapons they could save, and made for a river they had recently passed, as a possible route to safety. It was a nightmare journey of cold and hunger, during which more Cossacks died. Eventually, Dezhnev with ten or so fellow-survivors staggered into a tribal settlement by the river mouth. There, they forced the inhabitants to feed them, and began slowly to recover.

With their health restored, the Cossacks determined to stay and recoup their losses. They cobbled together an ostrog as best they could and remained for several years, hunting and exacting fur and ivory tributes from the tribesmen. Then they set off back towards the west, only to be robbed of most of their skins and furs, possibly by fellow-Cossacks, on the way.

Dezhnev got little recompense for his ordeal and it was only much later still that the true significance of his journey became clear. Prior to his shipwreck, he and his men had passed through the straits separating Siberia from Alaska, some 80 years before the man usually credited with discovering them and after whom they are named – the Danish navigator Vitus Bering.

The ostrog Dezhnev had founded on the River Anadyr became, in 1697, the starting-point for an expedition to the volcano-studded Kamchatka peninsula. Its members were Cossacks, but its leader was a storeman, Vladimir Atlasov.

At first, things went well. The Cossacks explored, collected furs and so impressed the native tribes that Atlasov was nominated as their high chief. In that position of power, he made the long journey to Moscow to present Kamchatka to the Tsar. But on the way back, he got into a brawl and was thrown into jail for four years.

In his absence, fighting flared up between the Cossacks and the natives, each side killing the other whenever they could. Atlasov, when he finally returned, could not quell the feud and disappeared, a broken man. The clashes went on for 30 years – one of the bloodiest episodes in the relatively bloodless annexation of Siberia.

Clipping the Eagles' Wings

Peter's Purge

Don Cossacks who helped Peter I's army and newly formed navy evict the Turks from Azov in 1696 could not have foreseen how swiftly the Tsar's appreciation of them would turn to anger. But Peter was an iron-willed autocrat with a mission to weld Russia into a modern European state, and careless of whom he offended in the process. Confrontations with the Cossacks were inevitable.

Lands on the middle reaches of the River Don, upstream from the long-established Cossack settlements, were the first flashpoint. Nominally inside Russian boundaries when Peter came to the throne, in reality they were still a lawless frontier zone, where Cossack settlements were springing up uncontrolled, providing havens for runaway peasants and serfs from the rest of Russia and the Ukraine. The fall of Azov brought the region under the Tsar's eye. He decided to tame it.

In 1700, Peter ordered the Cossacks in the new villages to return to their traditional areas lower down the Don, and to hand over the fugitives among them to Russian authority. Blithely, the Cossacks ignored the command – but with a man of Peter's temperament that was a mistake. First, he sent troops to round up the runaways. Men, women and children were hauled back in their hundreds to serfdom in Russia, while the Cossacks stood by helplessly. Then he punished the Cossacks, banning them from the upper levels of the Don and the area around Azov, and confiscating the fishing rights that had been theirs for centuries.

Once the initial fuss had died down, the Cossacks went back to their old ways as though Peter's restrictions did not exist. So in 1706 he sent another expedition to bring them to heel. Its aristocratic leader, Prince Yuri Dolgoruki, was remorseless. The new villages were burned, and anyone who tried to resist was summarily hanged. Hundreds more runaways were ferreted out. Again, most Cossack elders stood by while the Tsar's forces did their bloody work. But one of their number, Kondrati Bulavin, determined on revenge. With a band of followers, he laid an ambush for Dolgoruki, killing him and some of his men. The victorious Bulavin then called on all Don Cossacks to rise up against Moscow.

Below: Tsar Peter I (reigned 1682-1725) brought bloody retribution to the Cossacks of the Don.

Bulavin's revolt

To begin with, the uprising was a failure. The Don host's leaders, dependent on supplies from Moscow and fearful of Russian troops stationed at Azov, stayed loyal to Peter. Bulavin was forced to flee to the Dnieper, where the Zaporozhi Cossacks proved a readier audience for his fiery speeches. Several thousand Zaporozhi agreed to march with him back to the Don, and there many ordinary Don Cossacks joined the campaign.

Bulavin by now had an army large enough to defeat the Cossacks loyal to Peter, and to seize the Don capital of Cherkassk. The loyalist leadership was overthrown. Bulavin was chosen as ataman of the Don host.

In his new position, Bulavin seems to have tried to make peace with the Tsar. If so, Peter was certainly not listening. This time, the force he sent towards the Don was massive – perhaps 30,000 militia. Its orders were clear: kill the Cossacks and raze their settlements.

Bulavin was no tactician. He divided his forces, sending some north to meet the advancing Russians and others to besiege Azov. Both were routed. Bulavin himself retreated to Cherkassk, but many of his immediate followers had taken fright at the prospect of the Tsar's vengeance. They ousted Bulavin as ataman, and he killed himself rather than face Russian justice.

PETER THE GREAT

Boyhood contacts with Moscow's colony of western European craftsmen and military experts gave Peter I a taste for foreign women and a sense of his country's technical and social backwardness, which he determined to remedy when he came to the throne in 1689, aged 17. Naval matters, in particular, fascinated the Tsar. As part of his drive to make Russia a maritime power, he studied shipbuilding and naval gunnery in Holland and England in 1697-98, under the name of 'Peter Mihailov', an ordinary member of a diplomatic mission.

Peter's feeling of Russian inferiority was rubbed in on his tour, when he heard a smug European courtier refer to his shaggy-headed, bearded companions as 'baptised bears'. One of the Tsar's first acts on returning to Russia was to shave many of his nobles forcibly and to impose a beard tax. He also banned Russians from wearing traditional kaftans, insisting on western dress. These were symbolic changes. In his 36-year reign, Peter – a towering 2m (6ft 7in) tall and with restless energy revealed by an involuntary tic in his head and neck – forced through dozens of real and radical reforms. The army was reorganised, a navy created, taxation reshaped, the administration restructured and the Church brought under state control. All Russian citizens, from the nobility downwards, were made liable for state service. Nine out of ten of them were serfs; the rest were classified according to Peter's elaborate Table of Ranks.

War with Sweden gave Peter's Russia an outlet on the Baltic, and there he created his most enduring memorial, the city of St Petersburg. From 1713, it replaced Moscow as his capital.

Despite his respect for the west, Peter retained very Russian characteristics, participating personally in the torture and execution of some of those who resisted his will. In 1718, his own son and heir Alexis was put to death for treason. Peter died in 1725 after diving into an icy sea to rescue the occupants of an overturned boat.

Left: In his campaign to westernise Russia, Peter led the way by example, personally shearing the beards of his courtiers.

When the militia reached the main Cossack settlements around Cherkassk, the rebellion there had subsided, and the elders were once again ready to proclaim their obedience to Peter. That saved the Don Cossacks from total destruction. It did not save them from humiliation as rebel leaders were hunted down and executed, villages were put to the torch, the lands on the upper Don were handed over to Russian nobles and the whole Don region passed under Russian administrative control for the first time. It was all too much for many Don Cossacks. With their families, they trekked south towards the Caucasus, put themselves under the protection of the Turkish Sultan and settled along the Kuban River. Peter himself turned up in Cherkassk to accept the loyal oaths of the remaining leaders. The Don had been dealt with, but other Cossack strongholds remained.

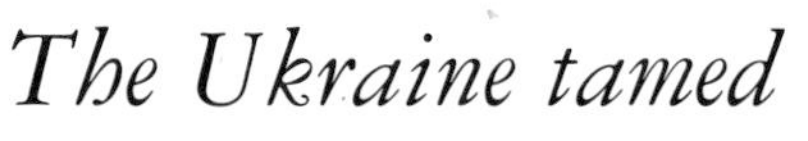

The Ukraine tamed

According to Peter the Great, Russia when he came to the throne was 'like a man with his shirt-sleeves sewn up', hemmed in from the sea not only by Turkey and its client Tartars in the south, but by the might of Sweden in the north. To a ruler who believed maritime power would help put his country at the centre of the European stage, the situation was an affront.

So after his initial successes against Turkey, Peter turned his gaze to Swedish territory on the Baltic coast, and in 1700 he began an armed campaign to secure it, in alliance with Poland and Denmark. In doing so, he pitted himself against the most brilliant military leader of his day – the young and dashing Charles XII of Sweden.

At first, everything went Charles's way. The Russians were crushed and humiliated at the Battle of Narva on the Gulf of Finland, and Denmark and Poland were subjugated. But in September 1708, the tide began to turn. Part of the Swedish army was defeated by the Russians at the Battle of Lesnaia. Charles, who had been preparing to march on Moscow itself, turned southwards instead, into the Cossack country of the Ukraine. There, he had been led to expect by secret negotiations, the Ukrainian Hetman Ivan Mazepa would cut his long connection with Moscow and raise a force of up to 80,000 Ukrainians in Sweden's support.

Mazepa proved a broken reed. In his time as hetman, his policies of repression had antagonised many of the poorer Ukrainian Cossacks, and they showed little inclination to follow him. Perhaps sensing that, he at first helped Charles only by refusing to fight for Peter. Then, when Peter realised Mazepa had been dealing with the Swedes and the Ukrainian leader was forced to declare himself for Charles, most of the elders stayed loyal to Moscow. Only a few hundred Ukrainian Cossacks joined Mazepa as he fled from his stronghold of Baturin to the Swedish ranks.

Further down the River Dnieper, the call to arms against Peter found a readier audience. The free Zaporozhi Cossacks under Ataman Ivan Gordienko threw in their lot with Mazepa and Charles, and Gordienko managed to raise many of the Ukrainian Cossacks where Mazepa had failed.

Victory at Poltava

Peter, with a reorganised army, was in no mood to put up with his unruly and treacherous borderers around the Dnieper, any more than he had been with Kondrati Bulavin's rebels on the Don. Towards the end of 1708, Russian troops stormed into Baturin, pillaged it and burnt it down. The Ukrainian elders quickly renounced the already-departed Mazepa; his replacement as hetman of the Ukraine, Ivan Skoropadsky, had Peter's approval.

In May 1709, the Zaporozhskaya Sich felt the Tsar's wrath. For three or four days, the Russians besieged the stronghold until it, too, fell and was set ablaze. Gordienko and some Zaporozhi escaped down the Dnieper to Tartar territory, where they claimed the protection of the Crimean Khan.

Then, in midsummer 1709, Peter gained his revenge on the Swedes for his defeat at Narva. At the Battle of Poltava, in the eastern Ukraine, the Swedish army was overwhelmed by the Russians, losing 10,000 men killed or captured. Charles and Mazepa, whose role in the battle is uncertain, managed to get away to the west.

The victory began a process which established Russia as a Baltic seaboard power, though it was not until the Peace of Nystad in 1721 that the war with Sweden ended. Poltava also brought the Ukraine more firmly under Russian control, with significant consequences for its Cossacks.

Below left: The Battle of Poltava in 1709 brought defeat for the Swedes and the downfall of the Ukrainian Cossack leader Mazepa. He sided with Sweden against Peter the Great's Russia, perhaps in the hope of creating an independent Ukraine.

Below right: Ivan Skoropadsky, successor to Mazepa as hetman of the Ukraine, was Peter the Great's placeman – but still a 'traitor' in the Tsar's eyes. On Skoropadsky's death, Peter refused to recognise his elected replacement, Paul Polobotuk, and imprisoned him for life.

NAKED ON THE STEPPE

As a young nobleman at the court of King John Casimir of Poland, Ivan Stepanovich Mazepa-Koledinsky had a prosperous future before him. But he jeopardised it all, according to tradition, in an unwise love affair with Theresa, wife of a count from his native region of Podolia. When the count discovered Theresa's infidelity, he and his henchmen seized Ivan, stripped him naked and lashed him to a wild horse which they then turned loose on the Ukrainian steppe. The youth would certainly have died, had he not been rescued from his plight by Cossacks, who sheltered him and eventually chose him as a leader.

The romantic tale, celebrated in Lord Byron's 1819 poem 'Mazeppa', may have a basis in fact. The real-life Mazepa was a noted womaniser and a born intriguer, whose family wealth enabled him to bribe his way to leadership of the Ukrainian Cossacks in 1687. For 20 years, he was ostensibly a faithful servant of Moscow, becoming a crony of Tsar Peter I and presiding over the final stage in changes which saw most Ukrainian Cossacks reduced to near-serfdom under Russian rule.

Mazepa's decision to switch allegiance to Charles XII of Sweden in 1708 has been seen by Russians, then and now, as treachery of the deepest hue, paid for by the promise of land and titles from the Swedes. In reality, like Bogdan Khmelnitsky several decades earlier, Mazepa was probably trying to secure the Ukraine's independence by playing neighbouring powers against each other.

News of Mazepa's impending defection was brought to Tsar Peter by Basil Kochubei, an official. Peter thought Kochubei was lying, and handed him over to Mazepa for execution. Then, in October 1708, Mazepa turned up with about 2,000 men at the Swedish outpost of Horki – and his change of sides became clear to all.

After the Swedish defeat at Poltava, Mazepa fled to Turkish territory. Though Peter put a price on his head, the Turks refused to hand him over. He died of natural causes in 1709.

Below left: Charles XII of Sweden, Peter the Great's opponent in the 21-year Nordic War. Russia's success made her a Baltic Sea power.

Below: On the Ukrainian steppe, young Mazepa pays the price for his illicit love affair.

Traitors all

'From Khmelnitsky to Skoropadsky, all Ukrainian hetmans have been traitors', declared Peter towards the end of his life. Given Mazepa's double-dealing, the Tsar's feeling was understandable, and he did his best to ensure the treachery was not repeated.

Skoropadsky, as the Tsar's placeling, was cemented into the Russian establishment by being forced to give his daughter in marriage to the Russian nobleman Peter Tolstoy. In 1722-23, most remaining vestiges of Ukrainian Cossack autonomy were swept away – a Russian army college was created to administer the Ukraine, and the Cossack regiments were put under Russian officers. Thousands of Ukrainian Cossacks were deported to Siberia in Peter's reign and immediately afterwards. With many of the Zaporozhi and Don Cossacks fled from their homelands or forcibly resettled, and the Yaik Cossacks subdued by a purge ordered in 1723, the Cossack way of life was altering dramatically. One act of Peter's sums up the change. In 1721, he decreed the Don, Yaik and Terek Cossacks should no longer deal with Moscow through its Foreign Ministry. Instead, they were placed under the War Ministry. From being a 'foreign power', they had become part of Russia's internal affairs.

A Changing Way Of Life

'In a man who tills the soil there is not a deed or thought which does not belong to the earth ... he is in complete bondage', says the Russian author Gleb Ouspensky. Early Cossack communities instinctively recognised the truth behind the statement. For 200 years they despised arable farming, which ties a man to his land for at least half the year, as being incompatible with the free life that they held so dear. But in the end, even death threats such as those issued around 1690 by Don Cossack leaders against would-be farmers in their ranks could not keep the Cossacks from the plough.

The continued influx of dispossessed peasants and runaway serfs was partly responsible for the change. Farming was the only thing many of the incomers knew, and the only way they could be fed. At the same time, Peter the Great's armed repressions reduced the opportunities for old-style Cossack piracy and freebooting.

By the early 18th century, Cossacks on the Don and Yaik were growing rye, buckwheat and other cereals on a three-strip rotation system which left one strip fallow as summer pasture for horses, cattle or sheep. Even some of the proud Zaporozhi, returning to their homelands on the Dnieper from their spell under Turkish protection, took to tilling the soil. Cossack farming flourished, despite a perennial shortage of labour when adult males were on military service for Russia. Dnieper and Don Cossacks were soon producing enough surplus grain to export to Russia, Poland and even Turkey, along with livestock, meat, hides and fish products. The Yaik could not grow enough grain for its own needs, but it, too, exported livestock, hides and many types of fish.

The proceeds of this trade, and payments in cash and kind from Russia to keep its borderers loyal, helped the Cossack communities to reach comparative prosperity by the mid-18th century. The number of Cossack villages increased, to more than 100 on the Don, for example. Stores, craftsmen's workshops and taverns were opened, churches and communal bath-houses were built – all signs that a sense of permanence was creeping into the Cossack way of life.

Below: Cossacks who had once despised farming increasingly took to it from the 18th century. But the men's military duties left women to do much of the farm work.

Rich and poor

The new wealth, however, was far from evenly spread. In keeping with tradition, the ataman and elders controlled the allocation of land, the distribution of payments from Russia and much of the trade. That gave them ample opportunities for lining their own pockets, and most did so with a will. Cossack leaders on the Dnieper, Don and Yaik all amassed huge herds of sheep, cattle and horses. They built themselves mansions, sometimes of stone, and furnished them lavishly. They and their families wore expensive clothes and jewellery.

All this was encouraged by the Russians. They reasoned that the richer the Cossack leaders became, the less likely they were to make trouble for the throne. Increasingly, the Russians intervened directly with armed force or economic sanctions to ensure candidates for high Cossack office were men of whom they approved, as they did by installing one Basil Pritkov as ataman of the Yaik Host in 1739. Increasingly, too, the leaders became more autocratic, drawn from an inner circle of the richest families, holding office for life and regarding themselves as answerable to no one in their communities for their decisions.

Many ordinary Cossacks did not seem to mind these departures from the old ways. Even those who farmed on the smallest scale – 'with half a man, a woman and a horse' as it has been called, because the man also had his military duties – prospered modestly. Their rough-hewn wooden huts, in which the family huddled around a stove on bleak nights, acquired framed icons and pictures, cushions and rugs. Outside grew cabbages and onions, with rye bread the staples of a poorer farmer's diet, and sunflowers, prized for their edible seeds as well as for their cheerful blooms.

Left: Harvest-time approaches in the Russian countryside.

Cossacks with larger holdings, or who fished or traded successfully, could afford greater luxuries – clocks, fine costumes for feast days and holidays, perhaps even a book or two for the few who could read. They could hire help, too, to work their land or in their businesses, or even to do military service in their place.

The underclass

However, not all Cossacks or the runaways who joined them could accumulate enough money to set up as farmers or fishermen on their own behalf. If they received pay for military service, much of it went on acquiring the necessary equipment. Some could not even afford horses and had to serve as foot-soldiers.

They might eke a living working other people's land for starvation wages, or in the fish-processing workshops which wealthier Cossacks were building on the rivers. But those were only seasonal occupations, not enough to support someone for the whole year.

To survive, dozens of the poorest steppe-dwellers turned, as their forebears had done, to pillage and theft. But by the mid-18th century, Cossackry had changed. Those time-honoured occupations brought the perpetrators into conflict with their now-respectable fellow-Cossacks, as well as with the Russian forces of law.

Below: Wayside encounter in an 18th-century Russian village.

The Bandits Ride

Gangs of penniless Cossacks from the Zaporozhskaya Sich, with no prospects of land or wealth at home, launched a reign of terror in the Ukraine in the 18th century. Their sole aim was plunder and any likely target would serve – Polish or Russian, Christian or Jew. Even fellow-Cossacks were fair game, if the bandits thought they could get away with it.

Their favourite roaming-ground was the Polish territory of the western Ukraine, which Poland, beset by political troubles, left poorly defended. Respectable Zaporozhi leaders turned a blind eye to the bandits' activities there. As on the Don in Stenka Razin's time, they judged it better to have disaffected Cossacks breaking the law somewhere else than causing trouble on their own soil.

Young Zaporozhi who had completed their miltary apprenticeships made up the hard core of the gangs, which had anything from a dozen to several hundred members. Around them, they collected the usual gaggle of criminals and runaways. From hideaways along the Dnieper, they burst out on lightning raids, returning to sell the spoils in the Cossack townships.

One of the bandits' biggest forays took place in 1768. A leader called Zelezhniak welded the gangs into what amounted to a small army, to rampage west from the Dnieper slaughtering landlords, estate managers and officials and raping their womenfolk. The bandits were strong enough to capture the Polish Ukrainian town of Uman, which they used as a base for attacks not only on Polish lands, but also into the Russian Ukraine. To the Russian authorities, Zelezhniak's activities had all the signs of a fullscale Cossack and peasant revolt.

The Russians acted quickly, sending troops against the bandits and forcing the respectable Zaporozhi to join the campaign, too. That swept the marauders back to the lower Dnieper, but did not immediately destroy them. In their homelands, the bandits promptly tried to foment an uprising of the poorer Cossacks against their wealthy leaders. The Zaporozhi elders, alarmed by these developments, called in the Russians to protect them, and the leading trouble-makers were either executed or flogged and then transported east to Siberia.

Nevertheless, enough escaped to continue the bandit raids, even attacking Russian military convoys. And the seeds of discontent had been sown. The rank-and-file Zaporozhi railed against both their own leaders and the Russian overlords to the extent that, in 1769, it proved difficult to raise Zaporozhi Cossack regiments to serve with the Russian army. These slights to Russia were eventually to bring her final retribution against all the Zaporozhi, respectable elders and bandits alike.

Right: Floggings with two or more knouts were generally reserved for serious offences in 18th-century Russia. Lesser misdemeanours might attract a beating with a lash or rod. But there were no hard-and-fast rules, and owners could administer whatever punishment they chose to their serfs.

Below: This line engraving, made in the middle of the 18th century, shows a Cossack attack on Prussian dragoons.

Trouble in the east

Bandit gangs appeared, too, from the Don and the Yaik, though none wreaked havoc on the scale of Zelezhniak and his ilk. But there was wider discontent among both hosts because of Russian attempts to impress hitherto–free Cossacks into regular army regiments.

That was particularly hateful to the many Old Believers in the Yaik host. In the army they would be forced to give up their distinctive religious customs, having their beards shaved and being compelled to make the sign of the cross with three fingers instead of two. They seethed and refused to be conscripted, bringing Russian reprisals in the form of mass floggings and the impressment of hundreds of Yaik Cossacks at gunpoint. Those who escaped plotted rebellion under a slogan which summed up their version of the Orthodox religion – 'For Cross and Beard'.

On the Don, Ataman Stepan Yefremov tried to thwart Russian plans for conscription. But in 1772 the government sent troops to enforce its will. Yefremov and his host mustered to defy them.

Rule Of The Knout

In 1756, a Russian land-owner called Saltikov died, leaving his widow Daria 600 serfs as part of his estate. Over the next seven years, she mercilessly thrashed them – men, women and children – for the slightest misdemeanour, such as coughing at the wrong time. More than 70 expired under the lash or from other forms of torture and mutilation the sadistic 'Saltichika' devised.

Even Russian society, where whippings of serfs by their masters were an everyday occurrence and deaths from floggings mostly went unpunished, was shocked. Daria was brought to trial, found guilty of murder and other crimes and banished for the rest of her life to a convent.

To be whipped in Russia was largely the dubious privilege of serfs. Nobles could be flogged, as part of a criminal sentence, until 1785, when a law was passed making exemption from corporal punishment one of the benefits of noble rank. But floggings were universally regarded as a mark of servitude, so those handed out by Russian soldiers to recalcitrant free Cossacks were considered a social humiliation for the recipients, as well as physical retribution.

Serf-masters and others who administered corporal punishment had a huge array of rods, staves and whips to choose from. The infamous Russian knout was originally simply a piece of rope with a knot at the business end, used by Cossacks and other riders in controlling their horses. But refinements were developed for human 'correction' – scourges with three or more knotted rope-ends spreading from a handle like a cat o'nine tails, or ropes where sharp pieces of bone or lead were tied into the knots.

Sometimes, leather thongs replaced rope. To improve their effectiveness they were wound round with wire. Men could die quickly from being flayed with those, and often did.

As the Cossacks became more organised militarily, they developed a semi-uniform style of whip, or nagaika, with a looped leather thong attached to a wooden handle. That was good enough for riding, but not really suitable for administering punishment or use as a supplementary weapon. For those purposes, some Cossacks were eventually equipped with a longer, single-thonged whip which had a small lead weight at the tip. It became both an instrument and a symbol of repression.

Below: Female serfs were as liable as males to receive the knout.

A Tsarina's Revenge

In the Russia of 1764, Cyril Razumovsky thought himself a very powerful man. His brother Alexis had been the lover of the late Tsarina Elizabeth, a family connection that obtained for Cyril the restored office of Hetman of the Russian Ukraine, with its opportunities for amassing vast wealth, and the post of colonel in the crack Ismailovski Lifeguard regiment. Using these positions, Cyril was a key figure in the plot which brought Catherine II to the Russian throne.

Like others before him, Cyril dreamed of an independent Ukrainian Cossack state, self-governing under Russian protection and with the Razumovsky family as hereditary rulers. He had reason to hope Catherine's gratitude would help him fulfil his grandiose ambition.

He could not have been more wrong. For the tough-minded Tsarina, once she felt secure, set about neutralising those who had gained her the crown. She also declared her aim of bringing Russia's turbulent border regions into the main body of the state. 'These provinces should be reduced to the point where they can be Russified and no longer look to the woods like wolves,' she told an adviser. Cyril was a target on both counts – and on a third. For his brother Alexis refused Catherine's efforts to make him testify he had been secretly married to the Tsarina Elizabeth. If Alexis had admitted to the union, which legend says took place, it would have created the precedent for Catherine to marry the commoner Gregory Orlov, a plan in which she was thwarted.

So when Cyril used discontent among the Ukrainians as an argument for more autonomy, Catherine was not prepared to listen. She turned the tables by forcing him to admit his own shortcomings as hetman and to resign. Then she abolished the post of hetman altogether, and sent a commission headed by a Russian general to rule the Ukraine. Cyril, who was not a fighting soldier, could do little.

Catherine's response was the first stage in a programme which, by 1783, integrated the eastern Ukraine wholly into Russia, reducing its Cossacks to the status of other Russians – that is, bondsmen. It served as a warning, too, of the Tsarina's general view of Cossackry. More tangible signs were soon to be forthcoming.

Dealing with the Don

Complaints among the Yaik Cossacks about conscription and their corrupt, Russian-backed leaders turned to open rebellion in 1772, when they murdered their ataman and Russian army officers deputed to protect him. Catherine, who had earlier rejected the allegations of corruption as fabrications, sent a large force to restore order on the Yaik and imposed a military government. Hundreds of Cossacks were found guilty of plotting against the state; dozens of the ringleaders were exiled to Siberia and elsewhere.

On the Don, Ataman Stepan Yefremov and Cossacks opposed to conscription assembled in Cherkassk, ready to do battle with Russian troops ordered by Catherine to bring them to heel. The uprising never really materialised. In a forerunner of modern 'snatch squad' tactics, a group of Russian dragoons managed to seize Yefremov and remove him from the area. Without his leadership, the Don Cossacks were swiftly subdued. Yefremov was deposed as ataman and joined the long procession of Cossacks going into enforced exile.

By the beginning of 1773, Catherine seemed to have tamed her frontier 'wolves' in the Ukraine, on the Don and on the Yaik. Only the Zaporozhi of the Dnieper, whose bandit gangs were again causing trouble, had not been fully dealt with in the Tsarina's name. But appearances were deceptive. The quiescent Yaik was ready to explode into the biggest Cossack rebellion since Stenka Razin's day. Its leader, like Razin, was a native of the Don – Emilion Pugachov.

Below: Catherine II (reigned 1762-96) in Moscow's Cathedral of the Assumption. Under her rule, most of the Cossack homelands were brought inside Russia's borders.

CATHERINE AND POTEMKIN

Russia's most famous woman ruler, Catherine II, was not Russian by birth, nor was she baptised Catherine. As Princess Sophia Augusta Frederika of the tiny German principality of Anhalt-Zerbst, she was betrothed to a grandson of Peter the Great, changing her name and adopting the Orthodox faith on marriage.

When her pock-marked, drunken and infantile husband came to the Russian throne as Peter III in 1761, Catherine swiftly contrived to depose and imprison him. The ring-leaders of the coup included Catherine's lover, Gregory Orlov, by whom she already had a child. In July 1762, the unfortunate Peter III was strangled by one of Orlov's brothers. In September the same year Catherine was crowned empress in her own right.

The Tsarina began her reign determined to reform Russian society according to principles advocated by liberal thinkers in France, Germany, Italy and England. She created an education system open to all social classes and reorganised local administration, but was less successful in trying to draw up a new legal code.

Even at the height of her reforming zeal, however, Catherine was no more than an 'enlightened despot' who had no intention of relinquishing her autocratic powers. The French Revolution of 1789, which sent shock waves through all the royal houses of Europe, brought an end to her experiments in liberalism. Under Catherine, Russian serfs lost their last vestiges of freedom and serfdom was fully extended to the lands of the Ukraine.

Above: Catherine consults her sometime lover and longterm favourite, Gregory Potemkin.

Catherine's private life was notorious. Before the handsome, vacuous soldier Gregory Orlov, her lovers included Sergei Saltikov – possibly the father of the heir to the throne, Tsarevich Paul – and Stanislas Poniatowski, later elected king of Poland with Catherine's backing. Orlov fell from favour in 1772, after his indiscriminate womanising became too much for the Tsarina to bear. Henceforth, Catherine changed her bed-mates every few years; as she grew older, they became younger. Of all her lovers, Catherine retained most affection for Gregory Potemkin, a gigantic one-eyed army officer who enjoyed her sexual favours for two years from 1774, and who apparently ended the liaison himself. Catherine made Potemkin, as commander of the armed forces, the most influential man in Russia until his death in 1791. He masterminded the campaigns against Turkey which added the whole of the Crimea and the Black Sea steppe to Russia.

In 1793-95, Russia annexed large slabs of Polish territory, including the western Ukraine and Lithuania. So by the time Catherine the Great died in 1796, at the age of 67 from a stroke suffered in the lavatory, most of the traditional Cossack homelands were inside Russia's borders.

Left: French philosopher Denis Diderot found Catherine the Great to have 'the charms of Cleopatra' when they met. Others thought she looked rather masculine.

TSAR PETER LIVES!

In November 1772, when Tsarina Catherine's deposed and murdered husband Peter III had been dead for a decade, an obscure Don Cossack in his thirties called Emilion Pugachov chose to take the biggest gamble of his life. He decided, perhaps at the instigation of friends, to pose as Tsar Peter, claiming to have miraculously thwarted the plot against him and gone into hiding, now to re-emerge to resume his rightful position.

The imposture, on the face of it, was laughable. Pugachov, who had fought in Russia's wars against Germany and Turkey before deserting and going on the run, was a short, stocky, battle-scarred illiterate. The late Tsar was lanky and stoop-shouldered, bad at speaking Russian because of his upbringing in Germany, and lettered enough to correspond with the French thinker Voltaire.

Russian history from the Time of Troubles held plenty of precedents for what Pugachov planned. Quite probably, he was aware of them only dimly, if at all. But he did know that, since 1765, five or six False Peters had already emerged in south-west Russia, among them an impostor called Bogomolov who led a Cossack uprising around Astrakhan. Their brief rebellions had been easily put down, but they had demonstrated that Peter's name could arouse the masses.

There were good reasons for that. Although Peter III is judged by most historians – and by his wife in particular – to have been weak and childish, he took some liberal measures in his six-month reign. They included establishing freedom of worship for the long-persecuted Old Believers, a ban on the buying of serfs by owners of Russia's workshops and mines, and the exemption of nobles from compulsory military service.

According to widespread rumours, Peter had intended to follow these innovations by emancipating the serfs and restoring Cossack freedoms. Instead, Catherine, though she paid lip-service to liberal principles, was drawing the chains tighter round both groups. Their disaffection was massive, and ripe for Pugachov to exploit. As an observer wrote: 'Everyone was bitter and waiting for an excuse to rebel; Pugachov provided it'.

Below: Playing the part of Tsar Peter III for all it is worth, the Cossack Pugachov holds court.

Making a prince

Pugachov opened his campaign as 'Tsar Peter' in September 1773, among the Yaik Cossacks who had been so harshly put down by Catherine's soldiers the previous year. The Cossacks knew he was an impostor; to them the truth of his claim was a matter of complete indifference. 'What do we care whether he is the Tsar or not – we can make a prince out of a piece of excrement', one of them boasted.

But Pugachov was determined to play his part to the hilt. Ringing declarations issued in the name of 'The Tsar Autocrat Peter Fedorovich' promised the Cossacks their ancient freedom of the steppe, money and goods. Other steppe peoples, such as the Kirghiz and Tartars, were to get the same. Peasants and serfs were offered liberation, the abolition of taxes and land 'to enjoy in peace for centuries'. Pugachov, not an Old Believer himself though he had posed as one in his past, pledged to restore the old religious forms.

Within a week or two, Pugachov's band of 80 Cossack followers had grown to several thousand, as towns and villages along the River Yaik went over to his cause with little or no resistance. Any of their inhabitants who remained loyal to Catherine were hanged or shot. By mid-October, the rebels were encamped outside the fortress of Orenburg, strongly garrisoned by Russian forces.

There Pugachov paused, hoping to starve the defenders out, while he mopped up the surrounding outposts. More reinforcements flocked to him, among them industrial workers from the Urals region under their own leader Khlopusha. He was a veteran of several previous uprisings, an escaped convict whose face had been hideously branded and whose nostrils had been torn off as punishments for past crimes.

Pugachov set about organising his rabble into an army, creating a 'war cabinet' of close advisers such as Khlopusha, and welding the men into approximations of regiments. Twice, the authorities sent troops to lift the siege of Orenburg. Twice, the rebels defeated them, killing dozens of officers and persuading ordinary soldiers to join the uprising.

When Catherine in St Petersburg first heard the news of Pugachov's rebellion, in October 1773, the court was celebrating the marriage of Catherine's son, the Tsarevich Paul, to Princess Wilhelmina of Hesse-Darmstadt, and a war with Turkey was in its delicate final stages. The Tsarina tried to hush up the insurrection, fearing word of it would damage her reputation outside Russia. But by mid-December, after the second attempt to relieve Orenburg had failed, she could no longer keep the matter secret. Grimly, she issued a manifesto denouncing Pugachov as an 'impertinent miscreant', and ordered her trusted adviser General Alexander Bibikov to bring him to account.

Left and below: The richly-bearded and stocky Pugachov bore no resemblance to the murdered Tsar he impersonated, the aristocratically lanky Peter III.

The Road to Kazan

As long winter dragged towards the spring of 1774, life was grim for the defenders of Orenburg. Pugachov's rebels had cut them off completely and were bombarding them daily with captured artillery. Soldiers and civilians were near starvation, reduced to scavenging for food. But Orenburg did not fall – and Pugachov, encamped outside, was growing impatient.

By now, 'Tsar Peter' had acquired the full trappings of the office he claimed, with a mock court and an array of 'ministers' and 'generals'. His 'regiments' were rampaging far to the north and east, gathering recruits from the peasantry and the steppe tribes all the time, while spreading slaughter and destruction. Pugachov himself, resplendent in red robes or a gold kaftan, was issuing proclamation after proclamation, many of them contradictory. In one, he said he did not want the Russian throne for himself, merely to remove the foreign usurper Catherine, with all the nobles, and to instal the Tsarevich Paul.

In February 1774, he sought to break the monotony by besieging the Cossack capital of Yaitsk, held by loyalists. That proved as resistant as Orenburg. The same month, he completed his parody of royal manners by marrying a poor Cossack girl whom he styled Tsarina. Meanwhile, General Bibikov was assembling a mixed force of the regular army and militia. Gradually, it drew a noose around the rebels.

Whatever his faults, Pugachov was no coward. When he learned that Russian divisions were once again moving towards Orenburg, he assembled several thousands of his best men and marched to head them off. In the battle that followed, the rebels fought doggedly, only to be overwhelmed. Two-thirds were killed or captured, but Pugachov managed to escape.

The rebels revived

For the next four or five months, 'Tsar Peter' twisted and turned with his remaining followers, moving east at one moment, west the next, north after that. Russian forces relieved Orenburg and Yaitsk, and nipped at the rebels' heels. But every time they seemed to have Pugachov at bay, he eluded them. Every time his forces were reduced, new bands of serfs, deserters and steppe tribesmen emerged to join him.

In May, he captured Troitsk, only to lose it almost immediately, with most of his men. In June, he was back with several thousand supporters to lay siege to the fortress at Osa, where the garrison went over to him.

There, 'Tsar Peter' agreed to the course his closest followers had long been urging on him – to march on Moscow. In early July, the rebel army, once again more than 15,000 strong, set out south-westwards across the River Kama towards Kazan, the first of its staging-posts en route to the former Russian capital.

The advance was as cruel as anything in Pugachov's career. Nobles' estates were pillaged and burned. Any noblemen who fell into the rebels' hands was put to death in the cruellest fashion, by flaying, dismemberment or burning. Noblewomen were raped before being slaughtered. Moscow was besieged by refugees fleeing ahead of the terror.

A Russian force sent to protect Kazan was easily swept aside and on July 12 Pugachov took the city. For three days, the rebels looted, raped and killed, finally burning most of Kazan to the ground.

Below: Russian winter, as seen by Nikifor Krylov (1802-31). For the starving defenders of Orenburg, it was far less of an idyll.

THE CAPTAIN'S DAUGHTER

'I cannot express what I felt on leaving this terrible man, a monster of evil to everyone but me. Why not admit it? I was drawn to him ... I wanted to drag him away from the criminals he led, and to save his head.'

The 'terrible man' is Pugachov, and the speaker is Peter Grinyov, army officer hero of 'The Captain's Daughter', one of the best-known prose tales by Russia's greatest poet, Alexander Pushkin (1799-1837). In the story, Grinyov encounters a Cossack on a wintry road and gives him a hareskin coat to protect him from the cold. Thereafter Grinyov's fate and that of the Cossack, later revealed to be Pugachov himself, are intertwined.

Grinyov is posted to the fortress of Belogorsky, where he falls in love with Masha, the captain's daughter of the title. Eventually, Belogorsky is captured by Pugachov's rebels. Masha's parents are killed, but Pugachov, remembering Grinyov's earlier kindness, spares him and allows him to ride to Orenburg, where he takes part in the siege.

Then, learning that Masha, who is still at Belogorsky, is in danger of violation by one of Pugachov's villainous henchmen, Grinyov sets off to rescue her. By appealing to Pugachov's better nature, Grinyov enlists the impostor's help. The lovers are briefly reunited, but undergo further setbacks, including Grinyov's banishment as an alleged traitor, before they are brought together permanently, this time by the personal intervention of Catherine the Great.

Pushkin's yarn is rich in descriptions of the terrors wrought during Pugachov's rebellion – the hangings of army officers who remained loyal to Catherine, the floating gallows on which the Russian authorities sent captured rebels down the Volga, the effects of torture by the state's Secret Commission in Kazan. It is rich, too, in human touches. Pugachov, offered a cup of tea in an inn, calls for vodka instead, declaring 'Tea is not a Cossack drink'. Subsequently, the fearsome rebel leader admits he can hardly control the uprising he has started: 'My men are thieves and too independent. At the first setback, they will buy their necks with my head'.

Pushkin had a hot-blooded temperament that brought him into conflict with the authorities of his own day and eventually led to his death from wounds received in a duel. His self-knowledge helped him, despite his noble ancestry, to make of the lowly Cossack Pugachov a not unsympathetic character – and to suggest, through his art, how the real-life Emilion Pugachov may have won the following he did.

Below: The Pushkin Monument in St Petersburg.

Far left: Alexander Pushkin, whose genius captured the very soul of a Cossack rebel.

Left: Pugachov leads Grinyov to Masha, in a scene from 'The Captain's Daughter'.

End of an Uprising

Within a few days of taking Kazan, Pugachov was on the run again, thrown back by a small Russian force as he set out on the next stage of his journey to Moscow. This time, with a few hundred surviving followers, he weaved south to Pensa and to Saratov on the Volga, using the same tactics he had employed after his earlier defeat outside Orenburg. His proclamations of land and freedom fell on receptive ears in territories which had once risen behind Stenka Razin.

But circumstances had changed since the spring. General Bibikov, Catherine's first choice to quell the rebels, had died. The war with Turkey was over, releasing the ablest Russian commanders and troops for internal duties, among them General Peter Panin. He was a national hero for his role in the Turkish campaign, though a personal enemy of the Tsarina. Nevertheless, she picked him as Bibikov's replacement.

As Pugachov moved south, a Russian force followed him, while other regiments were deployed in areas where it was thought the rebels might appear. Once again, a noose was being drawn round 'Tsar Peter'. He might have escaped it, had he been able to raise his fellow Don Cossacks to support him. He tried – but the Don elders were loyal to Catherine and too many of the rank-and-file knew his real identity to be readily impressed by his grandiose proclamations.

Giving the Don up as a bad job, Pugachov marched south-east to the Volga. There, in August 1774, he turned to face the Russians who had tracked him since Kazan. The rebels were still several thousand strong, but mostly peasants with little knowledge of warfare. Pugachov's band was slaughtered. Eel-like, 'Tsar Peter' escaped once more, fleeing with his bodyguard to the Yaik where his rebel career had started two years earlier. Now it was over. On September 14, 1774, a group of his former cronies, lured by the prospects of pardons and a reward, overpowered Pugachov, trussed him up and, the following day, dragged him before the Russian commander in Yaitsk.

The aftermath

With Pugachov removed, the last vestiges of his rebellion were easily put down by Panin and his fellow-generals. Hundreds of rebel ringleaders were executed, but that was not enough to assuage Catherine's wrath.

In an order of January 15, 1775, she quite literally expunged the word 'Yaik' from the map of Russia. The River Yaik became the Ural. Yaitsk became Uralsk. The Yaik Host, reorganised and heavily garrisoned by Russian troops, was renamed the Ural Host.

Other Cossacks did not escape. Those around the Volga were forcibly resettled en masse in the new frontier lands of the Caucasus ceded by Turkey. The Don Cossacks, who had largely resisted Pugachov's blandishments, were luckier; False Peter's home village on the Don was entirely destroyed, and then rebuilt by order of the authorities on the opposite bank of the river. It, too, received a new name, Potemkinskaya, after Catherine's current lover.

There still remained, however, the problem of the Zaporozhi.

Right: Betrayed by fellow-Cossacks, Pugachov is delivered in chains to the Russian commander at Yaitsk in 1774.

Fate Of A Pretender

The 'Marquis de Pugachov', as Catherine the Great dismissively called the rebel leader who caused so much destruction to Russia in her reign, gave up all pretence of being Tsar Peter III as soon as he was captured. Interrogated by the authorities in Yaitsk and Simbirsk, he declared his real identity and admitted his 'sinfulness before God and man' in claiming otherwise.

Catherine wanted to believe Pugachov was the agent of a foreign power. But an extensive investigation failed to produce any evidence of that. Pugachov at one stage maintained he had been a mere cat's paw of the Yaik Cossack leaders. It availed him nothing.

From Simbirsk, he was carted to Moscow in a cramped iron cage, and prepared for trial. When the hearing began, at the end of December 1774, he appeared mentally and physically broken, though on Catherine's orders he had not been put to the customary forms of torture. His conviction for treason was a foregone conclusion, and he was sentenced to have his arms and legs cut off before being beheaded and quartered.

On January 10, 1775, Pugachov and his principal supporters were led to a vast scaffold in Moscow's Red Square. An eye-witness describes him as shabby and nondescript, with barely the strength to cross himself. Contrary to his sentence, and to the expectations of the huge crowd, he was immediately decapitated, and only after that was his body hacked up. Catherine had apparently decided on a gesture of 'mercy'.

From her writings, Catherine seems to have been ambivalent about the man who said he was her husband. In one letter, to Voltaire, she remarks that Pugachov 'lived as a renegade and must die like a coward'. In another, she hints that, if it had not been for requirements of state, she might have pardoned the Cossack 'for his courage'. As part of her campaign to eradicate all traces of Pugachov's rebellion, she ordered that his name and deeds should never be mentioned.

Below: The iron cage in which Pugachov was brought to Moscow is now in the History Museum on Red Square. Contemporary pictures show the rebel leader, and the scaffold on which he was executed.

Right: One of Catherine the Great's most successful generals, Alexander Suvorov (1730-1800) brought her victories over Turks, Poles and Crimean Tartars as Russia expanded west and south.

Demise of the Zaporozhi

Renegade Zaporozhi Cossacks helped precipitate Russia's war with Turkey between 1768 and 1774. During their murderous forays under Zelezhniak, the bandits from the lower Dnieper ransacked villages on Turkish territory in south-eastern Europe, as well as in Poland and Russia. The Turks were already worried by Catherine the Great's designs on Poland. They used the raids as one of the pretexts for opening hostilities, even though the Russians had already stamped down extremely hard on the perpetrators.

The campaign began with an invasion of southern Russia by Turkey's Crimean Tartar clients. However, Russian generals such as Peter Rumiantsev, Basil Dolgoruki and Alexander Suvorov, with the help of loyalist Cossacks, delivered a stunning series of land victories, taking Catherine's armies south across the steppes and deep into the Crimea itself, as well as west to the banks of the River Danube. In 1770, a Russian fleet under the nominal command of Alexis Orlov, murderer of the real Tsar Peter III, destroyed Turkish sea power at the Battle of Tchesme.

Some Zaporozhi, as so often in the past, exploited the war for their own ends, preying on all sides. Though Zelezhniak's immediate followers had been executed or transported, other bandits emerged to take their place. A few eventually found their way east to join 'Tsar Peter' Pugachov's rising on the River Yaik. Many more operated, to the ostensible despair of the respectable Zaporozhi elders and the disgust of the Russians, around the Russian supply lines, attacking convoys to the Turkish front. This particular piece of brigandry and defiance was eventually to prove the final nail in the coffin.

Below: The Russian fleet defeats the Turks at Tchesme in 1770. Zaporozhian Cossacks were part-responsible for provoking the Russo-Turkish war of 1768-74. When it ended in Russian triumph, the day of reckoning for the Zaporozhskaya Sich finally arrived.

Invasion of the Sich

When a peace treaty was concluded with Turkey in July 1774, Catherine's immediate priority was to put down Pugachov's rebellion. Suvorov was one of the generals deputed to help. Though he came dashing from the Danube towards the Volga, he had not arrived by the time Pugachov was betrayed and surrendered to the authorities by his own men.

The Zaporozhi escaped the immediate wave of reprisals against Cossacks who had backed Pugachov. It was about the only crime of which they were not thoroughly guilty. But their endless list of other offences – piracy, brigandry, rebellion, refusal to supply levies, harbouring of fugitives and many more – had not been forgotten.

Catherine could afford to wait a little. The 1774 treaty gave Russia not only part of the Crimea and the much fought-over port of Azov, but enabled it to annex the Black Sea coast between the Rivers Bug and Dnieper. The Zaporozhskaya Sich, for more than 200 years the stronghold of the unruliest Cossacks of them all, was for the first time encircled by Russian territory. Though it took 17 years, two treaties and another war with Turkey to confirm it, the Black Sea steppe was a no man's land no more.

The blow against the Cossacks of the lower Dnieper finally fell in mid-summer 1775. A huge Russian army of veterans seasoned in the Turkish war and Pugachov's rebellion materialised in the Zaporozhi heartlands. The Cossacks were outnumbered and outgunned. For once, even the Zaporozhi had no stomach for a fight. Their 'respectable' leaders were dragged out of their opulent houses to exile in the furthest corners of Russia. The barracks and buildings of the Sich itself, on Khortitsa Island in the Dnieper, were burnt to the ground. The whole area was placed under Russian military rule and the final remnants of Zaporozhi self-government were obliterated.

Unable to countenance the new regime, some groups of Zaporozhi fled to the Danube, to seek protection from the Turkish Sultan, as their forebears had sought it from the Crimean Khan in 1709. Those who remained were moved around like pieces on a chessboard to fit the planning ideas of Gregory Potemkin – given or allowed to keep land, reduced to serfdom or raised to noble rank as it suited his purpose.

For Potemkin emerged from his spell as Catherine's lover to become virtual ruler of the newly acquired southlands, a position enhanced by Russia's annexation of the whole of the Crimea in 1783. It was he who sanctioned the mobilisation of some former Zaporozhi to take part in campaigns in the Crimea and in another war against Turkey from 1787. But their brief revival was under a new name – the Black Sea host.

Despite Potemkin's initial doubts about their trustworthiness, they served bravely and loyally. The reward was a grant of territory far away from the Dnieper, on the Kuban River beneath the mountains of the Caucasus.

Below: Zaporozhian Cossacks of the new Black Sea host fought alongside regular Russian troops in their successful siege of Ochakov, during the Russo-Turkish War of 1787-91. Suvorov directed the attack under Potemkin's overall command, and was seriously wounded. At the end of the campaign, Russia had pushed her frontier to the River Dniester, ousting the Turks from most of the Black Sea's north coast.

Reforming the Hosts

The 34-year reign of Catherine the Great transformed Cossackry, as it transformed Russia's frontiers and many aspects of Russian life. When the Tsarina died in 1796, military repression and resettlements had brought most of the unruly Cossack freebooters firmly under St Petersburg's thumb, forced to accept its authority to keep what remained of their liberties.

The Zaporozhi, like the Ukrainian Cossacks before them, had to all intents and purposes ceased to exist, swallowed up in the extension of Russian forms of social organisation to the south-western border regions. Only the names 'Zaporozhi' and 'Ukrainian' Cossack remained, to flicker in and out of Russian regimental lists for the next century or so in nods to tradition.

The other old free hosts fared less badly. Catherine seems to have had a soft spot for the Don Cossacks, who declined to join Pugachov's rebellion. She brought 200 of them to St Petersburg to serve as part of her Imperial Court Guard, and towards the end of her reign ceremonially confirmed their possession of their traditional homelands 'for ever'. Even so, there were clashes – for example, in 1791 over the enforced resettlement of several hundred Don families in the Caucasus. They refused to go at first. But though the Don could field 20,000 or more fighting men, its Cossacks were no longer a match for the Russian military machine, and by now they knew it. Eventually, they yielded to Catherine's will.

The Yaik (now the Ural) Cossacks, seriously depleted after Pugachov's uprising, also received a mark of royal favour. Catherine's heir Paul, whose relations with his mother were stormy, included some of them in his personal guard, the Gachino Corps. But the Ural host was falling under the shadow of the newer Orenburg host nearby.

That occupied territory straddling the Ural Mountains, and had been formed from a mixture of resettled Ural Cossacks and peasants transferred from western Russia with Cossack status. Its fighting capacity was strengthened by neighbouring Bashkyr tribesmen organised on traditional Cossack military lines.

The use of once-hostile steppe people as Cossack-style irregular light cavalry was copied elsewhere. The Kalmuks, from the region around Astrakhan, supplied a 'Cossack' regiment at the end of the 18th century. In sparsely populated Siberia, where anyone could obtain Cossack status by enlisting for state service as a town or border guard, Buryats and Tartars joined Russian exiles and adventurers in the Cossack ranks.

The new south

At the end of Catherine's reign, the lands of Ciscaucasia between the Sea of Azov and the Caspian had been wrested from Turkish control. For more than 200 years, there had been Cossack communities on their eastern fringes, along the River Terek. Old Believer Cossacks had pushed beyond those, to build villages in the Greben Mountains. The rest of the territory was wide open for settlement.

In the 1790s, 10,000 displaced 'Black Sea' Zaporozhi trekked there from their former homelands, at their own suggestion, but with

Below: Catherine the Great used Cossacks to create a cordon of farmer-soldiers to guard her new southern territories.

Cossack Ranks

By the end of the 18th century, the post of ataman in all Cossack hosts was firmly in the gift of the Russian monarch. For practical reasons, the choice had to be broadly acceptable to the Cossacks; in 1800, for example, an ataman who proved thoroughly unpopular with the Kuban host was ousted by the authorities. But the Cossacks themselves had less and less say in who led them, and in 1827 Tsar Nicholas I appointed his young son Alexander ataman of the Don and Ural hosts, underlining the fact that the job had become largely symbolic.

Other key figures in the administration – such as the host secretary, or adjutant – were also, directly or through the ataman, Russian appointees. Village elders, in most cases, were still elected by the Cossacks they were to represent, but the authorities needed to be assured of their loyalty to Russia before they were allowed to offer themselves as candidates. Effectively, that completed the concentration of Cossack political power in the hands of a few rich families. Nevertheless, ordinary Cossacks could occasionally break into the ruling circle if distinguished military service raised them to commissioned, and therefore noble, rank.

Military rank titles were one area in which Cossack tradition continued to prevail. Up to the level of lieutenant–colonel, the Cossacks used their own, not Russian, designations:-

British	Cossack	Russian
Private	Kazak	Nizhnichin
Corporal	Prikazni	Mladchi Unteroffizier
Sergeant	Uriadnik	Starsky Unteroffizier
Sergeant-Major	Vakhmistr	Vakhmistr
Lieutenant	Sotnik	Poruchik
Captain	Podesaul	Kapitan or Rotmistre
Major	Esaul	Maior
Lieut.-Colonel	Starshina	Podpolkovnik

Catherine's approval. The reluctant Cossacks from the Don were moved in, too. Catherine wanted to create a cordon of farmer-soldiers to guard her new southern frontier.

Land was plentiful, available to any Cossack signed up for 20 years of military service and ready to fight with gun or sabre to protect his holding from hostile hill-tribes, who waged a running battle against the incomers for more than half a century. The young Leo Tolstoy experienced this warfare first-hand in 1851; it gave him the material for his novel 'The Cossacks', the finest he wrote before 'War and Peace'.

The former Zaporozhi mostly settled in western Ciscaucasia, along the Kuban River, where they joined those Don Cossacks who had emigrated after Bulavin's revolt in 1706. Within a few years, the Kuban capital of Ekaterinodar (later Krasnodar) had become a thriving town, and the new Kuban Cossack elders grew rich from farming, fishing and trading, as their forebears had once done on the River Dnieper.

Prospects on the southern frontier were attractive to others, too. Catherine's controls on serfs in both Russia and the Ukraine were intended to prevent the mass wanderings of the poor and hungry that caused so much strife throughout Russian history. Nevertheless, runaways and army deserters still headed for Cossack frontier settlements, with the Caucasus replacing the Dnieper and Don as a destination. Once at the Kuban, they could expect a welcome; manpower on the frontier was in short supply.

Up the social scale

Naked force and economic subjection helped Catherine and Potemkin to complete the process of taming Russia's borderers begun by Peter the Great. But the wily Tsarina and her ministers used another weapon, too – the Cossack elders' desire for social respectability.

In 1775-85, Catherine adopted laws reforming the rights and duties of the Russian nobility, and for the first time Cossacks who reached senior military rank acquired with it the status of hereditary nobles. They became entitled to run their land-holdings as mini-Tsardoms, effectively reducing poorer Cossacks who lived and worked on their estates to serfs. Shortly after Catherine's death, similar privileges were extended to junior officers, and the serfdom of Cossack estate-workers was formally confirmed.

The reforms delivered the death–blow to democratic Cossackry, barely a century after enraged Cossacks had slaughtered the Ukrainian leader Ivan Briukhovetsky for presuming to become a serf-owner. Perhaps unnoticed by wealthy elders eager for ennoblement, they also ended the freelance fighting tradition of the Cossacks.

For Catherine's charter permitted nobles to enter the service of states other than Russia – but only if the states concerned were European and allied to Russia. Even that was permissible only if those concerned were not needed to serve Russia itself. No longer could a free Cossack ataman lead his host to side with Russia's enemies. The eagles' wings had finally been clipped.

On the World Stage

Dealing with the French

Don and Ural Cossacks formed the vanguard of an Austrian and Russian army which drove the forces of revolutionary France out of Italy in a lightning campaign during the summer of 1799. Victories on the Rivers Adda and Trebbia and at Novi fanned the Cossacks' reputation throughout western Europe as fearsome irregular cavalry – particularly in England, where newspapers showered praise on their 'knightly' military feats against the French enemy.

The Russians' venture into Italy was rich in ironies. Paul I, called the 'Tsar Madman' because of his violent changes of mood and his reversal of many of the reforms instituted by his mother Catherine the Great, had not wanted war with France. But a bizarre sequence of events led to the election of Paul, a pillar of the Orthodox Church, as Grand Master of the Roman Catholic Knights of St John. When the French occupied Malta, where the Knights of St John were based, Paul took Russia into alliance with Britain, Austria, Turkey and Naples against them.

Right: The memorial to Suvorov in the Summer Garden, St Petersburg. The great general is buried in the nearby Church of the Annunciation, beneath a simple slab with the terse inscription 'Here lies Suvorov'.

Below: The military exploits of Alexander Suvorov (1730-1800) brought him countless honours and made him a near-legend in his day. Virtually the whole population of St Petersburg attended his funeral.

To head the Russian army, Paul picked Alexander Suvorov, who had been deputed to help put down Pugachov's Cossack rebellion more than 25 years earlier. Although he was of noble birth, Suvorov had entered the Russian army as a private, rising through the ranks to become a field-marshal and covering himself with glory in the wars against Turkey. On campaign, he wore a rough peasant shirt instead of a splendid uniform, and ate the plain food of the ordinary soldier. He was no admirer of Cossack indiscipline – in the Turkish wars he ordered Cossacks to be flogged for pillaging. That contributed to his reputation for bringing the men under his command to top fighting trim.

By 1799, Suvorov was 70 years old and semi-retired. But the old general had lost none of his cunning and, employing his motto of 'Intuition, Speed and Impact', he fought some of the most brilliant battles of his life. He was ready to carry the war on into France itself when the unpredictable Paul gave him new orders – march into Switzerland to link up with other Austro-Russian forces and drive the French from there. Against his better judgment, Suvorov obeyed instructions, heading for Zurich with the long-coated, bearded Cossacks flanking the advance.

A Russian Hannibal

The diversion went well for Suvorov at first, as the Cossacks harried the French back, amid ferocious fighting, over the lofty St Gothard Pass and the Devil's Bridge (Teufelsbrucke) across the River Reuss at Schollenen. But near Altdorf, on the edge of Lake Lucerne, the pursuers were forced to halt. There was no route forward between the sheer cliffs and the lake, and the French had removed all the local boats.

Suvorov had to cast around eastwards to the River Muota, and that cost the Russians dearly. During the delay, the French commander Andre Masséna defeated the forces Suvorov was to join at Zurich, and promptly headed towards Suvorov himself with an army 80,000 strong.

That far outnumbered Suvorov's 18,000 soldiers and 5,000 Cossacks. He had no choice but to retreat through the Pragel Pass to the town of Glarus. Now, it was the French turn to harry. They nearly cut the Russians off at Glarus, but Suvorov managed to spirit his men to the village of Elm.

From there, with the Cossacks now providing a rearguard, the old field-marshal made the do-or-die effort to escape that earned him the nickname of the Russian Hannibal. In deep snow on October 6, 1799, he led his troops, exhausted and half-starving, on a perilous trek up the Panixer Pass through the 3,000 metre (9,000ft) mountains of the rugged Bundner Oberland.

The journey was sheer hell. The French attacked the Cossacks protecting the rear of the column, but fell back in the face of the conditions. The Russians, who had to go on, burnt the wooden stocks of their rifles and the shafts of their lances to combat the cold. Agonisingly, the strongest slipped and slithered to the summit of the pass, while dozens weakened by hunger succumbed to the cold.

Even over the crest, they were not safe. The trail downwards at one point veered sharply away from a plateau ending in a precipice. In the dark and snow, without guides, hundreds of soldiers and Cossacks missed the turning, to fall to their deaths from the cliffs. Nevertheless, when Suvorov finally reached the town of Chur near the Rhine, he brought 16,000 of his original force with him.

Above: Cossack courage helped the Russian army over the wintry mountains of Switzerland in 1799. The American writer J.T. Headley said in 1845 that Hannibal's crossing of the Alps was 'child's play' by comparison.

An effort wasted

Suvorov's gallant foray, which took the Cossack plainsmen over four Alpine passes in two weeks, fighting all the way, was to little military avail. Suvorov himself was disgusted with his Austrian allies, blaming them for the nearest thing to a defeat he had suffered in his long career. They in turn grew bitter over the depredations of Suvarov's Cossacks, to whom foraging at the expense of the local population was a way of life, in their winter quarters in Bohemia. In January 1800, Tsar Paul called the army home, rewarding Suvorov with the title of 'supreme general' and raising him virtually to the status of an equal – a unique honour which the old soldier lived only a few months to enjoy. Paul was unhappy with his allies, too – in particular, the British. An Anglo-Russian expedition, which included Cossacks, to fight the French in Holland had ended in mutual recriminations and no victories. Then in September 1800 Britain took Malta from the French and refused to hand it over to Paul.

In the meantime, Napoleon Bonaparte had seized power as First Consul in France, and was turning himself from an instrument of the revolution to an autocrat – a transformation of which the Russian Tsar naturally approved. As Napoleon and Paul moved towards a formal alliance against Britain, the 'Tsar Madman' devised the maddest scheme of his life. The luckless Don Cossacks were to carry it out.

To the Ganges!

Rich British possessions in India were a tempting target for Tsar Paul when he turned against his former allies and towards an accommodation with Napoleonic France. Once Napoleon had broken the Austrians at the Battle of Marengo, he warmed to the idea, too. It would give him the opportunity both to deal a blow to Britain and to recapture French holdings on the sub-continent lost half-a-century previously.

Napoleon prepared to send a corps under André Masséna, persecutor of Suvorov's Russians in Switzerland, to take part in the Indian adventure. But on January 12, 1801, long before Masséna was ready, Tsar Paul decided to move on his own.

The expedition was one of the worst conceived in military history. Basil Orlov, a relative of Catherine the Great's one-time favourite, was the nominal commander. The real leader was the seasoned Don Cossack Major-General Matvei Platov. In less than a month, he mustered 22,000 Don Cossacks and provisioned them as best he could in the depths of Russian winter.

The Cossacks' first destination was to be Bukhara, the trading centre on the ancient Silk Road across Asia. From there, they were to work their way through Afghanistan to northern India and the River Ganges. Altogether, they were expected to ride some 4,800km (3,000 miles) over steppe, deserts and mountains. But the precise routes and distances were uncertain; the Cossacks had not even been given maps.

Roads out of the Don region were all but impassable in the winter snows. The resigned Cossacks struggled along them to the frozen Volga and across the ice. It cracked in places, dropping dozens of men and horses into the swirling waters to drown in the depths.

The depleted expedition reeled on over the southern steppe and into the desert. Provisions were already beginning to dwindle, and even the Cossack ponies, as used to hardship as their masters, could find no suitable forage. The Cossacks seemed destined to leave their bones somewhere in the endless wastes of central Asia.

Reprieve came unexpectedly, three weeks into the trek. As the Cossacks staggered forward, messengers from Russia caught up with them. Tsar Paul had been assassinated and the attack on India had been abandoned. Wearily, the Cossacks turned back to their homelands.

At war again

With Paul dead and his son Alexander, who connived at the murder, on the throne, Russia hastened to make peace with both the British and the French. But it was barely four years before the Cossacks were back in action – the spearhead of a Russian army allied with England, Austria and Prussia to thwart the ambitions of Napoleon, now crowned Emperor of France.

Tsar Alexander used the interlude to increase his Cossack levies. He had more than 50 Cossack regiments with perhaps 50,000 men, more than half of them from the Don. Attempts were made to standardise their uniforms, though they still looked as scruffy as the shaggy ponies most of them rode in their traditional uncurbed style. Front-line mounted Cossacks were usually armed with a lance, a shoulder-slung carbine and a curved sabre. Some of those attached to guards regiments had pistols instead of carbines. Others served as infantry or horse artillery.

To Napoleon's soldierly eye, trained at France's starchy écoles militaires, the Cossack horse-soldiers must have looked a disgrace as they attacked, not in an orthodox cavalry charge, but in the twisting,

Below: The ancient central Asian city of Bukhara, now in Uzbekistan, was to be the first staging-post in the Cossack-led invasion of India in 1801. But the expedition was recalled soon after it had started. Bukhara eventually fell to the Russians in 1868.

Below right: Tsar Alexander I (reigned 1801-25). In his epoch, the Cossacks were finally transformed into bastions of the autocracy.

Above: Tsar Alexander presents 'Cossacks' to Napoleon after the two rulers had concluded their peace treaty in 1807. In fact, the troops shown are predominantly Kalmuk and Bashkir tribesmen, who had been organised militarily on Cossack lines.

swirling clouds perfected by their ancestors back to the Tartars. In 1805, though, he had no special reason to fear them.

For in Alexander's first forays against the French, his Cossacks were part of an outmoded army led by generals with none of Napoleon's battle-skills, flair and dash, and wracked by the mistrust between Russians and Austrians. When Napoleon advanced through Austria in November 1805, the Russian commander Michael Kutuzov favoured a cautious defensive strategy. He was over-ruled by Alexander and Emperor Francis II of Austria.

The Cossacks, attacking in their normal way and ahead of orthodox cavalry, had an early success, driving back the French advance guards and taking prisoner 50 dragoons. In the pitched encounter that followed at Austerlitz – described in all its bloody detail by Leo Tolstoy in his masterwork 'War and Peace' – the 90,000-strong army of Russia and her allies was outwitted and crushed.

On the eve of battle, Napoleon spread his troops out thinly, leading Alexander and Francis to believe he was over-stretched and victory was there for them to take. The Cossacks spent the night roistering in anticipation. But while they got drunk, Napoleon swiftly and silently regrouped. The next morning, as soon as the Russians committed themselves to an onslaught, the French hurled 70,000 men at the gap left in the Austro-Russian centre. In nine hours of struggle, 15,000 Russian soldiers and Cossacks were killed, 20,000 captured and 40 regimental standards lost. The rest of Kutuzov's force fled, throwing down its arms and abandoning 80 guns. Francis and a tearful Alexander, who had watched the terrible catastrophe unfold, joined the rout. Of the 7,000 French casualties, only a few hundred died. Napoleon later claimed that Austerlitz was the easiest battle he fought in his life.

Within a few days, Austria had sued for peace with France. The remnants of the Russian army struggled home. Reorganised, with its Cossacks once more in the van, it was to struggle with the French again and again – to defeat at Jena, to an inconclusive standstill at Eylau and to another bloody rout at Friedland.

In the retreat from Friedland in June 1807, the Cossacks once again operated as the rearguard. They, like the rest of the Russian troops, were near the end of their tethers. There could be no clearer evidence of that than the presence among them of Kalmuk 'cossacks', armed only with bows and arrows which they fired backwards over their shoulders in the ancient Parthian shot.

Shortly afterwards, Alexander called a ceasefire and wrote to Napoleon: 'An alliance of France with Russia has always been the object of my desires'. The two emperors met in July in a pavilion on a raft on the River Neman, near Tilsit (later Sovietsk) on Russia's north-west frontier. After dining together, the pair, who got on well, concluded a peace treaty effectively dividing Europe between them.

Moscow is Burning!

In June 1812, Napoleon was once again on the banks of the River Neman where, four years previously, he and Tsar Alexander had signed their peace treaty. Now the treaty was just paper, rendered useless by Russia's continued commercial and diplomatic dealings with Britain. The French emperor was determined to make Alexander pay in full for that treachery.

Around him, Napoleon had assembled the full might of his multinational Grand Armée – 575,000 troops from France, Italy, Poland, Holland, Switzerland and the German states. Nearly 60,000 of them were cavalrymen, light horse and the tightly disciplined central reserve whose heavy cuirassiers had delivered victory in so many battles. There were 1,200 pieces of cannon.

With this huge force, Napoleon was confident he could quickly crush the Russians, as he had done at Austerlitz and elsewhere. Their armies, divided into three under the commanders Barclay de Tolly, Peter Bagration and Alexander Tormasov, numbered no more than 220,000. When the French emperor moved across the Neman into Russia, the 420,000 men of the first-wave invasion had rations for only three weeks.

But the Russians would not stand still and fight. As the Grande Armée approached the city of Vilna, Napoleon's soldiers saw the sight that was to torment them throughout their advance – squadrons of Cossacks ghosting away on the horizon, having set ammunition and food stores ablaze.

That was the Russians' tactic. As their heavily out-numbered forces retreated east, a flying cavalry command, under the Don Ataman Matvei Platov and drawn from all the Cossack hosts, covered their rear, destroying everything the Grande Armée might use.

Not a village, not a town, not a grain field in the invaders' path escaped the Cossack torches. A plaintive eye-witness in the French ranks wrote afterwards: 'It was part of the Russian system to destroy everything they could not carry off, so the resources of the French were soon reduced to very little'. Napoleon was forced to send foraging parties 50km (30 miles) from his flanks in search of provender. They were easy targets for roving Cossack bands.

Through blazing heat punctuated by bursts of torrential rain, the trudge east went on, during July and into August. Men were now dying by the score of hunger, disease or at the hands of preying Cossacks. Starving horses dropped in their tracks. Occasionally the retreating Russians held their ground for a while, but they still avoided the fullscale battle Napoleon wanted.

That looked as if it might come at Smolensk, on the upper reaches of the River Dnieper, where Barclay de Tolly and Bagration joined forces on August 3. But after a vicious engagement Barclay withdrew. Tsar Alexander and his advisers, disturbed by Napoleon's progress towards Moscow, were furious. Barclay was ousted and Field-Marshal Prince Michael Kutuzov was made supreme commander. Egged on by the court and his generals, Kutuzov finally gave the Grande Armée the setpiece encounter it was seeking – west of Moscow, at Borodino.

Below: Don Cossacks were among the last Russian troops to quit the field at Borodino in 1812. Though the French claimed to have won the battle, the murderous losses they sustained meant they were facing defeat in the war.

The field of Borodino

As dawn broke in a clear sky on the morning of September 7, 1812, Napoleon told one of his aides: 'This is the sun of Austerlitz'. But if Napoleon was to remember the earlier battle as one of his easiest, he was to recall Borodino as the most terrible. The depredations of the long march had reduced his troops by nearly two-thirds – to a dismal array of 130,000 hungry and exhausted men. Half his cavalry no longer had mounts. Against him, the Russians fielded 112,000, not counting reserves and Platov's skirmishing Cossacks.

The French guns carried the day, raining round after round, mostly of grape shot, into the Russian ranks. Then, when the Russian guns were taken, those were turned on Kutuzov's forces too, cutting down infantry and cavalry like a hay-maker's scythe. By day's end, the Russians had lost nearly half their forces dead and wounded.

But the Grande Armée had paid its own terrible price – 57,000 casualties, with 47 generals among them. Although its remaining cavalry and crack infantry regiments gave chase as Kutuzov withdrew, a shield of Cossacks and other troops allowed the Russians to retreat in good order with their casualties, first to Moscow and then eastwards towards Riazan. On September 15, Napoleon entered Moscow, which had been left undefended

HERO FROM THE DON

Matvei Platov's part in mad Tsar Paul's abortive expedition to India brought him the highest honour a Don Cossack could hope for – to become ataman of the Don host. At the age of 50, after three decades of distinguished military service against the Tartars, Turks and Persians, General Platov might have been forgiven for resting on his laurels in his new post. He did not.

In the years between 1801 and 1812, he threw himself wholeheartedly behind Tsar Alexander's attempts to improve Russian military standards. By the time of Napoleon's invasion, the Don alone could field upwards of 50,000 Cossacks, approximately uniformed in a blue chekmen, or frock-coat, and cloak. After the loss of Moscow, Platov raised 15,000 more.

The events of 1812-14 made Platov a hero to the whole of Russia and much of Europe. First, at the head of a highly mobile division of Cossacks, he covered the Russian withdrawal to the east, 'scorching the earth' to impede the French advance. Then, when the old one-eyed Field Marshal Michael Kutuzov was given supreme command, Platov's division joined the main body of the army and fought gallantly at Borodino. As the French eventually withdrew, Platov's men led the pursuit which carried the Cossacks across the Rhine to Paris itself. Legend says he promised his daughter in marriage to any Cossack who captured Napoleon, though the pledge was never tested.

In recognition of Platov's achievements, Tsar Alexander made him a count. On a visit to London in June 1814, he was awarded a diamond studded portrait of the Prince Regent and other gifts. Under the influence of English admirers, he trimmed his flowing Cossack whiskers. Platov, the most renowned Cossack of his day died in 1818, aged 67.

Below: Don Cossack ataman, Matvei Platov (1751-1818). His exploits against the French became the stuff of legend – but only fate had stopped him from fighting the British in India.

and partly evacuated. As his weary soldiers began to seek billets or make bivouacs, thick plumes of smoke and flames were seen coming from the city's merchants' quarter. Moscow was ablaze, probably at Russian orders. For five days the terrible conflagration raged, spread by drunken Russian arsonists and fanned by strong winds. When the fire was finally extinguished, three-quarters of the ancient city had been destroyed.

Far left: Napoleon and his generals on the heights overlooking Borodino, 110km (70 miles) west of Moscow.

Left: Napoleon Bonaparte (1769-1821), Emperor of the French from 1804 to his downfall in 1815.

Slaughter in the Snows

Right: The stereotypical view of a Cossack bent on killing and plunder. During Napoleon's retreat, Cossacks lived up to the image. but they suffered hardship and death, too.

'It was the most grand, the most sublime and the most terrible sight the world ever saw', Napoleon said of the holocaust that enveloped Moscow soon after he entered the city. The little French emperor singed his own hair and eyebrows in fighting the blaze, and claimed its heat made the walls of buildings 5km (3 miles) away unbearable to touch. He also maintained for the rest of his life that it had prevented him from subduing Russia. He had counted on finding in Moscow supplies for a year or more, and thousands of serfs who, once he had proclaimed them free, would rally to his army.

The fire robbed him of much-needed provisions. The mass evacuation of Moscow robbed him of fresh troops. Tsar Alexander absolutely refused to negotiate a peace. And in early October, the Russians surprised a French force led by the dashing Marshal Joachim Murat, King of Naples, inflicting heavy casualties.

On October 19, 1812, calculating he had two months before the worst of the Russian winter set in, Napoleon began the withdrawal of his tattered Grande Armée – 80,000 men and perhaps 30,000 camp followers. Parts of the Kremlin were blown up, with other public buildings that had survived the fire.

When the exodus westward started, it was more like a holiday procession than a military retreat. The soldiers were laden down with booty pillaged from Russian cities; one carried a diamond-studded spittoon among the treasures in his knapsack. Waggon-trains stuffed with more plunder, with the wounded, with French and other civilians who had

been living in Moscow, rolled behind. The camp-followers, many with mobile canteens, roamed carelessly among the regimental columns. Horses and cursing men dragged heavy cannons Napoleon could not bear to leave behind.

It was a Cossack's dream. Soon the steppe-horsemen began to strike, appearing from nowhere as waggons stuck in the sandy roads, to kill the stragglers and plunder in their turn. The wily Kutuzov, who maintained he had been the victor at Borodino, was content to let the Cossacks do their deadly work. The Russian army shadowed the retreat, but avoided open battle with Napoleon's main force.

Napoleon's escape

At Malo-Yaroslavets, Platov and 6,000 Cossacks tried a large-scale assault under cover of fog. They were beaten back, 'howling like wolves' according to a French soldier, after they had come within inches of capturing Napoleon himself. The emperor was inspecting outer troop positions when the attack started, but went unrecognised by men from the Don bent on booty. The incident shook even Napoleon; if he still had doubts about quitting Russia, he lost them at Malo-Yaroslavets.

On October 30, the first snows fell. Soon the temperature began to plummet, far earlier than Napoleon had anticipated. The retreating column was spread out across miles of hostile, frozen terrain, and its horses were dropping dead in the cold; more than 30,000 succumbed in one night, according to Napoleon himself. Waggons, artillery and the wounded were gradually abandoned.

Always, the Cossacks were lurking, waiting to swoop on the stragglers with their terrible curved sabres flashing. Like the men of the Grande Armée, they were cold, hungry and dying in dozens. But the lust for plunder and killing kept them going.

Below: Through the ruins of Moscow, Napoleonic troops make their way from the Petrovsky Palace to the Kremlin.

Death at The Berezina

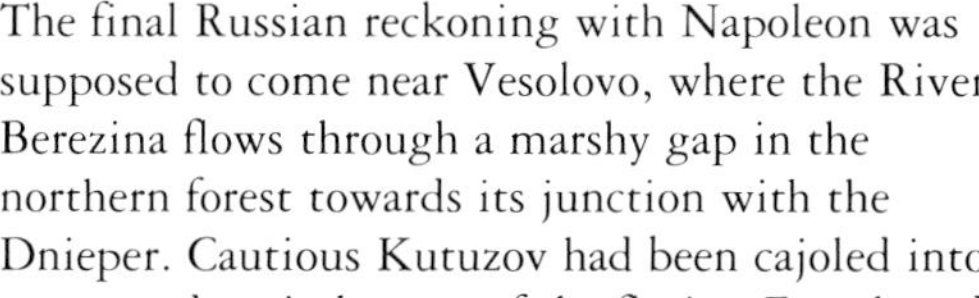

The final Russian reckoning with Napoleon was supposed to come near Vesolovo, where the River Berezina flows through a marshy gap in the northern forest towards its junction with the Dnieper. Cautious Kutuzov had been cajoled into an attempted encirclement of the fleeing French and their allies. All bridges across the river were down. Platov's Cossacks had a special role; they were to remedy their earlier oversight, and locate and take the emperor.

The scheme almost worked. On November 26, Napoleon arrived on the river bank with his much-depleted army, from which an entire corps had been lost to the Russians a few days before. In a masterly move, the French emperor divided his surviving force into two sections, and spread them several miles apart. In both sections, men hastily set to improvising bridges, up to their shoulders in icy water.

Then the Russians and Platov's Cossacks struck. They took one bridgehead, capturing the whole force around it, but eventually realised Napoleon was not there. The Cossacks were sent at full gallop to trace him.

Meanwhile, at the second bridgehead, spans had been thrown across the stream. Napoleon ordered a detachment to the other bank, and followed with his principal commanders. Losing all discipline, the rest of the soldiers hurled themselves in the emperor's footsteps, a teeming mass of half-frozen, desperate humanity. In the confusion, the Russian forces arrived.

Desperation turned to blind panic as men struggled to escape. They threw themselves into the waters, to be swept away to drown, or over the dead bodies piling up on the spans. Sabres swished and the bridges were torched, adding fire to the scene of frozen horror. At least 6,000 died in the horrific carnage at the River Berezina, and more than 15,000 prisoners were taken.

Of the 420,000 troops of the Grande Armée who had crossed the River Neman in June 1812, fewer than 40,000 survived. But Napoleon was among them, so the terrible pursuit had to go on, through the ever-deepening winter with the Cossacks, as ever, lurking.

Above: Napoleon in retreat – as seen by Russian film-makers.

Below: Cossacks in hot pursuit of the foe.

Onward to Paris

Right: The War of 1812 against Napoleon is commemorated in a triumphal arch in Moscow.

To the shattered survivors of the Berezina crossing, the spires of Vilna (now Vilnius, capital of Lithuania) were a magnet as they stumbled west over the snows with Platov's Cossacks still harrying them. When they entered the city in December 1812 under the protection of Marshal Michel Ney's rearguard, they dreamed of shelter, warmth, food – some, even of revenge on their Cossack persecutors.

It was an illusion, for the citizens were no lovers of Napoleon. Ostensibly welcoming the exhausted troops, they murdered them in scores to pillage the last items of booty in their knapsacks. Dozens more began to die as heat in their billets thawed frozen, gangrenous limbs. And the pursuing Russian army caught up quickly.

Within a few hours, those who could move were forced to do so again, towards the icy mountains just outside the city. On Mount Vaka, the commanders had to abandon the last of the baggage – and the Grande Armée's treasury, millions of francs in gold and silver preserved through all the death and destruction.

Almost as though they could smell the loot, the Cossacks were there scrabbling for it. As a French observer wrote later: 'All that had not previously been seized by the Russians, all that the Berezina had spared, fell into their hands'. Meanwhile, others of Platov's Cossacks were in Vilna itself, robbing and massacring the wounded left behind.

By then, Napoleon was on his way back to Paris via Warsaw and Dresden, his Russian adventure at its cruel end. Under Murat, his troops plodded on to the frontier.

The chase continues

'The bones of the audacious foreigners have been scattered from Moscow to the River Neman,' declared Platov in one of his orders of the day as the invaders left Russian soil. But his Cossacks were no respecters of frontiers. In their hundreds, they rode across the Neman ice into Prussia in hot pursuit. It took Tsar Alexander a month to decide the main Russian army should follow the trail they blazed, and months more to forge the military alliances necessary to defeat the new and powerful French forces Napoleon was already assembling.

From May 1813, Platov's Cossacks were in set battles again – Lutzen, Bautzen, the Napoleonic victory at Dresden, and the three days of slaughter at Leipzig in October which forced Napoleon back across the Rhine. An English cartoon of the time shows Platov as a huntsman leading the chase after the Napoleonic fox.

Below: Russian partisans lead away French prisoners-of-war in an illustration by D.A. Shmarinov for a Russian edition of Tolstoy's 'War and Peace'.

Then, the struggles were on French soil. Lack of liaison between the commanders ranged against him allowed Napoleon to score several local victories. But the Cossacks were still on his tail, and on January 30, 1814, they once again came close to taking him.

Ironically, the incident occurred at Brienne-le-Chateau in Champagne, the town where the future emperor attended military academy until he was 15 years old. As Napoleon was emerging from a wood with a small escort, a squadron of Cossacks attacked, one charging directly at him with lance lowered. A French aide managed to divert and kill the assailant, before French troops appeared to rescue their leader from the Cossacks' clutches.

It was a brief respite. By the end of March, Paris had capitulated. Tsar Alexander led the victorious Russian and Prussian armies into the capital, to begin the diplomatic process leading to Napoleon's abdication and exile to Elba, the 'Holy Alliance' between the rulers of Austria, Prussia and Russia, and agreements making most of Poland a constitutional kingdom – with the Tsar as king.

While the mighty worked out the future of Europe in marble halls, Platov's Cossacks and ordinary Russian troops turned the streets of Paris into one huge, sprawling bivouac. Their beards, raggedly exotic clothes, thievery and uncouth habits drew the disdain of respectable, if vanquished, Parisians. So did their Russian tongue with its deeply rolled 'r'. But when they began the trudge back to their motherland, their barbarous-seeming Russian language had, according to a popular legend at least, left a legacy to mellifluous French – the word 'bistro'. In France, it came to mean a bar or public house. To the liquor-loving Cossacks of 1814, though, it was an urgent command to drinks-waiters: 'Quick!'.

Above: Platov the huntsman after Napoleon the fox in an English cartoon of 1813.

Below: Russian troops bivouacking in Paris.

The Russian Columbus

Right: Gregory Shelekhov (1747-95) and his Cossack followers established the first permanent Russian settlements on the American mainland. His tomb is in the Siberian city of Irkutsk.

While Napoleon was conducting his disastrous sortie to Moscow in 1812, Russians and Cossacks were building a new ostrog, one more of the strongholds they had dotted over the vastness of Siberia since the 17th century. But this was no outpost in Siberian taiga, tundra or steppe. It was set amid foggy coastal canyons 9,600km (6,000 miles) as the eagle flies from Moscow – in California, 96km (60 miles) north-west of the Golden Gate.

The fort was a monument to the ambitions of two remarkable men, Gregory Shelekhov and Alexander Baranov. Shelekhov, remembered today as the 'Russian Columbus', was born in the Ukraine in 1747 and, like many from that troubled region, drifted east to the new frontier of Siberia as a young man. There, he grew wealthy, trapping and trading in lucrative furs from the Arctic fringes explored for Russia by Vitus Bering in 1728-41.

Shelekhov based himself in Irkutsk, but was soon roaming far afield to the Aleutians, the islands spreading like a necklace across the southern end of the Bering Sea. They were a bleak hell, where roving bands of Siberian Cossack trappers were slaughtering sea otters, seals and foxes by the thousands. Periodically, too, the trappers murdered each other and native Aleuts in their greed for furs.

The bloody competition for fast-dwindling pelts convinced Shelekhov to move east again, through the Aleutians towards Alaska, where the fur resources had hardly been touched. In the 1780s, he and band of Cossack frontiersmen made the perilous trek, to establish an ostrog at Three Saints Bay on Kodiak Island, beside the Alaska Peninsula. From that base, they explored the surrounding territory, creating the first permanent Russian settlements on the American mainland.

Below: Alexander Baranov (1746-1819) became governor of all Russian settlements in America. Under his leadership, a Russian expedition reached Hawaii and annexed the islands by treaty for the Tsar. But the arrangement was never officially ratified.

In the fur-rich Alaskan wilderness, Shelekhov conceived the idea of claiming the whole western American coast for Russia, and of securing a monopoly to exploit it. He recruited Baranov – whose own activities in the fur trade had run into trouble – as his deputy at Three Saints Bay, and set off in 1791 to promote his plan in Catherine the Great's St Petersburg. The Tsarina showed no interest, and in 1795 Shelekhov died, a disappointed man.

South to California

Four years later, Alexander Baranov had better luck than his predecessor. By then, the 'Tsar Madman' Paul I was on the throne and reversing many of the decisions of his mother. Paul created the Russian American Company, with a trade monopoly and the job of administering the Alaskan coastal regions on his behalf. The area under its jurisdiction ended almost exactly where Alaska's southernmost frontier runs today. Baranov was made general manager, virtual ruler of an icy Alaskan kingdom.

With dogged determination and keen business sense, Baranov seized the opportunity. He encouraged the immigration of Cossack trappers from the Aleutians, and imported native Aleuts as slaves to help with hunting and fishing. He moved the capital of his colony from Three Saints Bay, first to Fort St Michael, where it was sacked by local tribes, and then in 1804 to New Archangel – the site of present-day Sitka. He built ships, and began to explore the Pacific as far south as the island of Hawaii. Above all, he sent back to Russia furs in ever-growing quantities.

There were times of desperate hardship. In 1805-06, the tiny population of New Archangel came near to starvation. Ships were ordered south to try to obtain food, and put in to San Francisco Bay in Spanish California.

The governor, Jose Durio Arguello, was eager to trade grain for Alaskan furs, and also to involve the Russians in a plot to win California's independence from Spain, under the protection of

SEWARD'S 'FOLLY'

Colonisation of the northern Pacific basin by Siberian Cossacks and traders led to the first international dispute between Russia and the newly independent United States. The row started in 1821, when Russia claimed sole rights to trade, trap and fish along the western American seaboard north of Vancouver Island, and banned foreign vessels from coming within 160km (100 miles) of Russian settlements in Alaska and the Aleutian Islands.

President James Monroe and Secretary of State John Quincey Adams, who had previously been US representative at St Petersburg, suspected the Russians wanted to seize more territory in the Americas, including former Spanish possessions such as California. Quincey Adams denounced the Russian claim as contrary to international law, and it helped spur the president to set out his 'Monroe Doctrine' of 1823.

According to that, attempts by European powers to extend their hold anywhere in the western hemisphere endanger the peace and safety of the US, and the Americas are closed to future colonisation by any European nation.

Tsar Alexander I, who professed to being an admirer of the US Constitution, backed down in the face of Monroe's determination. A US-Russian treaty of 1824 restored freedom of shipping and fishing in the northern Pacific, and reduced the territory claimed by Russia to present-day Alaska and the Aleutians. Those lands remained in Russian hands, but a decline in the market for their furs and the realisation that they were militarily virtually impossible to defend made them an increasing worry for St Petersburg. In 1867-68, they were sold to the US for $7.2 million, or about 20c an acre.

The deal, negotiated on the American side by Secretary of State William Seward, was widely criticised in the US, where it was nicknamed 'Seward's Folly'. Within a few years, the discovery of gold near Juneau gave an indication of the vast natural resources the United States had acquired.

Below: Shelekhov's voyages with his band of Cossack trappers took him through the Aleutian Islands to the coast of Alaska. His ultimate aim was to secure the whole western seaboard of America for Russia. But the scheme petered out, and Russia's American holdings were sold to the US at 20 cents an acre.

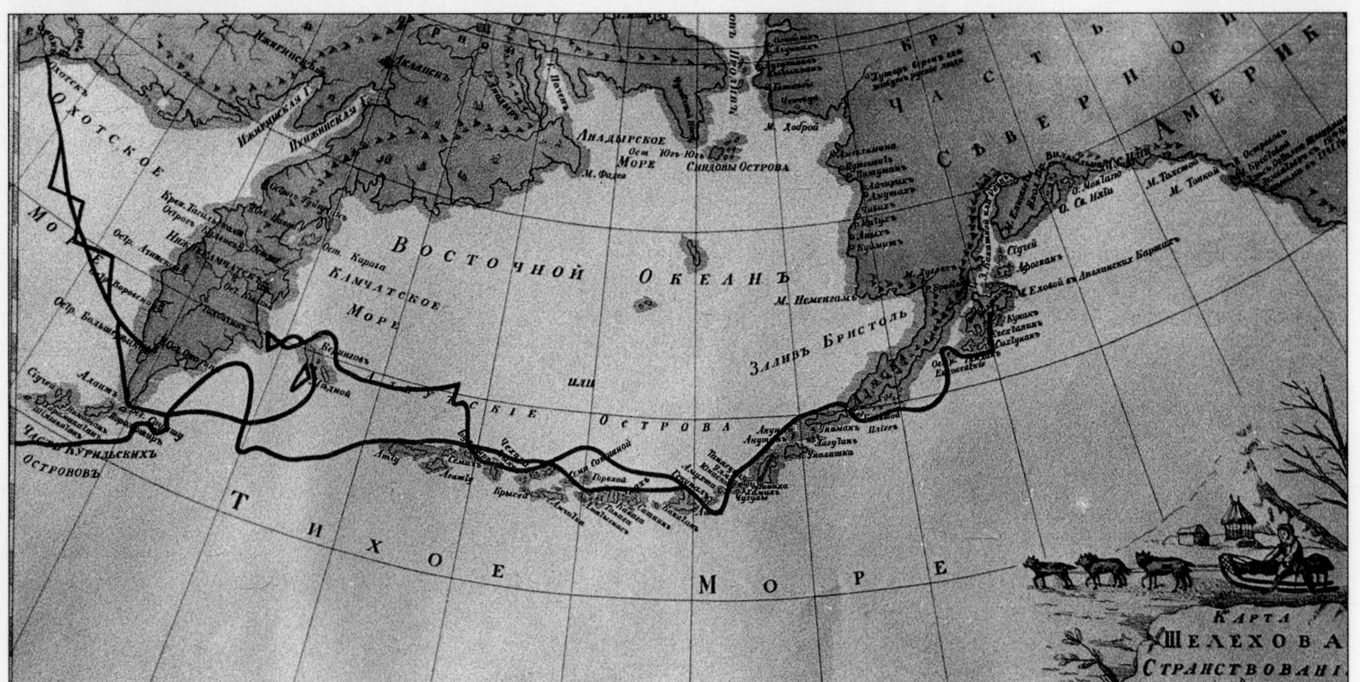

the Tsar. The scheme was helped along when Arguello's daughter, Consuela Conçepcion, fell in love with Nicholas Rezanov, one of Baranov's young officials. Rezanov was deputed first to return to Sitka with the much-needed supplies, and then to travel to St Petersburg with Arguello's proposals. However, on the Siberian leg of the journey to the Russian capital, Rezanov caught pneumonia and died – a fact not learnt in California until much later. The distraught Consuela spent her days gazing across San Francisco Bay awaiting her lover's return, while the idea of California as a Russian protectorate withered away.

These dramatic events made little difference to relations between the settlers. By 1812, the Spanish were ready to lease enough land to the Russians for them to build their Californian ostrog of stockade, blockhouses and tiny church.

Baranov was ousted from the Russian American Company in 1818 and died the following year. Russia gave up all her North American holdings in the middle of the 19th century as too remote and unimportant. The restored and preserved ostrog, at Fort Ross near Bodega Bay, is one of the few visible reminders that Russians and Cossacks once walked the soil of California.

LACK OF UNIFORMITY

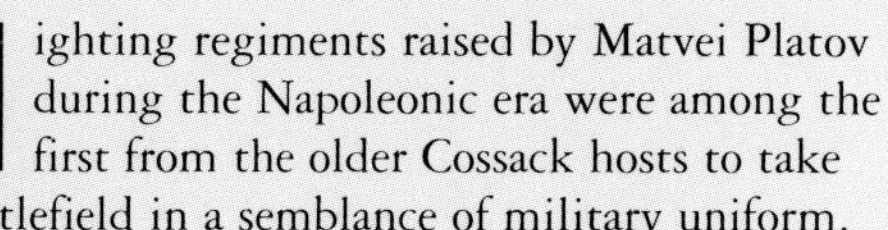

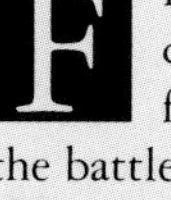

Fighting regiments raised by Matvei Platov during the Napoleonic era were among the first from the older Cossack hosts to take the battlefield in a semblance of military uniform. For unlike regular members of Russian armies, from Ivan the Terrible's streltsi onwards, free Cossacks had to supply their own clothes, along with horses and weaponry. So they wore what they chose.

Nevertheless, by the early 18th century – when regular Russian regiments adopted uniforms supposedly modelled on western European lines – some degree of regional conformity was already evident in Cossack battledress.

Ukrainian, Zaporozhi and Don Cossacks could be identified by the prevalence among them of the chekmen, a modified version of the kaftan. Terek Cossacks of the Caucasus favoured the cherkeska, a coat with sewn-on cartridge pockets. It was eventually taken up by their neighbours on the Kuban and, later still, by Don Cossacks who served in the Caucasian wars.

Cossacks from the Urals region wore far heavier coats and great wool or fur hats. So, too, did the Siberian Cossacks; they were recruited as individuals rather than en masse like the free Cossack hosts, and therefore had their clothing, weapons and horses provided by the state.

Right: The streltsi (fusiliers), created by Ivan the Terrible in the 16th century and abolished by Peter the Great in 1698, formed the core of Russia's earliest standing army. Like the Cossacks, they became a military caste, elected their own junior officers and combined soldiering with other occupations – usually crafts. But they were equipped by the state with regimental uniforms, based on the traditional kaftan, and were commanded by the appointees of the Tsar.

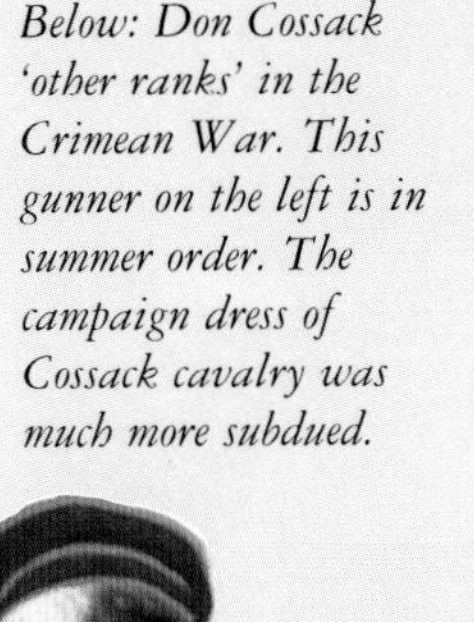

Left: Zaporozhian Cossack troops had a distinctly Tartar look, wearing baggy, practical clothes with turned-up shoes.

Within these broadly distinctive local styles, there were innumerable differences of colour, material and accoutrements. And the Cossack habit of stripping the dead of any items which took their fancy ensured that, even when all members of a squadron started a campaign dressed in roughly the same way, they often ended it looking very different from each other.

From Platov's day onwards, as the free hosts were assimilated more closely into the mainstream of Russian life, the authorities tried hard to persuade them to assume a better-disciplined, military appearance. It was sometimes an uphill effort. For example, all ranks in the crack Don Ataman Guards Regiment were ordered to wear belts – but because they provided their own, no particular colour or pattern could be specified, so their look was hardly enhanced.

As the 19th century progressed, conformity increased. By the time of the Crimean War (1853-56), battledress had been largely standardised, with only minor regional variations among the hosts. Ordinary Cossack horsemen wore tunics and trousers of brown-grey, at first with plentiful coloured facings. Those were eventually reduced or discarded in favour of all-over khaki or, for summer campaigns, a white tunic and dark trousers. That remained the style into the First World War.

Parade uniforms, though also standardised, were altogether more colourful, with clearer regional distinctions. The kaftan or chekmen had generally given way to a western-style tunic worn over dark, baggy trousers. It was usually of red, modelled on the dress of the Imperial Lifeguards, the most senior of the Cossack regiments. But the tunic of the Ataman Guards Regiment was a highly distinctive pale blue.

Cossacks of the Tsar's Own Convoy, raised in the Caucasus by Nicholas I as a personal escort, retained the traditional cherkeska and woollen hat particular to the region. With it, they carried both a sabre and a dagger.

Below: Don Cossack 'other ranks' in the Crimean War. This gunner on the left is in summer order. The campaign dress of Cossack cavalry was much more subdued.

The Decembrists

Army officers back from the war against Napoleon brought with them a desire to reform Russia along lines similar to the more open western European societies they had seen on their travels. Two of their main aims were to abolish serfdom, under which four-fifths of the population languished, and to end the autocratic powers of the Tsar. But they disagreed among themselves about ways of achieving these goals, and about the precise form of the new society they wanted to create. Some, looking back to previous chapters of Russian history, saw the rough and ready equality and democracy of early Cossack communities as a model.

Cliques of the most radical officers and their supporters, meeting in secret, plotted the overthrow of Tsar Alexander I. He had gradually abandoned the liberal principles he endorsed at the beginning of his reign, though ironically he, too, was seeking inspiration from the Cossacks. In Alexander's case, it was to create military colonies – self-supporting villages of soldier-farmers and their families which he dotted around Russia. At their height, they could supply more than 300,000 men-at-arms, surpassing in numbers the traditional Cossack hosts they in some respects resembled.

In November 1825, before the plot against him had been properly worked out, Alexander suddenly died. The succession should have gone to his brother Constantine, governor of Russian Poland, who renounced it in favour of a third brother, Nicholas. The plotters used the confusion this caused as a pretext for an attempted coup. But it was a half-baked affair.

Right: More than 100 of the Decembrists, aristocratic plotters against the Tsar, were banished to Siberia when their coup failed. Some were accompanied into exile by their wives, and added a gloss of high culture to Siberian frontier society.

Below: Cossack regiments in St Petersburg refused to join the 1825 uprising on Senate (later Decembrist) Square. But many of the participants believed an idealised version of Cossack self-government provided a pattern that Russia as a whole could copy.

On December 14, 1825, 3,000 soldiers gathered on Senate Square in St Petersburg, refusing to swear allegiance to the new Tsar. Significantly, the Cossack regiments were not among them. After some delay, Nicholas turned artillery on the crowd, and the uprising in the capital was over. An associated coup in the Ukraine was put down with the same efficiency. Nearly 300 conspirators were brought to trial. Five were hanged, and more than 100 were banished to forced labour in Siberia.

If Nicholas I ever had any liberal principles, the Decembrist uprising, as it came to be called, dispelled them. His 30-year reign was marked at home by despotic regimentation of the population to quasi-military standards under the eyes of his secret police, and attempts to eradicate minority languages and religions in the name of 'Russification'. Russian Poland suffered heavily; after a rebellion there in 1830, Nicholas stripped it of the last vestiges of its former autonomy, and reduced it to the status of a province. Abroad, the Tsar, who regarded himself as the 'gendarme of Europe', used Cossacks to suppress popular revolts in Hungary and Czechoslovakia.

'Second-class soldiers'

The Cossacks took no part in the abortive Decembrist revolt against Nicholas, fought loyally for Russia in his wars, and assisted him in applying his slogan of 'Orthodoxy, Autocracy and Nationalism' ruthlessly to Russian Poland after the 1830 rebellion. Yet the Tsar regarded his frontiersmen ambiguously.

On one hand, he visited the new Don capital of Novocherkassk amid great pomp to present his son as Don ataman, and to award charters and other signs of his favour. On the other, he complained that the Cossacks at the ceremony were poorly turned out, but refused to increase their pay so they could buy better equipment. And when, in 1830, he abolished flogging with the knout as a military punishment, Cossacks were specifically excluded from the ban.

DAY OF DISGRACE

While 673 British cavalrymen earned glory in the charge of the Light Brigade during Russia's Crimean War against Turkey, England and France in 1853-56, some of their Cossack enemies behaved shamefully, according to eye-witness accounts.

The charge, commemorated in one of Alfred Tennyson's best-known poems, took place on October 25, 1854, at the Battle of Balaclava. A sequence of misunderstandings sent the Light Brigade on an unsupported foray to capture 30 field-guns of the Don Cossack Third Horse Artillery Battery. The guns were positioned at the head of a valley, and protected by other emplacements along the encircling hills.

Losing men by the score in the murderous Russian crossfire, the Light Brigade scattered a shield of mounted Cossacks and reached the artillery, to hack down some of the gunners and put the rest to flight. Then the British turned to withdraw, under attack by Russian lancers.

At that point, the surviving Cossack gunners resumed their posts and opened fire again, indiscriminately hitting Russian and British cavalry alike. The war correspondent of 'The Times' newspaper, William Howard Russell, called the Cossacks' action in shooting when they were certain to hit fellow-countrymen an 'eternal disgrace' to Russia's name.

Once the Light Brigade had completed its withdrawal, with 303 men killed, wounded or captured and some 500 mounts lost, the Cossack horsemen who had earlier fled the field reappeared, swooping to grab any riderless English or Russian horses they could find. Later, they sold the mounts they had seized back to their own side to supplement their meagre pay.

The war, fought to curb Russian expansion at the expense of Turkey and thwart Tsar Nicholas I's supposed designs on India, cost 500,000 Russian lives. The allies lost about 150,000 men. Though Russia's naval base and stronghold of Sebastopol was captured after a siege lasting nearly a year, the victory was not pursued and the war ended inconclusively when Nicholas died, to be succeeded by his son as Tsar Alexander II. Nevertheless, Russia was weakened as a European power and the shortcomings of her autocracy were starkly revealed.

During the Crimean campaign, mounted Cossack regiments were used most frequently for reconnaissance. In set battles, their role was indistinguishable from that of regular cavalry – and they did not perform it well. Their horses were notably poor; as they provided their own, they saw no reason to risk good animals. Their firearms were often old and nearly useless, too. But for the first time their uniforms were largely standardised. Only small regional variations remained.

Below left: Tsar Nicholas I (reigned 1825-55) did not deliberately provoke the Crimean War. But Russia's territorial expansion in the Balkans and central Asia worried the British. It also gave the French a pretext to seek revenge for their humiliations of 1812-15.

Below: The charge of the Light Brigade at Balaclava brought futile glory to the British and shame to some of their Cossack adversaries.

Nicholas was a fanatical parade ground-style militarist, widely credited with designing the 'pickelhaube' spiked helmet that later came to symbolise Prussian militarism. The scruffy, thieving, ill-disciplined Cossacks probably appalled him as much as they had once appalled Napoleon. Increasingly, Nicholas and many of his commanders came to regard them, with the exception of a few crack regiments, as second-class soldiers. Treated that way, the Cossacks responded in kind, performing without distinction, for example, in the Crimean War.

Yet Russia's frontiers were expanding south and east, and Cossacks were still unequalled – and cheap – in their traditional fighter-settler role. It took a few mavericks of genius to recognise the fact, among them Nicholas Muraviev, governor of eastern Siberia from 1847.

One More Sigh ...

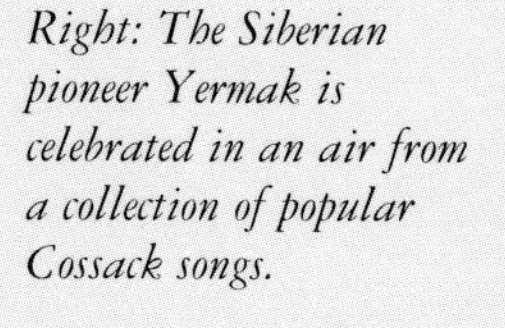

Right: The Siberian pioneer Yermak is celebrated in an air from a collection of popular Cossack songs.

Spectacular squats, kicks and leaps from agile dancers to the accompaniment of fast-thrumming balalaikas and resonant singing are everyone's epitome of Cossack musical entertainment, thanks to the Red Army Ensemble and the countless 'Cossack' troupes that have appeared outside the Soviet Union since the 1917 Revolution. But the Cossack musical heritage is far older, richer and more varied than haunting songs played on balalaikas, a 19th-century invention.

For, next to the drinking that usually accompanied them, music and dancing were favourite all-purpose Cossack pastimes for more than 400 years. They were a means of expressing sorrow as well as joy or triumph, or of alleviating loneliness or boredom as well as of celebrating.

They drew heavily on the traditions of Russia, the Ukraine and Poland, where most Cossacks once originated. But they also borrowed, indirectly or directly, from many other sources – among them Tartars, Turks, gipsies from the Balkans and Germany, and the peoples of the Caucasus. When Yeroshka, a central character in Tolstoy's novel 'The Cossacks', is in his cups and wants a 'real' song, he chooses a mournful Tartar ballad of death and destruction at Russian hands, with its refrain 'Alone I am left! Ai, dai, dalali!'

The instruments, at least until the 19th century, were relatively simple – among them the domra, the three-stringed, plucked forerunner of the balalaika, and the volinka, a version of bagpipes. There were whole arrays of horns, flutes, pipes, whistles and trumpets, and of tambourines, drums and rattles. The garmon, a concertina now usually replaced by accordeons, was a later addition.

Below: A musical interlude when Cossacks reached Paris in 1814.

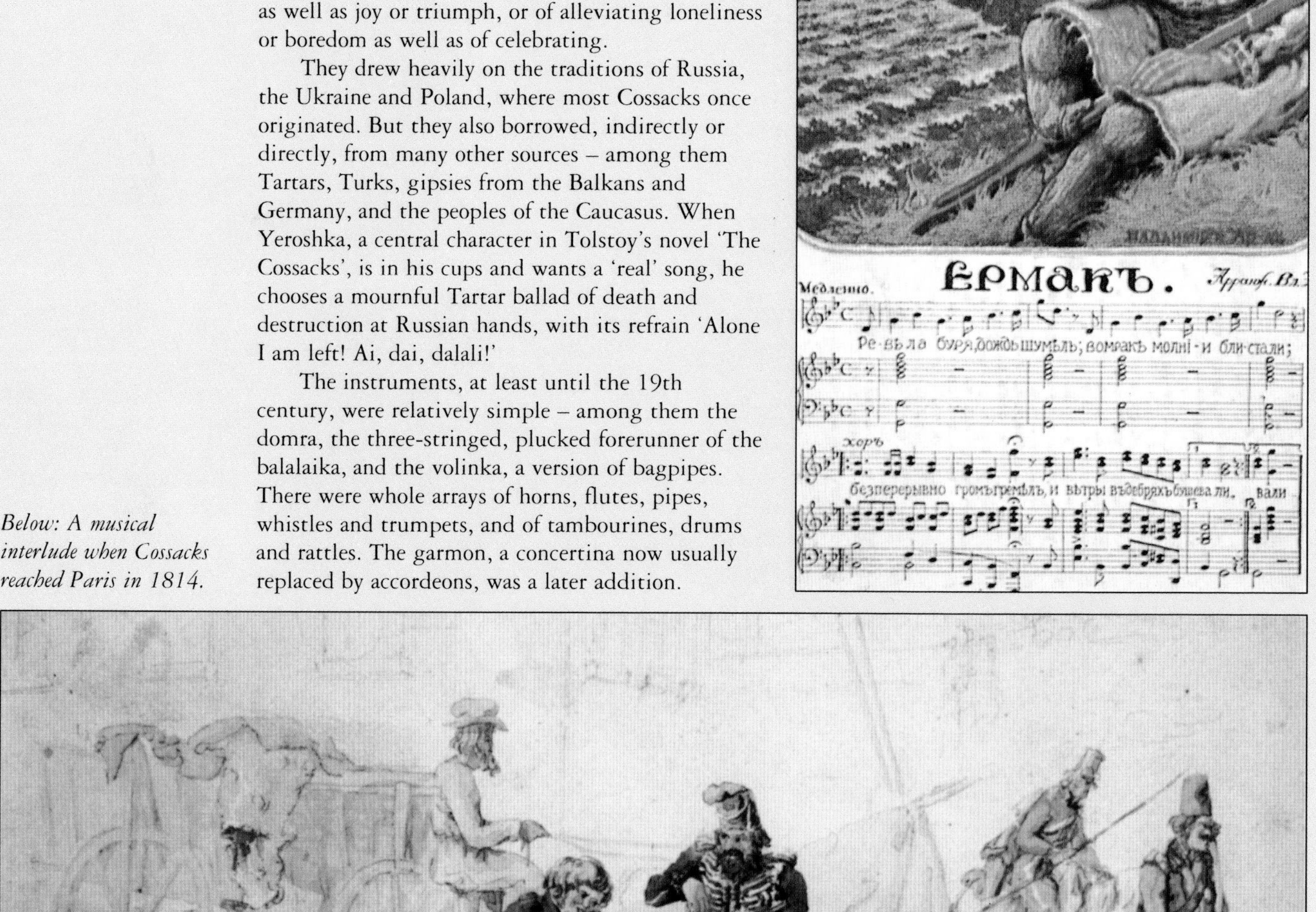

The songs

Epic ballads, telling tales of heroes in a song resembling the sacred chant of Orthodox Church music or of humorous characters at a faster pace, were a part of Russian folk music long before the first Cossack communities formed. One of their chief characteristics was the use of stock phrases to describe certain things – a heroine's hands, for example, were always 'fair and white'– making them easier to compose and remember.

The style developed in several ways. Spiritual songs told stories drawn from the Bible or the lives of the saints. Historical songs recorded past triumphs and disasters; the 'Ballad of Stenka Razin', for example, recalls one of the most famous Cossacks of all. Lyrical songs celebrated beauty, of a lover or of some natural feature such as a stream or pine-tree, or both together.

But the nearest descendants of the old epics were wedding songs – improvised using stock phrases to hymn the qualities of bride and groom during days of feasting, drinking, singing and dancing. The custom survives, or has been revived, in parts of eastern Europe today.

From at least the 18th century, work-songs, usually sung without instrumental accompaniment, began to evolve. The best-known outside Russia is 'The Volga Boatmen', with its yo-heave-ho refrain of 'ei ukhnyem' (one more sigh) to accompany the hauling of barges up the river. Thousands once warbled by Cossack frontier guards, soldiers, field-workers, even robber bands and Siberian prisoners, have been collected by folklorists.

As traditionally sung and played, Russian and Cossack folksongs tend to use natural minor and major modes, rather than the conventions of western music. In many modern arrangements, the harmonies are often westernised, but the distinctive, often plaintive-sounding, melody line remains.

The dances

Flamboyant Cossack dancing, too, has its roots north of the steppe. The khorovod, or round dance, and its counterparts pre-date Christianity in eastern Europe, and probably once formed part of pagan festivities to mark the coming of spring.

The khorovod was a complicated affair of dancing, singing and dramatic mime. At one moment it could involve the entire population of a village. At others, groups or individuals would play different parts in the whole – men and women separating, or the best dancers coming forward to perform their specialities to fast songs with lively, captivating rhythms.

The trepak – the stamping dance featured by Tchaikovsky in his 'Nutcracker Suite' – evolved as part of the round dance. So did a whole series of dances involving squatting with bent knees, leaping and kicking. The Cossacks took them to the steppe, and added refinements of their own devising or borrowed from the peoples they encountered. One potentially lethal addition was the inclusion of sabres as 'props'.

Top left: Carefree celebrations on the steppe towards the end of the 19th century.

Top and above: Thanks to state companies such as that from the Ukraine, the flamboyant leaps and knee-straining squats of Cossack dancing today thrill audiences all over the world.

The New Hosts

The treaty with which Alexander II ended the Crimean War in 1856 prevented Russia from expanding to the west. But in a restless drive for territory and trade, the Russians pushed out their boundaries to the south and east over the next three decades, with Cossacks in the vanguard again. As a result, five more Cossack hosts were created, while some of the smaller existing communities such as the Azov host, which no longer had a border role in their original locations, were resettled to protect the new frontiers.

The most dramatic developments came in Siberia. There, the old arrangements under which Cossacks had been hired individually for government service as everything from town guards to tax collectors were already in decay. Many Cossacks in remote areas where they served no military purpose were stripped of Cossack status. But in south-west Siberia, in the region around Omsk, the Cossacks were reorganised militarily in a Siberian host. With the Orenburg Cossacks to the west and the Ural Cossacks beyond those, they formed a cordon from the northern fringe of the Caspian Sea to the Altai Mountains.

Below: Cossacks charge into action in a scene by the 19th-century artist Franz Roubaud. Unlike many painters of the era, Roubaud here does not over-romanticise the Cossacks. As often in real life, their tunics do not match and their weaponry varies. The high saddles, absence of spurs and loose riding style are all authentic – and horrifying to the eyes of orthodox cavalrymen.

The cordon was in place when Nicholas Muraviev arrived in the Cossack-founded city of Irkutsk as governor of eastern Siberia. With him, he brought a plan – to win permanently for Russia the lands along the left bank of the Amur River, which flows for 4,350km (2,700 miles) from Mongolia to the Sea of Okhotsk and the Pacific Ocean. They had briefly been under Russian control two centuries previously, when Yerefei Khabarov's Cossacks had swept along the Amur. But those early settlers had been driven out by the Chinese, who laid claim to the territory without settling it themselves.

Between 1847 and 1851, Muraviev drafted Siberian Cossacks and Russian peasants by the thousands into the Irkutsk region, to establish the Transbaikal host. Local tribesmen were also given Cossack status.

Then, without reference to higher authority in St Petersburg, Muraviev led groups of Transbaikal Cossacks and regular troops posing as traders the length of the Amur to set up bases on the Pacific coast and the island of Sakhalin. With those established, Muraviev himself led expeditions back along the river to found settlements. Among these settlements was Khabarovsk, named for the 17th-century pioneer.

The Chinese, preoccupied by struggles with Britain and France, did nothing. From 1857, Muraviev shipped more and more Transbaikal Cossack families to sites he selected for villages all along the lower Amur. Each family was given provisions until it became self-supporting, a small wage, an allocation of timber and other essentials. In treaties of 1858-60, China ceded the whole left bank of the river to Russia. Soon, the Amur Cossack host was flourishing.

But Muraviev, whose initiative won belated approval from the Tsar, had his eye on yet more territory – the Pacific coastal strip below the mouth of the Amur and east of its tributary the Ussuri. The Chinese would agree only to share sovereignty with Russia over that area, so Muraviev, according to legend, resorted to a trick.

In confirming the treaties, he sent a map of the whole Amur region to the Chinese, with the disputed coastal strip shaded the same colour as the undisputed left bank of the Amur. The Chinese did not notice at first. By the time they did, Muraviev had transferred hundreds of Cossack settlers into the area, forming the Ussuri host, and Russian possession was a fait accompli. At Golden Horn Bay on the Pacific, he built a settlement whose boastful name summed up his pride in his achievement – Vladivostok, 'ruler of the east'.

Into central Asia

While Muraviev and his Cossack hosts were consolidating Russia's vast new territories in the east, other empire-builders were pushing out her southern frontiers. By 1859-64, Russian troops with Cossacks from the Don, the Kuban and the Terek had subjugated the whole of the Caucasus region between the Black and Caspian Seas. Once their task was completed with the defeat of the mountain tribes' leader Shamil, the men from the Don returned to their homelands, sporting as new features of their battledress crossed cartridge-belts copied from Caucasian styles. The Kuban and Terek hosts, enlarged and reorganised, remained as a military reserve.

East of the Caspian, a succession of armed forays by men such as Basil Perovsky, governor of

Liberation Of The Serfs

In 1861 – the same year that Abraham Lincoln was installed as President of the United States – Tsar Alexander II began to dismantle centuries of serfdom in Russia. The process was long, complicated and bloody; government troops were needed to put down 700 disturbances in the first five months after the reforms were announced. By the time they were theoretically complete, about 69 million people had become free at least in name. Of those, 30 million tilled land belonging to private owners, and a further 22 million toiled on state holdings. The rest mostly worked in factories or as house-servants.

While it was relatively easy to proclaim freedom, the accompanying land reforms posed endless problems. Under the arrangements eventually adopted, serfs working on private estates were given allocations which they had to buy from the owners over 49 years, at inflated prices and with much of the best land taken out of the sale. Many greeted the news with disbelief and violent protests, dealt with ruthlessly by government forces.

The storm hardly touched the Cossacks, among whom serfdom was rare. But the Don host had to give up about one-fifth of its traditional territory to freed serfs, at a time when its own population was growing rapidly.

Others of Alexander's changes had more direct impact on Cossackry. One was the introduction of the zemstvo system of provincial and county governments, which financed their public activities, such as welfare and road maintenance, by local taxes. Though zemstvos produced impressive results in much of Russia, they were bitterly resented on the Don. They duplicated existing Cossack institutions, put Cossack representatives on a par with the peasantry and imposed levies on land traditionally held tax-free. In the face of sustained complaints, the system was eventually abolished for the Don host.

The adjustment in military service requirements from 1875 was more welcome. The basic liability for most Cossacks was brought down to 20 years instead of 25 or 30, starting at the age of 18. Three years were spent in training, 12 on active call, and five in the reserve. But the arrangement was subject to variations and exemptions, depending among other things on the birth rate, and did not always work out to the Cossacks' liking.

Below left: The 'Tsar Liberator' Alexander II (reigned 1855-1881) and his Tsarina, formerly Princess Wilhelmina Maria of Hesse-Darmstadt in Germany. Between them stands the future Alexander III.

Below: An idealised view of Alexander freeing the serfs. In reality, the ensuing problems of land reform led to confusion, resentment and bloodshed.

Orenburg, and General C.P. von Kaufmann, took the Russians first to the borders of the Islamic Khanates of Kokand, Khiva and Bukhara, and then deep into their lands. Orenburg and Siberian Cossacks spearheaded the advance; Perovsky in particular spoke highly of their endurance and dedication. One by one, the great and ancient trading cities of central Asia fell to the Russian invaders – Tashkent in 1865, Bukhara and Samarkand in 1868. By 1885, Russia had annexed the whole region, expanding her territories right up to the frontiers of Persia, Afghanistan and China. To help hold these acquisitions, Siberian Cossacks were drafted south in the 1860s, forming the Semirechnie, or Seven Rivers, host. Its settlements were sprinkled parallel to the Chinese north-western border, from Lake Balkhash towards the Altai Mountains.

The Seven Rivers was the last big Cossack host to be established in a proud, 300-year line. For Russia's rapid expansion in the mid-19th century pushed her wilder frontiers to their limits. Henceforth, she was to turn increasingly inward in the process that took her from Tsarist autocracy to Marxist-Leninist dictatorship, and transformed the Cossack way of life.

Revolution and Civil War

Death of a Liberator

Radical political groups opposed to the autocracy made many attempts to assassinate the 'Tsar Liberator' Alexander II. Finally, on a spring evening in 1881, nihilists of the People's Will faction achieved their murderous goal.

After dinner with an aunt, Alexander was returning across St Petersburg to his palace with an escort of Cossacks for protection. As the royal carriage rolled along the bank of the Catherine Canal, a bystander hurled a bomb, injuring several Cossacks, but leaving the Tsar unscathed. He alighted to inspect the damage – and a second bomb was thrown. Mortally wounded, Alexander begged his Cossacks: 'Get me home to die'.

The murder of a ruler who had been liberal by the standards of time and place unleashed two decades of black repression across the Russian empire. The new Tsar, Alexander III, and Nicholas II, who came to the throne in 1894, reverted to the strongest form of autocracy, stamping on any sign of dissent and creating a non–stop flow of political prisoners to Siberia. Their main weapon was the secret police force of the notorious Third Section, with its vast underground network of informers and agents provocateurs.

Below: Alexander II's Cossack bodyguards rush to the aid of their Tsar, fatally wounded by an assassin's bomb.

In reserve, when dissent flickered into open protest, were government troops, with fiercely loyal Cossack horsemen as their vanguard. Students, workers, Polish patriots, all who assembled to express opposition, were broken and driven before the thundering hooves of Cossack horses and the lash of metal-tipped Cossack whips. The freedom-loving riders of the steppes had become 'monsters trampling on freedom', in the words of one socialist revolutionary of the day.

Jews, too felt the Cossack flail. As the 19th century passed into the 20th, a virulent wave of anti-semitism swept across Russia, fomented by nationalistic right-wing organisations which found their ultimate expression in the Union of the Russian People, otherwise known as the 'Black Hundreds'.

Cossack troops, as representatives of order, were supposed to help prevent pogroms – mob attacks on Jewish people and property. But they rarely did. More often, on instructions or through inclination, they stood by doing nothing. At Kishinev in Moldavia in 1903, for example, a mob was allowed to run riot for two days, sacking 1,300 Jewish-owned buildings and killing or wounding hundreds of Jews, before troops moved in. In some areas, the Cossacks joined the looting and murder.

Seeds of revolution

The apparatus of state terror prevented large-scale revolt in Russia for 20 or so years after the assassination of Alexander II. Nevertheless, underground political opposition grew – the Social Democrats, inspired by the works of Karl Marx, the Socialist Revolutionaries, anarchists and nihilists. A succession of poor grain harvests and a recession in the industry made discontent worse.

So did the war with Japan, provoked by Russia's continued expansion in the Far East, but started by a surprise Japanese attack in January 1904 on the Russian base of Port Arthur (now Lushun in China). Cossacks from the Transbaikal, Amur and Ussuri hosts were among the troops hastened to the front, to become bogged down in an initially inconclusive, costly struggle. Then, as the new year of 1905 dawned, Port Arthur surrendered, and the boil of popular anger burst.

On Sunday, January 9, 1905, a priest called Father Gapon led an orderly march of 120,000 workers to the Winter Palace in St Petersburg, seeking to present a petition to the Tsar. In

THE COSSACK PROVINCES

At the end of the 19th century, there were 11 recognised Cossack territories in the Russian empire, with their own systems of local administration under the Ministry of War in St Petersburg. Taken together, they had a population of 5.5 million, out of the empire's total of 120 million. But only 2.6 million of their inhabitants, including women and children, held Cossack status; the rest were mainly peasants or industrial workers. At any given time, about 300,000 male Cossacks were available for military service, mostly as horsemen.

The biggest concentration of Cossacks was in south–western Russia – on the Don, the Kuban, the Terek, around Astrakhan on the lower Volga and on the Ural. The Don, with its vast wheatfields and rapidly developing industry based on coal and iron, had a Cossack population of just under 1 million. The Cossacks still generally preferred to live in villages, shunning the more industrial environment of cities such as Rostov.

The lands of the Orenburg Cossacks stretched from the upper Ural into western Siberia. Beyond those, in a near-continuous fringe to the Pacific Ocean, were the provinces of the Siberian host, centred on Omsk, and the Transbaikal, Amur and Ussuri hosts founded at the instigation of Nicholas Muraviev. Cossacks of the Seven Rivers host lived in far-flung settlements east of Lake Balkhash, in present-day Kazakhstan.

Below: Cossacks beside the Trans-Siberian Railway, built between 1891 and 1917.

respectful, almost cringing terms, it asked for universal suffrage and improved working conditions and denounced the 'shameful' war. Units of Cossacks and hussars panicked in the face of the huge crowd. They opened fire, killing at least 130 people and wounding hundreds more.

The slaughter of 'Bloody Sunday' marked the final loss of trust in Tsar Nicholas II by those he ruled. Uprising after uprising followed in town and country, while the war against Japan turned from setbacks to humiliating defeat. The Tsar was forced to grant sweeping concessions – a new constitution, universal suffrage, a legislative assembly or Duma, the recognition of political parties. Later, as repression reasserted itself, these concessions were whittled down or revoked.

In the upheavals of 1905-06, the Cossacks served Nicholas loyally, and he rewarded those from the Don with a new badge of honour, a white ribbon on their uniforms. But even Cossacks soon began to chafe – over land shortages, lack of voting rights and constant orders to put down unrest among people with whom many of them sympathised. Only a call to defend the Russian motherland could stem their growing disaffection. It came in 1914.

Below left: As an arm of the autocracy, Cossacks break up a demonstration of students and workers on St Petersburg's Nevsky Prospect in 1901.

Below: In action again, to quell an anti-Tsarist protest about 1910.

At War with Germany

As Nicholas II mobilised his armies against Germany and Austria-Hungary, church bells rang and cheering crowds swarmed through the streets in cities across the Russian empire. Discontent with the Tsar and his ministers was largely forgotten in the orgy of patriotic emotion. Succumbing to the popular mood, Nicholas renamed his capital – Petrograd, in the Russian fashion, in place of Germanic Petersburg.

Few in the blazing August of 1914 opposed the war, declared ostensibly to protect Orthodox Christian Slavs in the Balkans. Most educated Russians expected that, with Britain and France as allies, Russia would win within four or five months.

One voice of caution belonged to Gregory Rasputin. The mysterious and dissipated wandering monk had insinuated himself into royal favour through his ability to control attacks of bleeding suffered by the haemophiliac heir to the throne, Tsarevich Alexis. Now Rasputin predicted: 'War will bring the end of Russia'.

In the Duma, the representative assembly Nicholas had reluctantly created, opposition came only from the Bolsheviks, a faction of the divided and permanently squabbling left. The other radical parties, Socialist Revolutionaries and Mensheviks, for once supported the Tsar.

The armies Nicholas put into the field against Germany and Austria were massive – 1.4 million regular troops and 3 million reservists in the first instance, including 350,000 Cossacks. But they were poorly supplied and hampered in their movement to the front by inadequate road and railway systems.

Nevertheless, what the British called the 'Russian steamroller' scored early successes. By mid-August, Cossack horsemen from the First Army under General E.K. Rennenkampf were rampaging across north-east Prussia, and in a set-piece battle Rennenkampf inflicted a partial defeat on the Germans that caused panic in Berlin.

Rennenkampf failed to press home his advantage, however, while a Second Army under General A.V. Samsonov struggled from the south to link up with him. The Germans, with Paul Von Hindenburg now in command, regrouped to smash Samsonov's forces at the Battle of Tannenberg, wiping out most of his Cossack contingents. Then they drove Rennenkampf back across the border. In a month, on one small section of the front, the Russians lost 300,000 men and 650 guns, though in doing so they occupied German troops who could otherwise have been used to telling effect against France and Britain.

Victory and defeat

In Galicia, near the Carpathian Mountains, the Russians fared better, with a succession of victories against the crack regiments of Austria and Hungary in 1914 and early 1915. The Russians' lack of artillery meant they often could not soften up the enemy in advance. 'My splendid Cossacks', as Nicholas II called them, astounded friend and foe with their ability to capture fixed positions under withering fire.

But Hindenburg was quietly grouping men and artillery in southern Poland, including eight divisions brought from France, and in May 1915 he struck back with a blow intended to drive Russia out of the war. The poorly armed Russians were no match for the devastating German guns. Entire divisions were annihilated in their trenches. Many of the reservists brought up in support had no weapons; they had to wait until armed comrades fell to seize rifles. 'Our army is drowning in its own blood,' wrote one Russian general.

Below: British and French depictions of their Cossack allies in the First World War. The caption to the picture on the right, from a Parisian magazine, said with more than a hint of sarcasm: 'The good Cossack – I'm for culture, too!'. French memories of Cossack behaviour in Paris a century earlier had evidently not died.

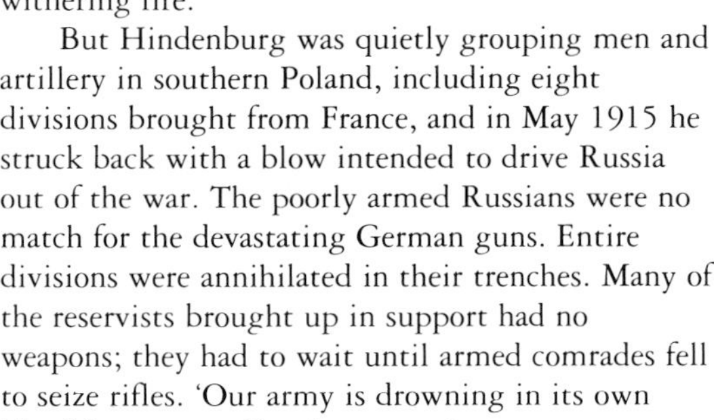

LAST DAYS OF CAVALRY

Fast-firing machine-guns, more than any other single military development, brought to an end the attacking role of cavalry in most forms of warfare. While infantrymen could at least seek cover from the sprays of bullets without abandoning an advance, horses and those in their saddles could not.

The lesson was swiftly taken by British, French and German generals in the First World War. The Russians were slower to learn. In part, that may have been because Vladimir Sukhomlinov, Minister of War in 1914-15, was a former cavalry officer who believed machine-guns were unworthy weapons for men of honour, and thus should be ignored. Thousands of Russian horsemen and their mounts died because of that opinion.

By 1914, Cossacks were treated as regular cavalry, mixed in divisions with dragoons, lancers and hussars. In his advance into east Prussia, General Rennenkampf, like Sukhomlinov a cavalryman, carelessly flung them against machine-guns and artillery, with horrendous losses. As late as 1916, Russian cavalry was still charging across ground cratered by shelling and through enfiladed fire towards Austrian gun emplacements protected by barbed wire. Cossacks were still used in their traditional role of scouts, too.

But as the war progressed, the steppe-horsemen, so renowned for their riding abilities, were increasingly turned into trench-bound infantry. Though most of them had not been trained to serve as foot-soldiers, they fought well and bravely, usually to the death. Proportionately, few Cossacks were taken prisoner.

Below: The horse's role in war was nearly over by the dawn of the 20th century – but not quite.

Under the German onslaught, there was nowhere to go but back – out of most of Galicia, then out of Poland and, when Hindenburg switched his line of attack, out of much of the Baltic region. Day and night the slaughter continued while the remnants of the Russian army trudged east. The roads were already choked with refugees ordered from their homes as the High Command attempted to repeat the 'scorched earth' policy used against Napoleon. It was bound to fail, because of the speed and breadth of the German advance.

But by September 1915, as Nicholas II took over the title of commander-in-chief, the German pursuit lost impetus. By winter it had halted altogether, along a line roughly 360km (200 miles) east of Warsaw. Believing Russia broken, Germany turned more of her attention to her western front, in particular to the French stronghold of Verdun.

With any other nation, the German assumption would have been valid. In the first 16 months of the war Russia had lost 3.4 million men dead, wounded or captured. The carnage reduced some Cossack regiments to one-quarter of their strength.

Behind the lines, there was chaos. The military call-up and the conversion of farm machinery factories to munitions work had slashed food production. Roads and railways were blocked by military traffic and refugees. Prices soared, provoking strikes and demonstrations that Cossacks were again called on to break. With the Tsar commanding the battle-front, his place as ruler at home was assumed by his wife, Alexandra. Born a German and openly influenced by Rasputin, she was becoming a figure of hate.

Below: Tsar Nicholas II (reigned 1894-1917), with his family.

The Spring Revolution

Right: Gregory Rasputin (?1871-1916), the semi-literate peasant from Siberia who exercised such a strong influence on Tsarina Alexandra. Although usually referred to as a monk, Rasputin was actually a starets – a peculiarly Russian type of wandering, self-styled holy man. His doctrine, such as it was, seems to have been based on sexual debauchery as a path to salvation. But his power over Alexandra came originally from his ability to help her haemophiliac son, perhaps through hypnosis.

Urged on by Britain, France and Italy, the Russian army resumed the offensive in 1916, despite its appalling losses the previous year. In June, General A.A. Brusilov's forces, with Cossack cavalry still in their ranks, broke through the Austrian lines in Galicia. Remorselessly, the 'steamroller' ground forward during the summer, inflicting stupendous casualties, but suffering them, too. For 1.4 million of the enemy dead, wounded or captured, the Russians sacrificed 2 million men, perhaps more. Their blood-soaked advance forced Germany to switch 18 divisions from France, and an allied victory for a moment looked possible.

The human cost staggered Tsarina Alexandra, who had herself nursed some of the wounded. More than ever, she was under Rasputin's spell, engineering the replacement of government ministers hostile to him. At Rasputin's prompting, she bombarded Tsar Nicholas with letters urging him to end the 'useless slaughter'. In September, Nicholas ordered Brusilov to halt.

That decision dealt another blow to Russian morale, which was collapsing as quickly as the country's war-stricken economy. Petrograd buzzed with loathing of Rasputin, widely held to be a German spy, and 'that German woman', the Tsarina. Officers who had once boasted they would reach Berlin in weeks did not bother to report for duty, but blithely drank the days away in Petrograd bars. Strikes spread – over food shortages, prices that had increased four- or five-fold since 1914 and wartime working conditions. Two infantry regiments called out by the Petrograd police to disperse strikers refused, turning their guns on the policemen. It took four regiments of Cossacks to squash the mutiny.

The countryside seethed, too. Secret police files bulged with reports of unrest, and on the Don a Cossack leader warned of an imminent Cossack rebellion. As the news of conditions at home reached the front, ordinary soldiers who had willingly charged machine-guns with only bayonets and prayers grew sullen and disobedient.

Below: Uprising in Petrograd (St Petersburg) in the summer of 1917.

Tsar Nicholas's relatives pleaded with him to remove Rasputin from the Tsarina's side and resume charge of home affairs himself. In the Duma, every political faction united to denounce 'the corrupt peasant' and the government ministers he had helped put in place. The Bolsheviks, most virulent critics of the war, were not there to take part. Their representatives had long since been banished to distant Siberia.

In December 1916, a group of conspirators including the wealthy young Prince Felix Yusupov and the monarchist Duma member Vladimir Purishkevich lured Rasputin to one of Yusupov's palaces to murder him. According to some accounts, he was fed poisoned cakes and wine, shot four times at close range and battered about the head with a heavy candlestick or club before being trussed and thrown into the icebound River Neva. His body was recovered three days later.

Alexandra and Nicholas were privately desolated, and had the monk buried at their estate of Tsarskoe Selo, outside Petrograd. But the Tsarina was consoled when the unbalanced Interior Minister Alexander Protopopov, a Rasputin protegé, revealed he could communicate with the monk's shade in his dreams. Less consolingly, Rasputin while alive had left various prophecies that the royal family's demise would follow his own. All too soon, his predictions were to come true.

The Cossacks stand back

When, in defiance of government warnings, a general strike and mass demonstration began in an unseasonally mild Petrograd on February 25, 1917, the behaviour of the Cossacks showed the protest was unusual. Ordered from their barracks, though forbidden to shoot, the two reserve regiments of Don Cossacks in the garrison displayed none of their habitual ferocity in crowd control. Their whips and sabres were not raised, and their horses were edged gently through the mass of people. As they heard the shouts of 'Down with the German woman, down with the war!' and the cheers, some Cossacks touched their caps and smiled or winked.

Just two days earlier, the same horsemen had been driving their foam-flecked mounts again and again at many of the same demonstrators. Now even the Cossacks had had enough. At first, they continued to obey their officers, though without hindering the demonstration. Then some rounded on mounted policemen who were using whips on the crowd. Finally, towards the end of the afternoon, a Cossack sabred down a police inspector – and a revolution was beginning.

Tsar Nicholas at his command headquarters was informed of disturbances in the capital. Brusquely he told the military commandant to restore calm. It was too late. On February 26, crowds again ignored orders to keep off the streets. Non-Cossack troops were sent against them, and some 200 people were shot. But the ordinary soldiers were, like the Cossacks, showing signs of discontent. The following day, one by one, the regiments mutinied. Among them was the Preobrazhensky Guard, of which the monarch, by tradition, was colonel.

Rampaging crowds of workers and soldiers stormed government buildings and police stations, setting them ablaze. The Petrograd Arsenal and the mighty Peter and Paul fortress fell. Prisoners were released from their cells. By the end of Monday, February 27, 66,000 out of the Petrograd garrison of 170,000 Cossacks and soldiers had joined the mob, while the rest melted away.

Above: Death of a policeman at the hands of revolutionaries, Petrograd 1917.

End of the Tsardom

In a last desperate attempt to head off disaster, Tsar Nicholas had ordered the Duma to be suspended. The assembly ignored the command, but it was suddenly faced with a rival set up by the revolutionaries themselves – the Council of Soldiers' and Workers' Deputies, or Soviet. Its vice-chairman was a personable liberal lawyer from Simbirsk on the Volga. His name was Alexander Kerensky, and he soon became the bridge between the Soviet and the Duma.

Events moved fast. Together, the Duma and the Soviet established the core of a provisional government and decided the Tsar must abdicate. Nicholas's generals agreed, leaving the Tsar no choice. On March 2, 1917, aboard his imperial train, Nicholas signed away his throne, at first in favour of his 12-year-old haemophiliac son Alexis, but subsequently in favour of his own brother, Grand Duke Michael. The Soviet opposed the choice, and the next day Michael abdicated, too – ending Tsardom in Russia and the Romanov dynasty that had begun 304 years previously with Michael's namesake.

Soon, 'Citizen Nicholas Romanov' was reunited with Alexandra and his family, prisoners on the estate at Tsarskoe Selo. In Petrograd, the urbane Kerensky was beginning the climb that would briefly make him new ruler of Russia. Another man from Simbirsk was also poised to enter the stage – Vladimir Ilyich Ulyanov, known as Lenin.

Left: Tsarina Alexandra, formerly Princess Alix of Hesse-Darmstadt, in 1901.

The Autumn Revolution

Petrograd's Winter Palace was a scene of frenzied disorder as two squadrons and a machine-gun crew of grizzled Ural Cossacks rode up to it on an autumn evening in 1917. Its former owner, ex-Tsar Nicholas II, and his family were far away, tightly guarded prisoners in Siberia. Its new master, Alexander Kerensky, president of the provisional government installed when Nicholas abdicated, was absent, too. In the echoing marble halls, Kerensky's fellow ministers debated endlessly, while instructors scurried around attempting to organise officer-cadets into a semblance of defence.

For the 2,000-room palace was the tottering government's last redoubt in a city swept by revolution for the second time in a year. Armed workers and thousands of soldiers defecting to the revolutionary cause had seized most of Petrograd's public buildings. In the Smolny Institute, a former girls' finishing school, the Bolshevik leader Vladimir Lenin and other politicians of the extreme left planned and argued over their final push on the Winter Palace itself, 5km (3 miles) across town. The scenes in the Smolny were chaotic, as agitators and organisers rushed to and fro or collapsed dog-tired to snatch sleep on the dirty, wet floors. 'Here', in the words of a participant, 'was the beating heart of revolution'.

Earlier, some senior Cossacks had come to Kerensky with an offer. They would mobilise the three Cossack regiments of the Petrograd garrison, sitting in their barracks in uneasy neutrality amid the upheavals, to put down the revolution. All they needed from Kerensky was a free hand and some seasoned infantry to help.

But neither side could deliver. Most foot-soldiers in Petrograd had long ago switched sides or deserted, so Kerensky left the Winter Palace by car in search of troops elsewhere. The Cossacks, despite their leaders' assurances, were divided over which side to fight on. They, too, wrangled interminably about what to do, refusing to move in any case without infantry support. The most they would offer for the moment were a few men from the Urals to protect the palace.

The veterans given the task were not impressed with the defence force they found – half-trained youngsters, some of them Jewish, crippled officers, and, later, an armed company of women. It was hardly what the old sweats understood by infantry. They grumbled and muttered, until the news came that the Cossack regiments had reached a decision; they would put themselves at the disposal of the revolutionaries, not as an attacking force, but to 'guard public property'. With that, the Ural Cossacks prepared to head back to their barracks.

Begged not to go, they looked scathingly round at the defenders, and one Cossack is said to have sneered: 'Yids and tarts! The Russian people stayed over there...with Lenin!'. As a gesture, the Cossacks left their machine-guns.

Below: A Soviet artist's romanticised view of the fall of the Winter Palace in autumn 1917. Though seizure of the palace is depicted in films and paintings as a titanic battle, in reality the ill-assorted defenders hardly put up a fight.

Above: Another example of Soviet myth-making shows Lenin arriving in Russia from exile in Switzerland in spring 1917, to a tumultuous reception from the revolutionaries awaiting his leadership. His speech at Petrograd's Finland Station in 1917 was actually badly received by many. The circulation of forged documents 'showing' he was in the pay of the Germans forced Lenin into hiding between July and October, when he re-emerged to begin his successful grab for supreme power.

A palace falls

The weapons were hardly needed. After the Cossacks had gone, revolutionaries infiltrated the palace through its dozens of entrances, persuading many defenders to slip out the same way. Then a crowd of about 400 marched across the square in front of the building, swarmed through it and accepted the government's surrender. Just six people were killed in the whole affair.

Within a day, a Soviet Federated Socialist Republic had been declared, governed by a Soviet of People's Commissars. Lenin was chairman and his co-revolutionary Leon Trotsky was in charge of foreign affairs. The Soviet's programme included immediate peace with Germany and the abolition of all private property rights in favour of the state.

When those proclamations were made, the Bolsheviks had control only of Petrograd, and precariously at that. The rest of Russia was a vast, stricken unknown. But Lenin, after more than 20 years preaching revolution, had his finger-tips on power. He was now set to grab with both hands.

Kerensky's last flourish

While the Winter Palace fell and his ministers were arrested, Kerensky was still seeking help. He found it at last at Pskov, more than 250km (156 miles) away, in the person of the Cossack General Peter Krasnov, commanding some 700 Don Cossack horsemen and a regiment of infantry. With this force, Kerensky moved back towards Petrograd.

On the outskirts of the city, they encountered the Bolsheviks' 'Red Guards' – armed workers, sailors, soldiers and garrison Cossacks. A few shots were fired, but Kerensky's men showed no zeal for a fight, and were ordered to retreat. As they did so, Bolshevik propagandists mingled with them, doing their work well. The men from the Don soon decided to go home. They rounded on Krasnov at gunpoint and turned him over to the Bolsheviks. Kerensky eluded them, escaping disguised in a sailor's coat to begin 50 years of exile.

Following Petrograd's lead, city after city went over to the Bolsheviks – nearly 50 in the space of two months, though in Moscow it took a week of bloody street-fighting. Nevertheless, Lenin's position was far from secure. He had quickly obtained an armistice with Germany, but the Germans were seeking harsh terms for a formal peace. Russian Poland and Finland were both plunged into civil war. An independence movement was spreading in the Ukraine. And much of Russia was starving.

The Cossacks presented their own problems. Those in Petrograd with Bolshevik sympathies were quickly drawn into the representative bodies of the new regime. A Commissar for Cossack Affairs and a Cossack Department were created. Almost their first job was to start demobilising the Cossack regiments at the front. Their second was to spread the message of Bolshevism and win support for it in the Cossack provinces of the south.

A DREAM OF KAZAKIA

Right: In a reversion to traditional Cossack ways, General Alexander Kaledin (1861-1918) was elected ataman by an assembly of the Don Cossack host after the spring revolution of 1917 deposed the Tsar. As a moderate republican, he soon fell foul of both monarchists and the revolutionary left.

The idea of an independent Cossack Republic, beholden to no one, was not new. Ivan Zarutsky had dreamed of it during the 'Time of Troubles'. So had Bogdan Khmelnitsky in the 17th-century Ukraine. During the revolutionary year of 1917, it came to life again – first as a spark, then as a flame.

In the heady days after the Spring Revolution, Cossacks from the Don to the Amur evicted leaders and officials imposed on them by the former autocracy. Free Cossack assemblies again chose their own atamans, such as General Alexander Kaledin of the Don.

The new Cossack dawn touched Petrograd, too. There, men from the steppe founded the Council of the Union of Cossacks, to be both parliament and spokesman for Cossackry. The political parties of Russia courted it.

Such developments seemed in tune with the times. All over the country, workers and peasants were establishing soviets to define and represent their interests. The old Cossack institutions now being revived were very similar. In the darkest days of 19th-century repression, radical thinkers such as Alexander Herzen and Leo Tolstoy had cited them as models for future Russian democracy. But there was a deep flaw in the revival.

Below: Lenin and Trotsky with delegates to the first Soviet congress of so-called 'working Cossacks' in 1920.

Who owns the land?

When the Spring Revolution erupted, there were 162 Cossack regiments and 171 independent Cossack squadrons on active service at the front or in garrisons – thousands of men, mostly young and poor, cut off from their homes. As host after host picked new leaders, the servicemen had no say in the choice. Many, already disaffected by their conditions, resented the way in which senior Cossacks such as Kaledin seemed to be grabbing more wealth and power. Bolshevik propagandists exploited the situation brilliantly, and the Cossack leaders could do little but watch.

The leaders did not help their own cause. The Cossack Council in Petrograd, dominated by the well-to-do, was preoccupied with what would happen to the Cossack territories under the provisional government. A redistribution of land seemed certain, and the Cossacks as a class stood to lose heavily. In the neighbouring provinces of the Don, the Kuban and the Terek, for example, the Cossack minority owned five times more land per head than the peasantry. Within the total Cossack holdings there were vast discrepancies – the rich on huge estates, the poor on tiny plots.

Citing precedents going back to Catherine the Great, the Council insisted the Cossacks held their territories inalienably, and distribution of them was their own affair. Ministers in the provisional government havered. Some talked of the Cossacks' right to 'their land', without saying what that

Above: Cossacks at the gallop through Russian streets. Their role in suppressing popular discontent made them figures of hate to many. But Marxist class analysis drew distinctions between officers and men, the well-to-do and the 'working Cossacks'.

meant. Others hinted the Cossacks would have 'to make a little room' for others.

The Cossack leaders did not like even those vague threats to the status quo. Still less did they like the Bolsheviks' programme, with its calls for land nationalisation and for poor 'working' Cossacks to throw the rich off their estates.

In August 1917, the Cossack commander-in-chief of the Russian Army, Lavrenty Kornilov, staged a coup against the provisional government. Some say it had the backing of the Cossack Council and the nationalist, right-wing Black Hundreds. To thwart it, President Kerensky had to enlist and arm the Bolsheviks – a manoeuvre that worked temporarily, but held the seeds of Kerensky's own downfall. It also brought a change of policy by the Cossack leaders.

Towards independence

Immediately after the Spring Revolution, only ataman Karaulov of the Terek Cossacks had called for total independence for his people. Kaledin and the rest seemed content with self-government within Russia. Once Kornilov's coup had failed and the Bolsheviks were in the ascendant, however, it was a different matter.

The movement towards secession and a free Cossack Republic seems to have taken hold even before the Bolsheviks seized power, when representatives from all the hosts took part in a congress of 'national minorities' in Kiev in September 1917. Following the Autumn Revolution, when the Bolsheviks abolished the Cossack Council in favour of their own soviet of 'working Cossacks', it gathered speed. By the end of 1917, Kaledin of the Don, Karaulov of the Terek and Colonel A.P. Dutov of Orenburg had met the leaders of the Kuban and Ural hosts to lay the foundations of a breakaway state.

It was easy for the Bolsheviks to depict the plan as another by the rich to hang on to what they held. In a long proclamation designed to reassure 'working Cossacks' they would not suffer from the land reform, the Soviet government denounced Kaledin, Karaulov and Dutov by name. It spread stories that Kaledin, asked by some Don troopers if he would divide up the great estates, had replied: 'Over my dead body'.

In fact, Kaledin showed, by the policies he briefly tried to follow on the Don, that he was both sensitive to the views of its non-Cossack population and prepared to give the political left its say. But in the times, there was no room for such moderation. The anti-Bolshevik forces – Whites, as they came to be known – were rallying, some of them on the Don itself around Lavrenty Kornilov. They had no truck with dreams of an independent Kazakia. They saw the Cossacks in their ancient role of kingmakers, to recreate a reunified, Bolshevik-free Russian empire.

Between the opposing aims of Red and White, Kaledin became an irrelevance unable to command his host. Early in 1918, in despair, he shot himself.

A Nation Torn

In the terrible, blood-drenched, chaotic years immediately after 1917, Lenin's Soviet Russia was besieged on all sides by counter-revolutionary Whites and the foreign powers supporting them. More than a dozen nations were involved, at first divided between Germany and her allies on one hand and Britain, France, the US and theirs on the other. Under their onslaughts in 1918-19, the Bolsheviks' Red Army with its many peasant conscripts was at times penned into an enclave occupying no more than a quarter of Russia's territory. At its heart was Moscow, which Lenin restored to its ancient status of capital.

But as the battles of the Civil War raged back and forth, great tracts of land changed hands again and again. One was the area around Ekaterinburg in western Siberia, where, in July 1918, the imprisoned ex-Tsar Nicholas II and his immediate family were shot by order of a Bolshevik court, as White forces approached.

In the Cossack heartlands, brother fought brother for control. Early in 1918, the Reds secured the main centres on Don, the Kuban and the Terek, as well as the Cossack capitals of Orenburg and Uralsk. They promptly began a campaign of murder and looting that turned many previously uncommitted Cossacks against them.

So when the newly elected Don ataman General Peter Krasnov set about forming an army to drive them out, he quickly assembled thousands of men. With money and supplies from the Germans, at that time controlling most of the Ukraine, Krasnov pushed the Reds back towards the right bank of the Volga, conducting mass executions of Cossacks who had helped them. Krasnov's drive to the 'Mother of Rivers' was halted at Tsaritsyn, where the young Joseph Stalin masterminded the Red defence of the city that later bore the name Stalingrad. There were bloody reprisals, too, as White Russians and Cossacks threw the Reds out of the Kuban and ataman Dutov's Orenburg Cossacks, with their counterparts from the Ural and Astrakhan, forced them towards the left bank of the Volga. But the various Cossack armies could not link up at the river. The Volga corridor, through which vital oil and grain supplies reached Soviet Russia, remained in Red hands.

Below: The young Joseph Stalin reviews the Bolsheviks' First Cavalry Army in 1919. Many of its members were Cossacks who threw in their lot with the Reds.

Fateful year

When the First World War ended in the defeat of Germany and her allies in November 1918, the victors increased their help to the Whites. British, Americans, French and Italians assisted the attack on Soviet Russia from the north. A Polish White Army moved in from the west. From the east, Admiral Alexander Kolchak's White Guard, supplied with men and materials by 14 nations including the US and Japan, swept across Siberia to the middle Volga.

Some of the bitterest fighting came in the south, where Germany's collapse created a vacuum into which the Red Army galloped. Though Britain, France and others sent troops, Krasnov's heavily outnumbered Don Cossacks bore the brunt of the first assaults, and could not hold them. Wooed by clever Bolshevik propaganda, they deserted in droves to the Reds or back to the Don. Krasnov was forced to merge his remaining men with the White Russian Army led by General Anton Denikin, to yield his command and to resign as ataman.

For most of 1919, Denikin scored success after success, driving north to within 160km (100 miles) of Moscow itself. However, the Reds pumped in reinforcements at the rate of 25,000 a month, increased partisan activity behind the White lines and finally turned the tide. As Denikin retreated, he was harried mercilessly by a new Red weapon – the First Cavalry Army. It included Don and Kuban Cossacks and, ironically, one of its commanders, Semyon Budenny, had been a Cossack sergeant in Tsarist days.

Retreat through Siberia

Many of the Red reinforcements used against Denikin came from the eastern front. There, the Reds had gone over to the counter-attack in May, smashing the Ural, Astrakhan and Orenburg Cossacks under Dutov through a combination of a frontal onslaught and partisan attacks from the rear. The Cossacks' collapse forced Kolchak, supreme leader of the Whites, to retreat with his forces along the path of the Trans-Siberian railway. The Reds eventually cut them off at Irkutsk, capturing Kolchak himself, torturing and killing him. Somewhere along the line, the Whites reputedly hid their huge treasury of gold and coin. Its fate has never been satisfactorily explained.

Before his death, Kolchak had passed supreme command to Denikin. But at the end of 1919

WHITE KNIGHTS OF THE DON

The fates of Cossack generals Lavrenty Kornilov and Peter Krasnov were tightly twisted together in the early days of revolution and civil war. Yet though they shared a similar military background and had both escaped from captivity to rally anti-Bolshevik forces on the Don, in many ways they were very different.

Kornilov, the younger by a year, was the senior in rank and an unashamed populist. In his abortive coup against the provisional government in mid-1917, he boasted he had peasant blood. By contrast, Krasnov was a stiff-necked autocrat who cared little for others' opinions, and regarded non-Cossacks with contempt.

Their war aims were different, too. As a co-founder of the White Volunteer Army, Kornilov wanted what amounted to the restoration of the Russian empire, with the Cossacks as an integral part. Krasnov took a more complex, federalist view. Briefly in 1918, with German aid, he ran an independent Don Cossack fief.

The same year, Kornilov was killed by a shell in an unsuccessful bid to oust the Reds from the Kuban capital of Ekaterinodar. His hastily concealed body was found the next day by Bolsheviks and dragged through the town. Kornilov's place at the head of the volunteers was taken by Anton Denikin, a non-Cossack who put Russia above Cossackry.

Kornilov's background, reputation and popularity might have kept the Cossacks together behind the White cause, vague and ambiguous though it was. Krasnov's arrogance alienated the non-Cossacks and eventually drove many of his own men to the Reds. Denikin, and later Peter Wrangel, lacked the means and appeal to restore unity. Krasnov eventually fled to exile in Germany, later to reappear dramatically in Cossack affairs.

Below (centre): General Lavrenty Kornilov (1870-1918) was a popular hero, renowned for courage and integrity. But his quarrels with Kerensky and abortive 'mutiny' helped his Bolshevik enemies to power.

Denikin resigned, and the job went to General Peter Wrangel, known to the Bolsheviks as the 'Black Baron'. He had inherited a hopeless task. On the northern front, the Whites were driven out of Archangel and Murmansk. In the west, the White Poles were pushed back by an army that included Budenny's Red Cossacks. Though Poland later regained some territory, including the western Ukraine, she was forced to sue for peace. So by the autumn of 1920, Wrangel and his remaining Russian and Cossack forces were the major threat to the Reds, who redoubled their efforts against him.

To make matters worse for the Whites, their foreign allies had lost interest in the campaign. Wrangel was beaten back into the Crimea and forced to evacuate it by sea, taking the last of the White Army towards Turkey. In Russia, though, the chaos continued.

Below left: Red Cossack commander Semyon Budenny.

Below: Traditional style, 20th-century subject. 'Red Cavalrymen' as seen by the Soviet painter K.S. Semaikin.

Right: Requisitioning food in a Russian village during the terrible years of the Civil War.

The Bandits Ride!

War, famine, pestilence, death – the Four Horsemen of the Apocalypse galloped across the Russia of 1917-22 as hard as they have ever done anywhere. In their hoofprints, as always in Russia, came the bandits.

They struck in the Ukraine, where independence flickered briefly as Germans, Poles and Russians warred over it. They struck in the Russian Far East, where the armies of 14 nations were encamped for four years. They struck everywhere in the vastness between.

There were thousands of them – great gangs of deserters from White and Red Armies, escaped prisoners, displaced peasants, the desperate, the greedy, the plain mad. They feared nothing, certainly not the bullets of authority or the typhus that left unburied bodies scattered like logs across the width of a continent. There were plenty of Cossacks, past-masters of banditry, among them.

Some dressed their activities up with a kind of rationale. One was Nestor Makhno, a Ukrainian anarchist who, under the banner of peasants' rights, attacked both Whites and Reds in the south-west, as well as Ukrainian nationalists. However, Jews were the favourite targets of his followers, deserters from both sides wearing bandoliers over women's fur coats and reeking of vodka and onions. They robbed and murdered Jewish men, women and children in their dozens. Makhno eventually fled the country, dying in Paris in 1935.

Another was a Siberian Cossack called Annenkov, who led a small army of deserters on a rampage through Central Asia and into China, ostensibly in the White cause. But the sheer insanity of the times is summed up by the career of Gregory Semenov and his nominally anti-Bolshevik gang in Siberia.

Below: The stark face of famine in the emergent Soviet Union.

The beasts of Transbaikal

Semenov killed for fun. On the half-caste Cossack warlord's own admission, the day did not start properly until he had someone's blood on his hands, and his leading henchmen felt the same. Among them was Ungern von Sternberg, from a family bearing one of the proudest names in Baltic history, a descendant of the Teutonic Knights. Von Sternberg's idol was Genghis Khan.

Semenov's ragtag private army of Cossack renegades and Buryat misfits were well-paid for their macabre pleasures. Somehow, in the chaos after 1917, Semenov persuaded the Japanese he was just the man to advance their interests in eastern Siberia, which they had half a mind to annex. So he took gold from Japan and booty from his victims. There were thousands of those as Semonov rampaged up and down the Trans-Siberian Railway east of Lake Baikal. He wiped out entire villages, to the point where even he and von Sternberg grew almost bored with the killing. They set about ways to make it more interesting.

A favourite diversion in winter was to strip their captives, line them up in the sub-zero Siberian cold and drench them with water to freeze to death. Once the corpses were frozen solid, bits could be snapped off as grisly souvenirs.

In early 1920, Semenov and his men took 1,800 prisoners to a spot near the Chinese border, divided them into five batches, and spent five days murdering them. On the first day, in a leisurely way, the first group was shot. On the next, another 360 prisoners were beheaded. So the murders progressed, through a day of poisoning and a day of suffocation until the climax, when the rest were burned alive.

The atrocity was one of Semenov's last. As the Reds advanced eastwards, he was defeated and killed. Von Sternberg and others escaped.

RAILS OF TERROR

The Trans-Siberian Railway, built between 1891 and 1917 and running more than 9,000km (5,625 miles) from Moscow to Vladivostok, was the key to the Civil War in Siberia, the only way of moving men and weapons with any semblance of speed between east and west.

In mid-1918, all its key points east of the Urals were seized for the anti-Bolshevik cause by men of the Czechoslovak Legion, a 40,000-strong force of prisoners of war who had undertaken to fight with the Russians against Austro-Hungary for Czechoslovakia's freedom. Along it, Admiral Alexander Kolchak's White Army advanced from the Pacific to threaten the Soviet heartlands.

But Kolchak's defeat and the refusal of the Czechoslovaks to fight the Reds once the First World War had ended left vast stretches of the railway a no man's land. On its rails lumbered bronoviks, heavily armed and armoured trains of Reds, Whites and freebooters such as Gregory Semenov. Around it lurked well-organised Red Siberian partisans, irregulars and bandit gangs.

Semonov had several bronoviks, which he gave names such as 'The Destroyer'. Each included one or two luxurious passenger carriages, where Semonov and his lieutenants could eat, drink and sleep in comfort when they were not fighting. In an attack on a trackside village, artillery pieces and horsemen already in their saddles could be swiftly unleashed from drop-sided wagons, while machine-gunners and riflemen gave covering fire from the train roof.

The trains were vulnerable to ambushes if tracks were blocked or lifted. But as the permanent way was a lifeline to all, no one destroyed it completely.

Below: Armoured trains bristling with firepower played a key part in the Civil War, particularly in the vastness of Siberia. This one was operated by the Reds.

A Mongolian kingdom

Over the frontier in Mongolia, von Sternberg rallied the local population around him in a rising against their Chinese overlords, and succeeded in throwing them out of the region. The victory drove him madder than he had been before. He announced himself to be, among other things, the living Buddha, the rightful heir to the throne of China and the man who would restore Genghis Khan's Mongolian Empire in its fullest extent, from Austria to India.

The Mongols did not seem to mind his delusions of grandeur. But von Sternberg's cruelty, well-practised with Semenov, appalled them. Once the Red Army had cleared most of eastern Siberia of Whites and their supporters in 1922, it came to settle scores with the megalomanic Baltic Baron in his new kingdom.

The Reds found him in the desert, alone and trussed up, where his long-suffering 'subjects' had mutinied and left him. He was shot in due course for anti-Soviet crimes.

Below left: Cossacks of the Red Army, engaged against Polish nationalists in 1920.

Below: A crack Red Army regiment on the march.

Into Far Exile

Right: The Crimean coast. For many Cossacks fleeing across the Black Sea with the defeated White forces of General Wrangel, it was their last glimpse of Russia. Some took Russian soil with them – a tiny bagful worn on a thong round the neck.

Across an autumnal Black Sea, the convoy ploughed its way towards the minarets of Constantinople on the skyline. There were ships of all kinds, from great battle cruisers to pleasure steamers and rusting coasters – more than 100 in all. Apprehensive, shivering men huddled together on their decks, in their cabins and holds. Many of the smaller vessels, wallowing with the weight of their human cargo, were near to sinking.

As the ragged fleet manoeuvred to anchor in the straits of the Bosphorus, hundreds of tiny boats buzzed around. From those, Greek and Turkish merchants proffered bread and figs. A few men in the convoy had money, kolokolchik ('little bell') notes issued by the White authorities in southern Russia. They were worthless. A loaf of bread cost a gold wedding ring, the merchants insisted. For a pistol, they would add some Turkish sweetmeat called halva. Cossacks and soldiers, unfed for three or four days, wrestled with each other to buy.

So, in a scramble for over-priced food, the defeated White forces of General Peter Wrangel began their exile. They were the last in a long, long procession across the Black Sea which had started the previous autumn, as the Red Army gradually took control of the south.

In Constantinople, occupied by French, British and Italians, firstcomers with money and influence had snapped up every spare room. The rest – fighting men and civilian refugees, including some women and children – were herded into a military camp in the desert. Conditions there, poor from the beginning, became appalling as more and more

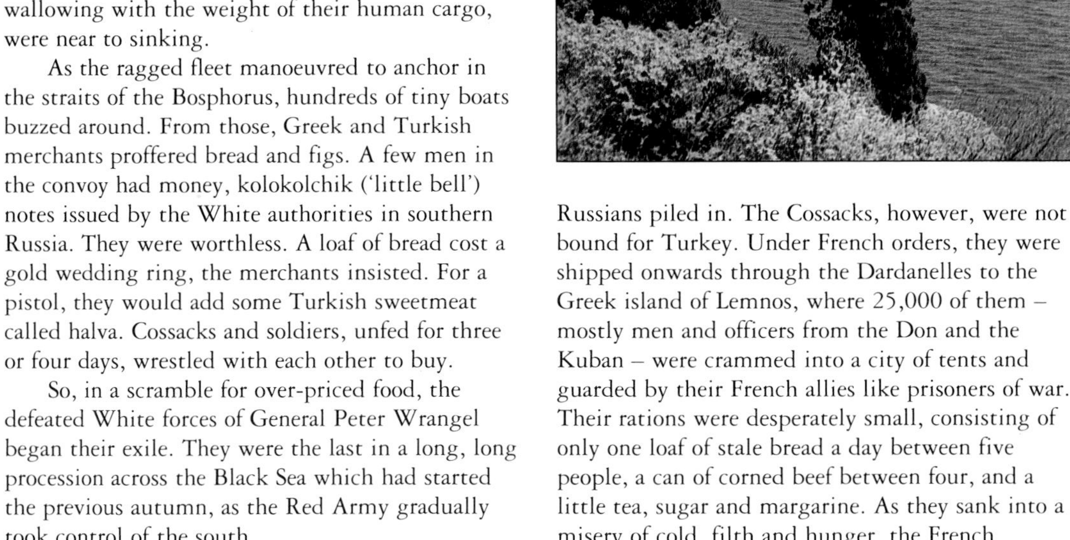

Russians piled in. The Cossacks, however, were not bound for Turkey. Under French orders, they were shipped onwards through the Dardanelles to the Greek island of Lemnos, where 25,000 of them – mostly men and officers from the Don and the Kuban – were crammed into a city of tents and guarded by their French allies like prisoners of war. Their rations were desperately small, consisting of only one loaf of stale bread a day between five people, a can of corned beef between four, and a little tea, sugar and margarine. As they sank into a misery of cold, filth and hunger, the French announced even that food was to be cut off – though volunteers would be accepted for the French Foreign Legion. About 3,000 accepted the offer and went to fight in North Africa. Several thousand more, in despair, took the opportunity of a Soviet amnesty to return to Russia, not sure what they would find, but certain it would be preferable.

Below: The advancing Red Army enters Irkutsk in 1920. Siberians who fled before the Reds created a thriving Russian community across the Chinese border in Harbin. Nearby, new Cossack settlements sprang up.

To Harbin

The exodus of Cossacks and Russians from south-western Russia was mirrored by another in the east as the Bolsheviks advanced through Siberia. The first destination for most of these eastern refugees was Harbin in Manchuria – on Chinese soil, but largely taken over by Russians since the building of the Trans-Siberian Railway had been completed. Although the Reds held Harbin briefly in 1917, once they had been driven out by the Whites they gave up all claim on the town.

In the space of a few months in 1919-20, the already considerable Russian population of Harbin was swollen by 200,000 immigrants. There was hardship at first, but the incomers were soon moved into cheap, quick-to-build houses of clay brick with board linings. Huge suburbs of them surrounded the old town. They were freezing in winter, the roads were not paved and many districts did not have running water. But the conditions were still far better than the filthy camps at Constantinople and Lemnos – and in Harbin, an important trade centre, there were opportunities both to work and to enjoy life. The cream of Russia's pre-revolutionary artistic talent put on concerts, plays, even circuses.

On the forest steppe of Manchuria outside Harbin, whole families of Transbaikal Cossacks established villages and farmsteads almost identical to those they had left across the Russian border. The area was largely empty, and the Chinese authorities were unconcerned.

The Cossacks fan out

Aid from organisations such as the Red Cross and deep-rooted Cossack loyalties helped the remaining refugees escape 'the island of death', as the Greek locals at that time called Lemnos. In large and small groups, they fanned out – to the newly liberated countries of the Balkans, to Paris and Berlin, to London and Brussels, to South America.

In their new homes, often unable to speak the language, many had to take menial jobs. Proud Cossack warriors became male nurses in Bulgaria, porters in Paris, nightclub doormen in Berlin. Those with riding, musical or dancing skills could, if they were lucky, turn to show business. From Yugoslavia, ataman I.G. Naumenko organised the Kuban Cossack chorus to provide employment and raise funds for Cossack causes. It was a success.

Unlike the unfortunates of Constantinople and Lemnos, few of the Cossacks who reached Manchuria felt the need to move on at first. Some with the resources to do so went south to Shanghai or across the Pacific to Canada and the United States, joining others who had left from Vladivostok as the Reds completed their sweep east. The rest had a brief interlude of peace before the Asian power-struggles of the 1930s and 1940s forced them once again to flee or die.

Above: Black humour from the Reds satirises White military leaders. The upper cartoon shows Denikin, Kolchak and Yudenich – 'early birds singing as the cat ate them'. The lower one depicts Denikin and Yudenich strangled by the proletarian dictatorship.

Left: Starving and sick, the Russian people quit the land. An Italian magazine illustration that appeared in 1921.

A Flickering Candle

The Steel Broom

At the end of 1920, Russia was a nation in ruin. Industrial production had collapsed to barely one-tenth of its 1913 level. Grain output was only a fraction of what it had once been. The country's livestock was devastated. The Cossack homelands of the south-west, scenes of some of the most brutal exchanges in the Civil War, bore more than their share of destruction.

On the Don alone, less than half of the arable land was still under the plough, with the rest a tangled mass of weeds. Two-thirds of the horses, nearly half the cattle, sheep and pigs in their thousands had perished, or did so during the winter famine of 1920-21. Even at full strength, the Cossack communities would have been hard-pressed to repair the damage. As it was, they had lost thousands of their able-bodied men in the Civil War and the White exodus. And there were other problems to contend with.

For the new rulers of Soviet Russia had no liking for Cossacks. Partly, it was gut-hatred, a legacy of the Cossacks' role as instruments of Tsarist repression and the association of many of them with the anti-Bolshevik cause. But the hatred was also ideological. In the new proletarian state, there was no room for a military class with land privileges and a mind of its own.

So Lenin and his followers set about breaking it up. The Cossack territories were abolished as such. Cossack assemblies were stripped of their power. Fighting men were denied their age-old right to bear arms and wear their traditional clothes. Land was arbitrarily reallocated.

Adding insult to injury, the Cossacks were reclassified in the same way as the peasantry they had so long despised – divided into three categories on the basis of their wealth and treated accordingly. Poor Cossacks, with nothing or little of their own, were regarded as friends of the new state, to be helped by it. The richest Cossacks, many of whom had in any case fled with the Whites, were designated 'kulaks', class enemies eventually to be extirpated en masse.

That left the majority of 'middling' Cossacks, who had a small surplus income from farming or other activities. They made up somewhere between half and two-thirds of the Cossack population and, according to Lenin, were to be encouraged into supporting the new state. But in the aftermath of civil war, with old enmities still burning, theirs was a rough wooing.

Deprived of some of their best leaders, the Cossacks hardly resisted the changes, though they were sulky and uncooperative. A few gangs took to roaming the steppe, stealing what they could to live on. However, that was banditry, not rebellion. Like their land, the Cossacks were exhausted.

Below: Weighing the grain on a state farm in 1920. Grain production was only a fraction of what it had been prior to 1914, and famine stalked even the once-prosperous Cossack lands of the Don.

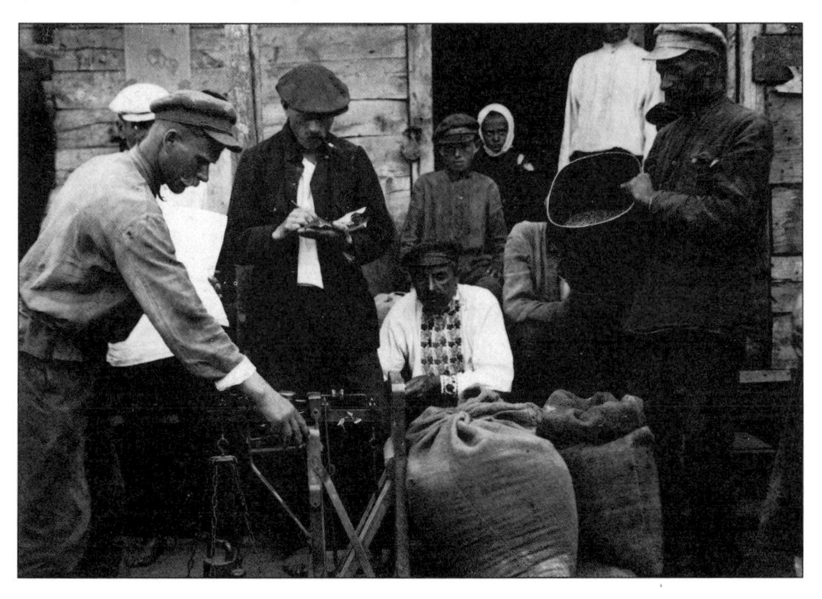

A short respite

Throughout 1921, the Cossacks were under the lash. When they failed to meet grain quotas, their barns were raided and even their precious seed-corn was seized by government officials. Any who showed defiance risked death, enforced resettlement or a long spell at hard labour as enemies of the people. Old scores were paid off in the guise of revolutionary justice.

But the results did not help the stricken national economy. Lenin and his colleagues were forced to rethink their attitude towards agriculture, and the 'New Economic Policy' which came into full operation from 1922 onwards gave farmers, including Cossacks, a welcome breathing space. The tax system was changed, allowing producers to keep more of their crops and to sell their surpluses on the open market. The tax burden was still heavy, fixed at more than 30 per cent, and the land reallocations continued, with more and more peasants being drafted into the Cossack regions. Nevertheless, as agriculture recovered, some Cossacks again began to prosper.

Red Class-Enemy

There were roughly 4 million kulaks – well-to-do peasants and Cossacks – in the Soviet Union of the 1920s. They made up just 5 per cent of the rural population, but produced about 12 per cent of the country's grain.

The definition of a kulak was elastic. It included anyone who regularly hired labour, who owned power-driven machinery such as a mill, or who had unearned income from any source. By that reckoning, virtually every Cossack elder came into the category.

Radical thinkers had been denouncing kulaks as ignorant, money-grubbing exploiters and parasites since the middle of the 19th century. Lenin, and later Stalin, raised the abusive rhetoric against them almost to an art form. But for the first few years after the Civil War, kulak knowhow and output were needed to help feed the country, and the heavy taxes levied on them contributed to the restoration of industry.

So although kulaks were deprived of the right to vote and some were dispossessed, they were tolerated up to a point between 1922 and 1927. Then the criminal code was invoked to seize their grain surpluses for the state. By 1930, Stalin had ordered their liquidation as a class, and he did not stop there. According to him, the Soviet Union had to rid itself of the 'kulak mentality' – the individual desire to enrich oneself. That diktat ensured collectivisation would be a bloody and cruel affair.

Below: 'Liquidate the kulaks as a class', ordered Stalin. The banner echoes his words.

There were other changes, too. The amnesty of 1922 allowed rank-and-file Cossacks who had left Russia with the Whites to return. Several thousand did. After Lenin's death in 1924, the yoke was lifted further. Cossacks were no longer forbidden to wear their distinctive dress, and even the kulaks among them were less rigorously persecuted.

The respite lasted five or six years. By then, Joseph Stalin, 'man of steel' and Red hero at Tsaritsyn during the Civil War, had consolidated his hold on the newly named Soviet Union. The first stage of economic recovery had been completed.

It was time for the next move towards communism. The Communist Party congress of 1927 called for agriculture to be collectivised – worked cooperatively on behalf of the state. At the start of 1930, a timetable for the operation was announced. Farms in the Cossack heartlands of the Don, the Kuban and the Terek were to be collectivised by spring 1931. Some of those in the Urals and Siberia would follow a year later, and the Seven Rivers territory of central Asia would be dealt with a year after that. In the process, the last distinctive vestiges of Cossackry were to be stamped out.

Below left: Joseph Stalin (1879-1953), blood-drenched heir to Lenin.

Below: Russian haymakers painted in 1917. Such idyllic scenes, if they ever existed, were soon to vanish as a result of civil war and Red terror.

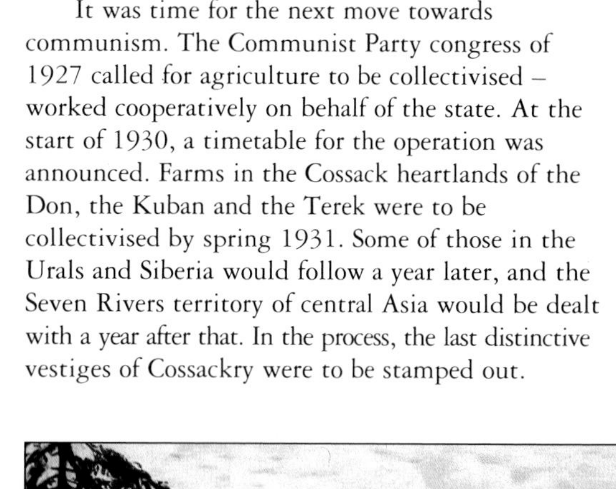

The Unquiet Don

Right: Mikhail Sholokhov (1905-84), author of 'The Quiet Don', at a meeting of Don Cossacks in Rostov in 1975. His novels chronicle the conflicts of loyalties set off among the Cossacks by the Bolshevik revolution, the Russian Civil War and their aftermath.

As Cossackry faced its demise under Stalin, a communist from the Don village of Veshenskaya wrote movingly in its praise. 'I am devilishly fond of the Don, of all that old, age-old style of Cossack life. I love my Cossacks and the Cossack women. I love them all! I want to weep when I smell the scent of steppe wormwood... and when the sunflower blossoms and the perfume of the rain-washed grapevines is in the air, I love it all so deeply and painfully.'

The author was Mikhail Sholokhov, and the words come from his most famous novel, which appeared in the Soviet Union between 1928 and 1940. In English-language editions, the first half of the book is called 'And Quiet Flows the Don', the second half 'The Don Flows Home to the Sea'. But in Russian Sholokhov chose a title from the stock phrases of folk songs and stories. Just as, in those, the Kuban is always swift and the Terek is always stormy, so Sholokhov's native river is always 'The Quiet Don'.

No nickname can have been less appropriate throughout most of Cossack history, and certainly not in the period Sholokhov's works cover. 'The Quiet Don' deals with the impact of the Bolshevik Revolution and the Civil War on Don Cossackry, and traces the waverings of its hero, the Cossack Gregor Melekhov, between the Red and White causes. Surprisingly for a work published in the Stalinist era, even by its end the hero is not a fully-committed communist.

With its masterly descriptions of Cossack life, the novel brought Sholokhov fame, fortune and, in 1965, the Nobel Prize for literature. Nothing he wrote afterwards equalled it. Nevertheless, two of his later works, 'Virgin Soil Upturned' and 'Harvest on the Don', allow glimpses of the true miseries of enforced collectivisation.

And miseries there were in plenty. From February 1930, thousands of communist officials and factory workers descended on the rural regions.

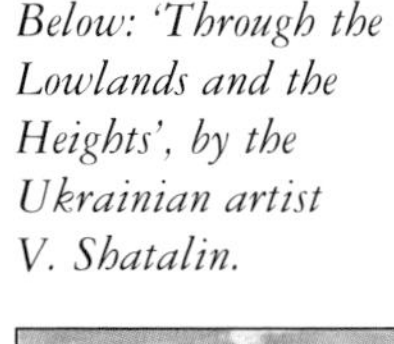

Below: 'Through the Lowlands and the Heights', by the Ukrainian artist V. Shatalin.

About 1 million kulaks in the western Soviet Union were thrown off their lands, which then passed to the collectives, and banished into hard labour. The poor and middling Cossacks and peasants were forced into collective farms by argument, threats and violence. Those that resisted were either murdered or shipped to labour camps. Within three months, around half the farms on the Don and Kuban had been collectivised; within six months, nearly all had, at least on paper.

Resistance grows

The methods used by some activists to impose collectivisation struck even Stalin as too harsh, and he ordered them to tone down their approach. In 'Virgin Soil Upturned', the communist organiser Semyon Davidovich is instructed to 'go easy' on the middling Don Cossacks, and to be 'cautious' in squeezing the kulaks. But in practice, in most areas, the violence and intimidation continued.

Rumours spread that the pooling of land, agricultural equipment, horses and oxen was only the first step in a process towards holding all property, including womenfolk, in common. That was too much for many Cossacks and peasants. They slaughtered their livestock rather than hand it over to the collective and stuffed their bellies with the meat through the summer of 1930. Some then fled, joining bands of uprooted peasants roaming the countryside as they had done so often in Russia's past. By 1933, there were 3 million wanderers.

Others turned to armed resistance, egged on – according to Stalin and Sholokhov – by White agents inside and outside the Soviet Union. Rifles and sabres hidden from confiscation ten or so years earlier were dragged out, and there were uprisings involving Cossacks on the Don, in the Caucasus and elsewhere in the early 1930s. The biggest embroiled much of the land between the Kuban and the Terek, and ended in the defeat of several thousand rebels by the Red Army in a pitched encounter near the town of Pyatigorsk.

The insurgents were treated ruthlessly. Hundreds were executed and thousands more were dragged off to forced labour. Whole villages were wiped out, and either left empty to rot or burnt to the ground.

THE DNIEPER TAMED

As Stalin ground the surviving remnants of the Cossack hosts under his heel, he also obliterated the environment in which the wildest Cossacks of all once flourished. As part of the Soviet Union's first five-year plan, launched in 1929, the lower reaches of the River Dnieper, home of the long-dispersed Zaporozhi, were tamed and harnessed in order to provide electric power and a continuous navigation.

In a vast project devised with the help of US and other foreign engineers, the river was dammed below Ekaterinoslav (later renamed Dnepropetrovsk). The lake created behind the dam, which was named after Lenin, covered the rapids and whirlpools which had protected the Zaporozhi and given them their name. The hydro-electric plant itself was sited next to one of the river islands that the Dnieper Cossacks had traditionally used as bases. During the 1930s, the plant proved its worth and produced more electricity than all the power stations in pre-revolutionary Russia.

The final phase

By 1933, three-quarters of the Soviet Union's arable land had been collectivised. Soviet leaders felt able to state that the kulak class had been liquidated and defeated in open battle. And Sholokhov could allow one of his Don Cossacks to think: 'Since 1921, the grain has been marvellous. All nature is on the Soviet government's side'.

It might have been, but the government was not on the Cossacks' side. As a result of Stalin's policies, including an increase in grain exports to earn hard currency, famine was again rearing its head, above all in the Ukraine and the Cossack homelands. Eye-witnesses described villages on the Don, the Kuban, the Terek and in Orenburg in 1933-34 with farmyards empty and equipment rusting in neglected fields, as the inhabitants slowly starved to death. Across the Soviet Union, up to 7 million people perished.

A scapegoat had to been found. Suddenly it was 'discovered' the kulaks had not been defeated at all. They had merely changed their tactics, infiltrating the collectives to wreck them from within. Stalin and his creatures promptly launched a purge against anyone who could be accused of kulak tendencies, and again the Cossacks suffered. Thousands whose only crimes were to try to feed themselves and their families were tortured, executed or transported. Even Sholokhov, who loyally depicted some of his Don collective farmers as secret wreckers, was moved to protest at the atrocities. Stalin ignored him and the purge went on until 1936. By then, reduced by terror and hunger to a shadow of its old Cossack self, the Don was truly quiet.

Below left: Victims of Stalinist repression, Ruthenian 'rebels' were imprisoned in the Ukraine of the 1930s.

Below: Passers-by ignore the bodies of famine victims in the Ukraine, 1932. The 'bread-basket of Russia' was reduced to starvation by Stalin's harsh policies, quite probably deliberately.

Right: The Cossack spirit rides on . . . Red Army cavalry in action during the Second World War.

In Battle Again

It could have been 1812. As invading troops drove eastwards towards the Russian heartlands, mounted Cossacks in patrol or company strength appeared from woods and cornfields to harass their lengthening supply lines. Fearlessly, the caped horsemen whirled in to deal death with rifle and sabre, before ghosting away into the morning mists as swiftly as they had come.

But this was the summer of 1941, and the invader was the mighty German army whose blitzkrieg tactics had already made Adolf Hitler and his Nazis masters of most of Europe. Breaking a two-year-old non-aggression pact with the Soviet Union, the Germans and their allies came pounding remorsely forward on a 3,200km (2,000 miles) front from the Baltic to the Black Sea – 3 million soldiers, 600,000 vehicles, 3,500 tanks, 7,000 guns and nearly 2,000 aircraft. By the end of the year, they occupied half of the USSR west of the Urals and were perched on the lower Don, though they had been driven back from Moscow.

The Cossacks, as so often before, were in the front line of resistance. In 1936-37, after more than a decade of persecuting them, Joseph Stalin had finally relented a little, reinstating the names of Cossack cavalry regiments and opening recruitment to all on the Don, the Kuban and the Terek. Some 100,000 Cossacks were serving in the Red Army as Hitler invaded. Tens of thousands more were conscripted as the war progressed.

Many of their lives were thrown away. Used as scouts, saboteurs, guerrillas and harriers while the ill-prepared Red Army retreated, Cossack horsemen performed splendidly to slow the Germans' advance and disrupt their rear echelons. In huge tracts of western Russia hardly touched by roads and railways, the horse was still king. So well did the Cossacks prove the point that the German army, which entered the Soviet Union with only one cavalry brigade, copied them. Eventually, the Germans had 2.5 million mounts on their books on the eastern front – to the annoyance of Hitler, who hated horses and horsemen.

Below: A German tank crosses the River Don in the summer of 1942. By then, Hitler's war machine had over-run much of the Cossack country north of the Black Sea and in the north-western Caucasus. Most of the area was under German military rule, but already there were plans to create civilian administrations, puppets of the 'thousand-year' German Reich.

However, Russian generals also insisted on staging the type of setpiece cavalry actions that had proved so gloriously futile in the First World War. A German non-commissioned officer described how, in autumn 1941, he watched incredulously as Cossack companies coalesced to attack a German force of tanks, heavy artillery and infantry in entrenched positions.

The Cossacks, a division strong and with no support, formed up in three widely spaced lines for a charge. Their first line was mown down by artillery and machine-guns hundreds of metres before it reached its objective. The second wave followed, over the mangled bodies of the first, to be brought crashing to destruction a little further forward. Then the third line charged, to meet the same fate. The Germans, endangered only by riderless horses galloping in a frenzy of fear and pain across their positions, had just four men wounded as virtually the entire Cossack division was wiped out before their eyes.

Time of terror

By the autumn of 1942, the Germans had pushed deep into the Caucasus, over-running the Kuban, but failing to reach the lower Terek and, beyond it, the oilfields of Baku. Although the territory they had conquered was a source of vital raw materials and contained much of the Soviet Union's heavy industry, the invaders were unable to exploit it to the full. Some industrial plants had been removed or destroyed as the Red Army retreated, in a new version of the ancient scorched earth policy. Others were persistently sabotaged by bands of partisans living rough behind enemy lines. Few were more skilful at that form of warfare than the Don and Kuban Cossacks who ignored the blandishments of deserting comrades and remained faithful to the Soviet cause.

It was a time of perpetual terror. Nazi racial policies and Stalin's own refusal to endorse international conventions on the treatment of prisoners combined to ensure that captured Russian troops received little mercy. They were deliberately starved to death, shot or hanged on the flimsiest pretexts, or none at all. Civilians fared as badly; hundreds of thousands were killed in reprisals for partisan activity or transported as forced labour to Germany, and hundreds of villages were burnt to the ground. Jews fared worst of all; not even the worst excesses of Cossack anti-Semitism could hold a candle to the clinical, efficient racial extermination programme of the Nazis.

But the tide was turning. Unable to take Moscow by frontal assault, the Germans tried to approach it along the classic route used in their times by the Cossack rebels of Stenka Razin and Emilion Pugachov – northwards up the Volga. They were halted at Stalingrad, formerly Tsaritsyn. For five months, from September 1942 to February 1943, the city defied Hitler's might. It was almost totally destroyed, and at one point its defenders, including Cossacks fighting as infantry, clung on to only a small central area. Nevertheless, the delay enabled the Red Army to regroup, surround the besiegers and force their surrender as the deadly cold of the Russian winter did its work. Historians still argue over the numbers of Germans captured or killed. Russian sources claim that there were 300,000, of whom between 100,000 and 200,000 were taken prisoner. Fewer than 5,000 eventually returned home.

In January 1943, the 900-day German siege of Leningrad, formerly St Petersburg, had also been lifted, and by the summer the Red Army was advancing westwards along the whole front. Gradually, the Germans were driven back – out of the Caucasus and off the Don, then across the Dnieper and, by November 1943, out of Kiev.

As with Napoleon's retreat in 1812, it was a procession of horror. The Red Army in its brutal turn allowed few prisoners to live, while partisans stepped up their murderous activities. And again pursuit did not stop at the Russian frontier. With planes, tanks and Cossack cavalry, the Russians pressed on in a remorseless frenzy of slaughter, rape and looting, through Romania, Bulgaria, the Baltic states, Poland, Hungary and Austria and into Germany itself.

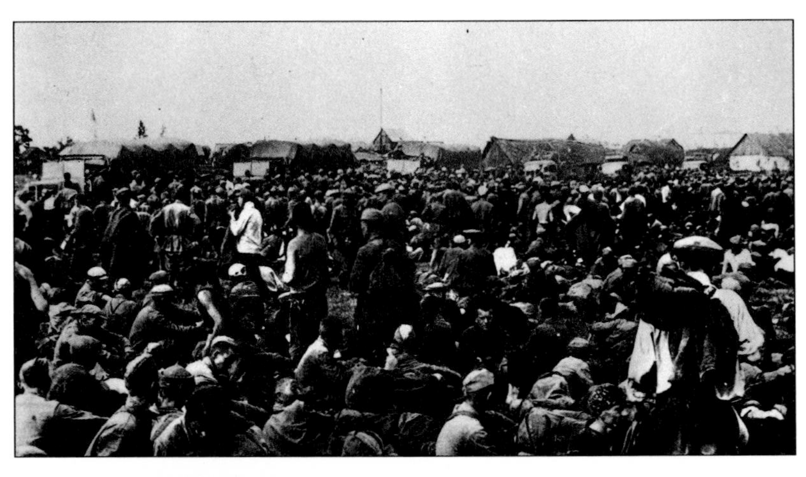

Top: Russian prisoners of the Germans in 1941.

Above: Death in the snow, on the approaches to Moscow, December 1941.

There, in east Prussia, with its memories of earlier Cossack incursions, the Red terror reached new heights of madness. Soldiers and civilians alike were killed indiscriminately – shot, sabred or crushed beneath armoured vehicles as they tried to flee. Women were gang-raped to the point of death by troopers riddled with venereal disease, carrying out Stalin's orders to 'smash for ever the fascist beast in his lair'. It was revenge redoubled for the 10.5 million Russian war-dead, half the collective fatalities suffered by all nations caught up in the Second World War in Europe, excluding the 6 million Jews who perished in the Nazi holocaust.

As the atrocities mounted, US, British and other allied troops, sweeping north from Italy and east through France and the Low Countries, linked up with the Russians and closed the vice on Nazi Germany, forcing her unconditional surrender on May 8, 1945. But Stalin's vengeance was not over. With the European fighting for the most part done, the 'man of steel' turned his attention to those he considered traitors. Among them were the Cossacks' ancient enemies, the Crimean Tartars, forcibly resettled in and around the Russian Arctic, the Kalmuks of the Volga region, moved far into Siberia – and several thousand Cossacks who had dreamed a dangerous old dream.

Last Throw of the Whites

When Nazi Germany's military machine thundered across the western Soviet Union in 1941-42, not all Cossacks regarded the invasion with patriotic hatred. Some saw it as an opportunity to throw off Red rule and restore old Cossack powers and freedoms. They were encouraged in that view by German plans to establish seven or eight new client-states on conquered Soviet territory – among them a 'Greater Ukraine', a 'Greater Caucasia', possibly even a 'Kazakia'.

Several White Cossack leaders in exile since the Civil War could identify with that ambition. They included Vyacheslav Naumenko and Andrei Shkuro of the Kuban and, above all, the aged General Peter Krasnov, who with German aid had briefly ruled the Don as an independent territory in 1918. Now he emerged as the figurehead of the Cossack pro-German movement.

There were pro-German Cossacks across the Soviet border, too. The Red Army Major Ivan Kononov was one of the first to declare himself. In August 1941, he defected with his entire regiment to the oncoming German forces. Then, as the conquest of the Don and the Kuban proceeded, Cossack collaborators began to appear. Among them was a group led by a Don Cossack military engineer, Sergei Pavlov.

The Germans' policy towards 'their' Cossacks was complicated and inconsistent. However after the horrors of Stalingrad, two clear strands appeared. Cossacks who had front-line experience or potential were to be welded into a cavalry corps. The rest were to accompany the German army's retreat, to be resettled away from the front. Pavlov led this group, which included women and children. Krasnov and his henchmen maintained close ties with both.

Below: General Helmuth von Pannwitz (centre) welded a mixture of Cossack emigrés, refugees and deserters into crack mounted regiments for the German cause.

The site of Pavlov's new community changed several times as the withdrawal from Russia continued. Eventually it came to rest for a while at Novogroduk in Byelorussia. There, the Cossacks – at this point about 10,000 strong – built a church, school and hospital, and White emigrés came regularly to inspect their progress or to join them in the new settlement.

The settlers formed several lightly armed militia regiments to protect themselves against Red partisans. In the course of one foray, Pavlov was killed, and his place as leader was taken by the former Red Army Major Timothy Domanov.

Meanwhile, the Cossack cavalry corps was being drilled into shape at Mlawa, north of Warsaw, under Major-General Helmuth von Pannwitz and other German officers. It was a difficult process at first, as Teutonic and Slav wills and temperaments clashed. But morale improved when von Pannwitz gave Cossack traditions a looser rein. His well-disciplined, smartly turned-out regiments of Don, Kuban, Terek and Siberian Cossacks fought fiercely in the mountains of Yugoslavia against Tito's Red partisans. Some also appeared in France, conducting operations against the Resistance.

As the tide of war flowed against Hitler in 1944, the Cossacks of Novogroduk were moved westward again with their horses, cattle, camels and laden carts. Their final destination was the town of Tolmezzo in northern Italy, designated by Berlin as the new Cossack 'homeland'. Nearby, at Paluzza, several thousand similar refugees from the Soviet Caucasus were also resettled.

End of a journey

For eight months, the Cossacks of Tolmezzo tried to recreate their steppe way of life on Italian soil, giving local inhabitants more than a taste of Cossack-style plunder and killing while they were there. But by April 1945 British troops were closing on the region and the time had come to move once more. Led by Domanov's mounted militia, with Krasnov following in a car, a long, weary procession of Cossacks and Caucasians straggled through rain and snow, under partisan fire, over the mountains towards Austria in a last bid for survival. On May 4, the column arrived at the town of Lienz, setting up a sprawling camp in the surrounding fields.

Von Pannwitz's cavalry, too, was retreating on Austria, with Bulgarian forces in pursuit. By May 9, the day after the Nazis finally capitulated, most of the Cossack corps was encamped near Wolfsberg, some 160km (100 miles) east of Lienz. Unlike Domanov's ragged and disorderly followers, von Pannwitz's men were in full parade-ground order when both Cossack groups formally surrendered to the British. Controversy over what followed is still raging furiously.

Under agreements previously reached between Britain and the Soviet Union, each country undertook to repatriate nationals of the other found on territories taken from Germany at the end of the

OLD WOLF OF THE KUBAN

Of the White Cossack leaders who sided with Nazi Germany, none was more colourful than little Andrei Shkuro. In contrast to the patrician Peter Krasnov, Shkuro was an earthy throwback to the early days of Cossackry – hard drinking, fond of dirty jokes and a good singer of the old Cossack ballads. He was also a cruel killer with more than a touch of the brigand.

He proved that in the Civil War when, at the head of a band of 400 Kuban Cossacks, he conducted a ferocious campaign against the Reds in the northern Caucasus, forcibly collecting 'donations' from wealthy civilians to help finance the fight. Shkuro and his followers wore wolfskin caps instead of the traditional woollen ones, and his personal armoured train was painted with pictures of a wolfpack in full cry. He looked a bit like a wolf himself, with shaggy hair and a long sandy moustache. Starchier officers among the exiles did not much care for 'Daddy' Shkuro, whose capacity for liquor and bawdy humour was undiminished in middle age. In the German-backed Cossack forces, he was given charge of a training regiment – a good pretext for yarning and drinking with the rank-and-file who worshipped him. When he was handed over to the Soviet Army in May 1945 for eventual execution, his Red military guards found him as entertaining a character as his own men had done. According to Count Nikolai Tolstoy, who has chronicled in great detail the transfer of the Cossacks from British to Russian authority, special care was taken to isolate Shkuro beforehand. The British, evidently feared the Kuban wolf might, even at the last, slip the trap.

Below: Shkuro, in full Cossack fig, and his German ally von Pannwitz admire a Cossack dance.

war. None of the Cossacks would have willingly submitted to the transfer, and the deal did not ostensibly cover an estimated 3,000 White emigrés such as Krasnov and Shkuro, who had never been Soviet citizens by most interpretations of the term. Certainly it did not cover von Pannwitz, a German.

Nevertheless, many White emigrés were with the Cossacks of Soviet origin when the handovers from British to Soviet authority took place, amid pleading, protests, confrontations and suicides. The first batch to be transferred included Krasnov, Shkuro and Domanov. Von Pannwitz joined them shortly afterwards. Since the surrender of his corps, his men had formally elected him ataman – a singular Cossack honour for a foreigner. Now, he repaid it by declaring he would share the bad times with the troops as he had shared the good, and declined various opportunities to escape. He died with Krasnov, Shkuro and Domanov on a Soviet gallows around the beginning of 1947.

Other less-exalted Cossacks were summarily killed as soon as they were in Red hands, or sent to the living hell of the labour camps. There, in their suffering, they found brother-Cossacks – loyal Reds captured and interned by their enemies and then reimprisoned on release by orders of Stalin.

Several thousand Cossacks managed to evade the shipments by fleeing or showing they were White emigrés; not all British officers interpreted the handover order in the same fashion. Most, but not all, of the women, children and old men were spared. Even so, 70,000 Cossacks, Caucasians and Yugoslavs were transferred by their British captors to Stalin's terrible vengeance.

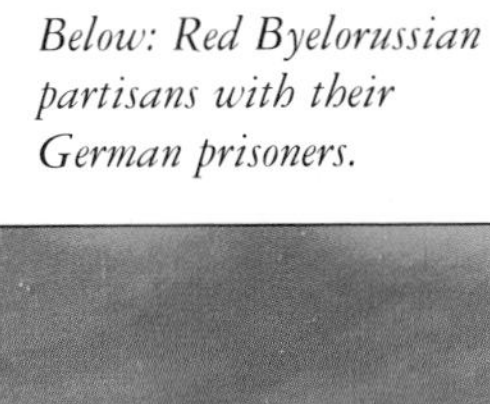

Below: Red Byelorussian partisans with their German prisoners.

ART OF THE DZHIGITOVKA

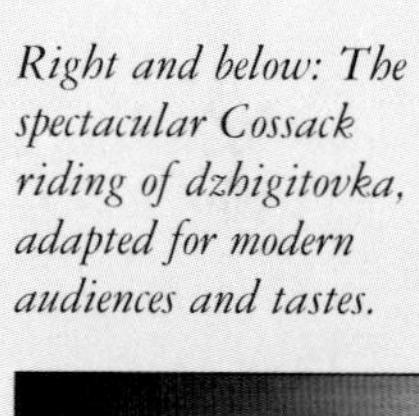

Breath-taking feats of daring horsemanship performed at the gallop in a tiny ring are the highlight of any visit to a Russian–style circus, still the most popular public entertainment in the former USSR. As the audience gasps at each new tour de force by mounts and riders, it is watching a living slice of history.

For this is the dzhigitovka, the trick-riding style that generations of Cossacks have raised to an art. It has few equals for audacity and skill.

Riders in colourful blouses and baggy trousers leap on and off their horses. They balance on their saddles to somersault, do headstands or make pyramids. Then they turn to repeat the performance facing backwards. They throw and catch sharp-edged sabres or lances. They swing right under the horse's belly, or so close to the ground a slip would dash their brains out. They do it all, and much more, at full tilt. Finally, in suitable arenas, they exit inch-perfectly up narrow gangways through the crowd – the nearest the flinching watchers will come to experiencing a Cossack charge in all its terrifying power.

Right and below: The spectacular Cossack riding of dzhigitovka, adapted for modern audiences and tastes.

Left: Equestrian skills could mean life or death for Cossacks in battle.

Below: Formal mounted drill stressed the practical side of dzhigitovka – here in rescuing the wounded.

The dzhigitovka takes its name from the dzhigits, warriors of the Chechen people in the Caucasus whom Cossacks and Russian troops long struggled to subdue in the 19th century. There was a mutual respect between Cossacks and the Caucasian braves, as Leo Tolstoy witnessed.

But, though the dzhigits undoubtedly taught the incomers some new riding tricks, the Cossack repertoire was already extensive, inherited from the Tartars and earlier steppe-horsemen. Most of it originally had a serious purpose – for example, to rescue an unhorsed comrade in battle, to use the horse's body as cover from enemy fire or to mount swiftly if suddenly attacked.

The dzhigitovka was also a recreation and entertainment, like polo and tent-pegging among horse-soldiers of other armies. Cossacks high and low regularly burnished their skills. One notable adept was the rumbustious Kuban White Cossack General Andrei Shkuro. In exile in Yugoslavia and Germany after the Civil War, he at one stage took to appearing in circuses – probably the only holder of the British Order of the Bath to do so!

Envoi: Cossacks Today

Cheap badges pinned to moth-eaten blue frock coats carried a dramatic legend. 'Liberty or Death' they read, in a flash of Cossack bravado rarely seen on Soviet soil since the age of Joseph Stalin.

Bemedalled greybeards and ear-ringed youngsters sported the slogan in the summer of 1990, at meetings in Moscow and at a rally on the River Dnieper near the old haunts of the Zaporozhi. Officially, the occasion was the 500th anniversary of Cossackry, though any year since 1900 would have served as well, or as badly. The first Cossacks kept no written records, and their early history was recorded by others.

None of that mattered to the badge-wearers. In the new USSR of Mikhail Gorbachev, reputed himself to have Cossack blood, the descendants of the hosts were at last being allowed to parade the shreds of their identity beyond the confines of theatres and circus-rings.

On the Dnieper, the gathering was a celebration. Cossacks in traditional costume with sabres and daggers displayed their riding skills and sang their old songs. But even Stalin in his more generous moods permitted them that occasionally. The real business was in Moscow.

There, 250 Cossacks from the Don and the Caucasus, the Urals and Siberia, took part in the first meetings of a Great Cossack Assembly. An ataman was elected, a Cossack Union formed, a Cossack newspaper launched. The future may dispel the echoes of similar, but ill-starred, events in spring and summer 1917.

The participants were optimistic, though. Their suitably named spokesman Kazakov declared the assembly was a landmark on the way to uniting all Cossacks in the Soviet Union (as in 1990 it still was) and abroad. It is an ambitious aim.

Right: The age-old partnership between man and horse is maintained in the modern Caucasus.

A people scattered

Wars, revolutions, famines and persecution have driven Cossacks in their tens of thousands all over the globe. Men and women whose forebears roamed the steppe now ride the prairies of North America, the pampas of South America, the veldt of southern Africa, the grasslands of Australia. They are found in cities from Milan to Montreal, in jungles and deserts, forests and frozen wastes. Some, from necessity or choice, are assimilated almost beyond recognition in their new lives. There are still in China the descendants of the Cossacks of Albazin, captured and imprisoned by the Chinese in the 17th century. Until the communist revolution of 1946-49, they lived in Peking; by that time, they were outwardly indistinguishable from their Chinese neighbours, but they maintained the Orthodox faith throughout. In the former Soviet Union itself, somewhere, are the offspring of the Trekhrech

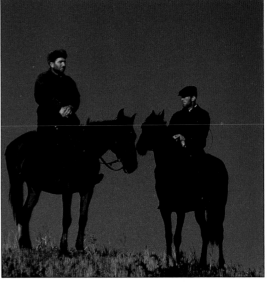

Below: Once again, the Cossacks don their flamboyant garb to march and sing – in strictly peaceful celebration.

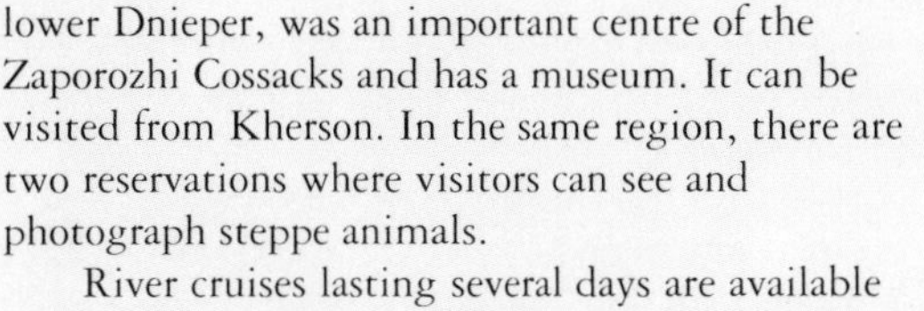

What To See Of Cossackry

Aspects of the Cossack heritage are on show in museums, galleries and other sites throughout the former Soviet Union. However, travel restrictions and reorganisations of exhibits make it difficult to specify what can be seen where. Local offices of the worldwide travel organisation Intourist or its successors may have more precise details.

Of the major cities, Moscow has weapons and military accoutrements dating back to the 13th century in the Kremlin Armoury, while the iron cage in which Emilion Pugachov was brought for execution is in the History Museum. St Petersburg's Hermitage/Winter Palace complex contains relics and artefacts from the time of the Scythians onwards, a section devoted to the Caucasus, and military uniforms and medals; the Russian Museum contains some paintings of Cossack subjects. Among the splendours of Kiev is the folk art collection in the History Museum, part of the Monastery of the Caves; on the same site there are graves of Cossacks executed by Ivan Mazepa. Kiev has a Museum of Folk Architecture too.

In the Cossack heartlands, Rostov-on-Don's History Museum contains uniforms, weapons and other items relating to local Cossackry. From Rostov, it is normally possible to make day trips to the former Don Cossack capital of Novocherkassk, where there is also a museum. Nikopol, on the lower Dnieper, was an important centre of the Zaporozhi Cossacks and has a museum. It can be visited from Kherson. In the same region, there are two reservations where visitors can see and photograph steppe animals.

River cruises lasting several days are available on the Cossack waterways of the Don, the Volga and the Dnieper. Shipping lines of several nations operate cruises on the Black Sea.

Below: 'The Cossack went to the war', by the Ukrainian M. Krivenko. Museums and art galleries across the former Soviet Union are rich in treasures associated with the Cossack heritage.

Cossacks, who moved into Manchuria from around Lake Baikal as the Bolsheviks came to power, and created an entire colony there. Unwisely, they chose not to join the Russian emigrés' exodus to Shanghai after the Japanese occupation of Manchuria in 1932. Their decision had fatal consequences. In August 1945, the Red Army hauled them back to be consigned to Soviet labour camps – a plight that has been largely unsung among the many Cossack victims of Stalin.

Other groups of emigré Cossacks retain open links with their past. There are associations of them in western Europe, the Americas and elsewhere. Not all their members have forgotten feuds with roots in old wars.

The very name 'Cossack' has been, to put it at its kindest, borrowed by others, though that is a long-established practice. In the Russian colonisation of Siberia and central Asia, almost anyone could buy it with service. In the 19th century, the Tsars used it for Ukrainian horse regiments with few discernible Cossacks in their ranks. Stalin's and Hitler's Cossack cavalry took all–comers from the old Cossack territories, by then heavily repopulated. Musicians and dancers, actors and acrobats all appropriate the term for its redolence and romance.

Retying these multifarious strands of Cossackry, therefore, would be a complicated task. Perhaps it is better just to remember the Cossack legacy, in all its aspects, and to heed the words of a participant in the Dnieper-side rally in 1990. Pointing out that one meaning of the word Cossack is 'free man', he added simply: 'That's what we all want to be'.

Left: Three ages of Cossackry and five centuries of tradition. Participants in the Cossack festival on the River Dnieper, 1990.

Glossary

Russian words in English-language editions of this book are spelled in the way thought to be most helpful to non-specialist readers, rather than transliterated from Russian with strict consistency.

There are fashions in transliteration that may affect the spellings. Where no general precedents exist, the simplest spelling has been preferred.

Ataman	Cossack leader
Boyar	Member of order of nobility abolished by Peter the Great
Bronovik	Armoured train
Burka	Caucasian cape
Chaika	Smallish Cossack boat (literally, 'seagull')
Chekmen	Cossack frock-coat with hook-fastenings
Cherkeska	Cossack coat with sewn-on cartridge pouches
Decembrists	Participants in unsuccessful revolt of 1825
Duma	National legislative assembly in Russia 1905-17
Dzhigitovka	Trick riding
Gaidamak	Rebel or bandit in Ukraine (Ukrainian 'haidamak')
Hetman	Variant of ataman (qv), specifically used of certain Cossack leaders in the eastern Ukraine.
Host	English translation of Russian 'voisko', denoting the Cossacks of a given territory (eg. the Don host)
Icon	Holy image, chiefly painted
Kaftan	Or 'caftan'. Various types of coat-like garments, long and often belted
Kazakia	Term for a unified, autonomous all-Cossack state. It almost came into existence in 1917.
Kinzhal	Cossack dagger
Klich	Type of curved sabre
Knout	Whip
Krug	Cossack assembly
Kubanska	Fur cap of Kuban style
Kulak	Wealthy peasant or Cossack
Kvas	Beer-like drink
Mir	Village assembly
Muzhik	Peasant
Nagaika	Cossack riding-whip
Old Believers	Opponents of 17th-century Church reforms who swelled the ranks of the Cossacks, particularly on the Yaik (Ural) and Terek rivers.
Oprichnik	Member of Ivan the Terrible's terror squads
Ostrog	Wooden fort
Preobrazhenski Regiment	Senior regiment of the Russian regular army, founded by Peter the Great
Red Cossacks	Members of Soviet (Red) cavalry and associated forces. Many individuals were not of Cossack origins
Shashka	Caucasian sword
Sotnik	Cossack lieutenant in command of a sotnia of (roughly) 100 men
Stanitsa	Fortified Cossack village
Streltsi	Members of standing army formed by Ivan the Terrible
Tabor	Defensive waggon-circle
Tsar	Emperor
Tsarina	Empress
Tsarevitch	Son of Tsar (especially eldest)
Voisko	Army or Cossack host
Voivod	Early Russian term for a military commander
White Cossacks	Members of anti-Bolshevik forces (Whites) in or after the Civil War
Zemstvo	Elective district council after about 1864

Bibliography

Many sources have been used in the compilation of this book. The author acknowledges his particular debts to the following works:-

Russian History Atlas, Martin Gilbert, Weidenfeld & Nicolson, London 1972.

Information USSR, ed. Robert Maxwell, Macmillan, New York 1962.

The Russian Empire 1801-1917, Hugh Seton-Watson, Oxford University Press, 1967.

Cambridge Encyclopaedia of Russia and the Soviet Union, Cambridge University Press 1982.

The Mongols, David Morgan, Basil Blackwell, Oxford 1986.

The Cossacks, Philip Longworth, Constable, London 1969.

The Despised and the Damned, Jules Koslow, Macmillan/Collier Macmillan, London and New York 1972.

The Other Russia, Michael Glenny and Norman Stone, Faber & Faber, Boston and London 1990.

Uniforms of the Russian Imperial Army, Boris Mollo and John Mollo, Blandford Press, Poole 1979.

Napoleon's Enemies, Richard Warner, Osprey, London 1977.

Life in Russia under Catherine the Great, Miriam Kochan, B.T.Batsford, London/ G.P. Putnam's Sons, New York 1969.

Russia, M.T.Florinsky, Macmillan, New York 1953.

Russia Tsarist and Communist, Anatole G. Mazour.

The Evolution of Russia, Otto Hoetzsch, Thames & Hudson, London 1966.

The Russian Chronicles, Random Century, 1990.

The Third Reich, James Lucas, Arms & Armour Press, London 1990.

Victims of Yalta, Nikolai Tolstoy, Hodder & Stoughton, London 1977.

Stormy Petrel, Dan Levin, Frederick Muller, London 1965.

References in italic refer to captions to illustrations.

Index

A

Adams, John Quincey, 103
Akhmad, Khan, 25
Alaska, 103
Alabazin, 70
alcohol, love of, 27
Aleutians, 102, 103
Alexander I, *94,* 103, 106
  wars against Napoleon, 94-6, *95,* 98, 100-1
Alexander II, 91, 107, 111, *111,* 112, *112*
Alexander III, *111,* 112
Alexanderskaya Sloboda, 30
Alexandra, Tsarina, 115, 116, *116, 117*
Alexis, Tsar, 45, 51, 60
Alexis, Tsarevich (d. 1718), 73
Alexis, Tsarevich (d. 1918), 114, 117
America, 102-3
Amur host, 110, 112, 113
Andrusovo, Peace of, 52
anti-semitism, 49, 51, 112, 124, 133
Arguello, Jose Durio, 102-3
Asia, 110-11
Astrakhan, 32, 64, *64,* 113
ataman, 29, 46, 77, 91
Atlasov, Vladimir, 71
Austerlitz, battle of, 95
Autumn Revolution, 118-19, *118*
Azov, 56-7, *56,* 72, 89, 110

B

Bagration, Peter, 96
Baikal, Lake, 70
Balotnikov, Ivan, 42
bandits, 77-8, 88, 124
Baranov, Alexander, 102, *102,* 103,
Bariatinsky, Prince, 65
Basil II, 24, 25, 27
Basil III, 30
Basil IV (Shuisky), 41, 42
Basil, Emperor, 18
Batory, King Stephen, 34, 35
battle tactics, 12, 20, 55
Batu, 21
Belorussia (White Russia), 24
Berezina, 99
Bering Straits, 71
Bibikov, Alexander, 83, 84, 86
Black Sea host, 89, 90-1
'Bloody Sunday', 112-13
Bolsheviks, 114, 116, 122, *122, 123, 125,* 135
  Autumn Revolution, 118-19
  Civil War, 122-5
  collectivisation, 129, 130-1
  Trans-Siberian Railway, 125, *125*
  treatment of Cossacks, 128-9
Bonaparte, Napoleon *see* Napoleon Bonaparte
Boris, Prince, *18*
Borodino, battle of, 96, *97*
bridlery, 13, *13,* 55
Briukhovetsky, Ivan, 52-3
Bronze Age, 10, *10, 11*
Brusilov, A.A., 116
Budenny, Semyon, 122, *123*
Bulavin, Kondrati, 72

C

California, 102-3
Captain's Daughter, The (Pushkin), 85
Catherine II (the Great), *80, 81,* 82, 89, 90, *90,* 102
  Pugachov's rebellion, 83, 87, 89
cavalry, 11, 115
chaiki ('seagulls'), 58-9, *63*
Chancellor, Sir Richard, 34
chariots, 10, 11, *11*
Charles X of Sweden, 52
Charles XII of Sweden, 74, 75, *75*
Cherkassk, 72-3
China, 110, 127
Christianity, 17, 18
Cimmerians, 12
Civil War, 122-6, 135
collectivisation, 129, 130-1
communism, 129
  see also Bolsheviks
Conçepcion, Consuela, 103
conscription, 78, 80
Constantine, Emperor, 18
Constantinople, 17, 24, *24,* 59, 126
Cossack Council, 120, 121
Cossack Department, 119
Cossack Union, 138
Council of Soldiers' and Workers' Deputies, 117
Crimea, 69, 89
Crimean War, 107, 110

D

dances and dancing, *6,* 108-9, *108, 109*
Darius, King, 12
Davidovich, Semyon, 130
Decembrists, 106, *106*
Denikin, Anton, 122-3, *127*
Dezhnev, Semyon, 71
Dmitri, False *see* False Dmitri
Dmitri, Prince, 40, 41
Dmitri Donskoi, Grand Prince, *22, 23, 23*
Dnieper, river, *9,* 16, 17, *29,* 131
Dnieper Cossacks, 28-9
  see also Zaporozhi
Dnieper festival, 138, *139*
Dolgoruki, Basil, 88
Dolgoruki, Yuri, 19
Dolgoruki, Prince Yuri, 72
Domanov, Timothy, 134, 135
Don Cossacks, 28, 29, *42,* 60, 65, 86, 90, 113
  and the Turks, 56, 57, 59
  bandits, 78
  collectivisation, 129-31
  Indian expedition, 93-4
  Michael I favours, 45-7
  prosperity, 76-7
Don Cossacks (cont'd)
  revolts, 41-4, 72-3, 80, 122
  The Quiet Don, 130
  uniform, 104, *105*
Doroshenko, Peter, 52-3
drinking clubs, *27*
Duma, 113, 114, 116, 117
Dutov, A.P., 121
dwellings, 28, *29*
dzhigitovka, 136-7, *136, 137*

E

Elizabeth I, 34
Eurasia, 8-9
exodus, 126-7

F

False Dmitri (the first), 41, *41,* 43
False Dmitri (the second), 42, 43
famines, 40, 45, *124, 128,* 131, *131*
farming, 46, 76, *76, 77,* 77, 128, *128, 129*
  collectivisation, 129, 130-1
Feodor I, Prince, 35, 40
Filaret, Patriarch, 45, *45,* 60
First Cavalry Army, 122, *122*
floggings, *78,* 79, *79,* 106
folksongs, *108,* 109
France
  wars with, 92-3, 94-6
Francis II of Austria, 95
free Cossacks, 33, 34-5, 42
fur trade and traders, 70-1, 102

G

Galicia, 114-16
Gapon, Father, 112
'gathering of the lands', 25
Genghis Khan, 20, *20,* 21
Germany
  pro-German movement, 134-5
  wars with, 114-15, *114,* 119, 132-5, *133*
Gleb, Prince, *18*
Gogol, Nikolai, 53, *53*
Golden Horde, *20,* 21-6, *21,* 27, 32, 56
Golitsin, Prince Basil, 69
Gorbachev, Mikhail, 138
Gordienko, Ivan, 74
Gorki, Maxim, 66, *67*
Goths, 13
Great Cossack Assembly, 138
Great Horde, 24
Gudonov, Boris, 40-1, *40,* 45

H

Harbin, 127
Hindenburg, Paul Von, 114-15
Hitler, Adolf, 132
horse-herders, 10
horsebreeding, 12
horsemanship, 11, 13, 55
  bridlery, 13, *13,* 55
  dzhigitovka, 136-7, *136, 137*
horses, wild, 10, 11
Horsey, Sir Jerome, *34*
hosts, 29, 110, 128
Huns, 13
hydro-electric plant, 131

I

icons, 61, *61*
independence, 120-1
India
  expedition to, 94, *94*
Indo-Europeans, 10
Irkutsk, *38,* 70, 110, *126*
Islam, 18, 23
Ivan I (Kalita), 22-3
Ivan III (the Great), 24-5, *25*
Ivan IV (the Terrible), 30-6, *30, 33, 34, 35,* 37
Ivan Ivanovich, 35, *35*
Ivan Vorenok, 43

J

Jan III of Poland, 68, *68*
Janissaries, Corps of, *56*, 57
Japan, 113, 124
Jesuits, 49
Joasaphat of Tobolsk, Archbishop, 49
Judaism, 17, 18, 49
see also anti-Semitism

K

Kaledin, Alexander, 6, 120, *120*, 121
Kalita, Ivan, 22-3
Kalka, battle of, 21
Kalmuks, 90, 95, *95*, 133
Karaulov, ataman, 121
Kasim, Khan, 27
Kaufmann, C.P. von, 111
Kazachok, 6
Kazakia, 43, 120-1
Kazaks, 26
Kazan, battle of, 32, 84
Kazan, Khanate of, 24
Kerensky, Alexander, 117, 118, 119, 121
Khabarov, Yerofei, 70
Khan, Genghis *see* Genghis Khan
Khan Kasim *see* Kasim, Khan
Khan Mamai *see* Mamai, Khan
Khazars, 13, 17
Khmelnitsky, Bogdan, 50-1, *50*, *51*, 52, 120
Khmelnitsky, Michael, 50
Khmelnitsky, Yuri, 52
Khorovod, 109
Kiev, 17, 19, *21*, 22-3, 52, 139
Kievan Rus, 18-19, 24
kingmakers, 41, 44, 83, 121
knout, *78*, 79, *79*, 106
Kochubei, Basil, 75
Kolchak, Alexander, 122, 125, *127*
Kononov, Ivan, 134
Kornilov, Lavrenty, 121, 123, *123*
Krasnov, Peter, 119, 122, 123, 134, 135
Kremlin, *23*, *33*, 98
Kuban Cossacks, 91, 110, 113, 126, 133
collectivisation, 129, 130
Kublai Khan, *20*, 21
Kuchum Khan, 36, 37, 39
Kul-Oba, 13, 14, *14*
kulaks, 128, 129, *129*, 130, 131
Kulikovo, battle of, *22*, 23
Kurbsky, Prince Andrei, 32
kurgans, 14
Kutuzov, Michael, 95, 96, 97, 98, 99

L

landowners, 25, 31, 120-1
Lavryentevich, Atashka, 39
Lemnos, 126, 127
Lenin, Vladimir Ilyich, 117, 118, 119, *119*, *120*, 128, 129
Leningrad *see* Petrograd; St Petersburg
Liapunov, Prokopy, 43
Light Brigade, charge of the, 107, *107*
Lithuania, 23, 24
see also Poland

M

Magyars, 13
Makhno, Nestor, 124
Mamai, Khan, 23
Martha, Sister, 45
Marx, Karl, 112
Massena, André, 93, 94
Mazepa, Ivan, 69, 74, *74*, 75, *75*
Mengli Girai, 24
mercenaries, 12, 26-7, 34, 54
Mezhakov, Ataman, 44
Michael, Grand Duke, 117
Michael I, 44-5, *44*, 46, 47
middle classes, 31, 43
Minayel, Frol, 60
Minin, Kuzma, *42*, 43
Mniszek, Marina, 40, 42, 43, *43*
Mnogogreshny, Demian, 71
Mohammed IV of Turkey, 68, *68*, 69
Mongolia, 125
Mongols, 20-1, *25*
see also Tartars
Monroe, James, 103
Monroe Doctrine, 103
Moscow, 22, *23*, 24, *24*, *64*, 73, 96-8, *98*, 122, 139
Mstislav, Prince, 19
Murat, Joachim, 98, 100
Muraviev, Nicholas, 107, 110, 113
Muscovy, 24, 25, *28*
museums, 139
music and dancing, 6, 108-9, *108*, *109*

N

Napoleon Bonaparte, 6, 93, 94-101, *95*, *97*
national assembly, 91
Naumenko, I.G., 127
Naumenko, Vyacheslav, 134
Neapol-Skifskii, 12
Nevsky, Alexander, 22
New Economic Policy, 128
Ney, Michel, 100
Nicholas I, 91, 106-7, *107*
Nicholas II, 112, 113, *115*, 118, 122
Spring Revolution, 116-17
war with Germany, 114-16
Nikon, Patriarch, 60, 61, *61*
nobility, 91
nomadic tribes, 8-9, *8*, 10
Novgorod, 17, 19, 21, 22, 24, 25
Novogroduk, 134

O

Ogedei, 21
Old Believers, 60, 64, 78, 82, 90
Oleg the Seer, *16*, 17
oprichniki, 30, 34
Orenburg, siege of, 83-4
Orenburg host, 90, 110, 113, 122, 131
Orlov, Alexis, 88
Orlov, Basil, 94
Orlov, Gregory, 80, 81
Orthodox Church, 18, 19, 22, *24*, 49, *49*, 60-1
Otrepev, Grigori, 41, *41*
Ottoman Turks, 24, *24*, 56

P

Palaeologus, Sophia, 24-5, *24*, *25*
Panin, Peter, 86
Pannwitz, Helmuth von, 134, *134*, 135, *135*
Paris, 101, *101*
Parthians, 12-13
Paul, Tsarevich, 81, 83, 90
Paul I (Tsar Madman), 92, 93, 94, 102
Pavlov, Sergei, 134
peasants, 31, 40, 45, *46*, 76, 130
Pechenegs, 13, 17
Perovsky, Basil, 110-11
Persia
attacks on, 63
Peter I (the Great), 72, *72*, 73, *73*, 74, 75
Peter III, 81, 82
see also Pugachov, Emilion
Petrograd, 114, *116*, 117, 118, 119
see also St Petersburg
piracy, 56, 58-9, *59*, 63
Platov, Matvei, 94, 96-100, *97*, 101
Poland, 24, *48*, 53, 68-9, 81, 123
Cossack regiments, 34-5
invasion of Moscow, 42-3
repression of Ukranian Cossacks, 47-8
Polobotuk, Paul, *74*
Poltava, battle of, 74, *74*
Poniatowski, Stanislav, 81
Potemkin, Gregory, 81, *81*, 89
Pozharsky, Dmitri, *42*, 43
Pritkov, Basil, 77
Protopopov, Alexander, 116
Pugachov, Emilion, 66-7, 80, 82-4, *82*, *83*, 86-7, 86
Purishkevich, Vladimir, 116
Pushkin, Alexander, 85, *85*

Q

Quiet Don, The, 130

R

raskolniki, 60
Rasputin, Gregory, 114, 116, *116*
Razin, Frol, 62, 65, *65*
Razin, Ivan Timofeyevich, 62
Razin, Stepan Timofeyevich (Stenka), 62-7, *62*, *63*, *65*, *67*
Razumovsky, Alexis, 80
Razumovsky, Cyril, 80
Red Army, 122, *125*, *126*, 132-3, *132*, 139
Reds *see* Bolsheviks
reforms, 73, 81, 82, 91, 111, 113, 128-9
registered Cossacks, 28, 33, 34, 51, 52
religion, 18, 24, 29, 49
Rennenkampf, E.K., 114
Repin, Ilya Efimovich, 69
Revolution, Autumn, 118-19, *118*
Revolution, Spring, 116-17, *116*, *117*
Rezanov, Nicholas, 103
Riazan, 21, 26-7
Riazan, Grand Duke of, 26-7
ritsari, 46
Roman Catholicism, 18, 49
Romanov, Anastasia, 30, 34
Romanov, Feodor, 45
Romanov, Grand Duke Michael, 117
Romanov, Martha, 45

Romanov, Michael *see* Michael I
Rublev, Andrei, 61
Ruin, The, 53
Rumiantsev, Peter, 88
Rurik, Prince, *16*, 17
Rusi, 17
Russell, William Howard, 107
Russia, 17, *28*
Russian American Company, 102
'Russification', 80, 106
ryabchiks, 9, *9*

S

sable, 70, *70*
Sahaidachny, Peter, *47*, 48, 49
saiga antelopes, 9, *9*
Saltikov, Sergei, 81
Samoilovich, Ivan, 69, 71
Samsonov, A.V., 114
Sarai, 20, 21
Sarmatians, 13, 14, 15
Scythians, 11-15, *12, 13, 14, 15*
'seagulls' (chaiki), 58-9, *63*
Semenov, Gregory, 124, 125
serfs and serfdom, 62, 73, 76, 81, 91, 106
  liberation, 111
  punishment, 79
Sergei of Radonezh, *22*, 23
Sergievo, Abbot of, 44
Seven Rivers host, 111, 113, 129
Seward, William, 103
Shakhovskoi, Grigori, 42
Shelekhov, Gregory, 102, *102*, *103*
Shkuro, Andrei, 134, 135, *135*, 137
Sholokhev, Mikhail, 130, *130*, 131
Shuisky, Prince Andrei, 30
Shuisky, Basil, 41, 42
Siberia, 33, 36-7, *37*, 70-1, *71*, 90, 110
Siberian Cossacks, 71, 90, 104, 129, 134, 138
Siberian host, 110, 113
Simbirsk, 65
Sirko, Ivan, 6
Skoropadsky, Ivan, 74, *74*, 75
Slavs, 16, *16*, 17, 27, *27*
Sobieski, Jan, *see* Jan III of Poland
Social Democrats, 112
Socialist Revolutionaries, 112, 114
Sophia Palaeologus, 24-5, *24, 25*
Soviet Federated Socialist Republic, 119
Soviet of People's Commissars, 19
Spring Revolution, 116-17, *116, 117*
St Basil's Cathedral, 32, *32*
St Petersburg, 73
  see also Petrograd
St Sophia's Cathedral, 19, *19*
Stalin, Joseph, 122, *122*, 129, *129*, 131, 132, 133
Stalingrad, 133
  see also Tsaritsyn
stanitsi, 28
staroveri, 60
steppes, 8-9, *8, 9*
Sternberg, Ungern von, 124-5
streltsi, 33, *104*
Stroganov family, 36-7
Sukhomlinov, Vladimir, 115
susliks, 9, *9*
Suvorov, Alexander, 88, *88*, 89, *89*, 92-3, *92*
Svyatopolk, Prince, *18*
Sweden, 42, 74, 75
Switzerland, 93, *93*

Tamerlane *see* Timur
Taras Bulba (Gogol), *7*, *52*, 53, *53*, *54*
Tartar Cossacks, 26-7
Tartars, 21-4, 25, *25*, 31-3, 36-7, 51, 56, 133
Terek Cossacks, 29, 46, 47, 110, 113, 122, 134
  collectivisation, 129, 130
  Old Believers, 60
  uniform, 104
territories, Cossack, 113, 120-1, 128
Third Section, 112
Tigin, Chief, 70
'Time of Troubles', 40-3
Timofeyevich, Yermak, 32, 37, *37*, 38-9, *38*, *108*
Timur (Tamerlane), 21, *21*, 23
Tobolsk, *39*
Tokhtamysh, 23
Tolly, Barclay de, 96
Tolmezzo, 134
Tolstoy, Leo, 27, *66*, 91, 95
Tolstoy, Peter, 75
tombs, Scythian, *13*, 14-15, *14, 15*
Tormasev, Alexander, 96
Trans-Siberian Railway, *113*, 125, *125*
Transbaikal host, 110, 112, 113, 127
Trekhrech Cossacks, 138
Trotsky, Leon, 119, *120*
Tsar of all the Russias, 30, 44
Tsaritsyn, 64
  see also Stalingrad
Turkey, 56-7, 59, 68-9, 88-9, *88*
Tyumen, 37

U

Ukraine, 24, *50*, 52, 68, 74
Ukranian Cossacks, 34-5, 47, 48-53, 60, 74-5, 80, 90
Ulyanov, Vladimir Ilyich, 117
  see also Lenin, Vladimir Ilyich
Uniates, 49
uniforms, military, *34, 55*, 104-5, *105*
Ural Cossacks, 90, 92, 104, 110, 113, 118, 122, 129
  see also Yaik Cossacks
Ussuri host, 110, 112, 113

Varangians, 16
Vikings, 16, 17
Vilna, 40, 52, 100
Vladimir I, 18-19, *18*
Vladimir (city), 21
Vladislav, Tsar, 42
Volga, river, 16, 32, *62*
Vygovsky, Ivan, 52

War, Ministry of, 75, 113
warriors, 10, 54-5
  see also Scythians
westernisation, 73
Whites, 121, *127*, 130, 134, 135
  Civil War, 122-5
  exile, 126-7, *127*
  Trans-Siberian Railway, 125, *125*
wildlife, 9, *9*
Winter Palace
  fall of, 118-19, *118*
women, 29, 46, *76*
Wrangel, Peter, 123, *126*

Yaik Cossacks, 29, 45-6, 47, 60, 75-7
  rebellion, 78, 80, 83-4, 86
  see also Ural Cossacks
Yakuts, 70
Yaroslav the Wise, Prince, *18*, 19, *19*
Yefremov, Stepan, 78, 80
Yermak Timofeyevich *see* Timofeyevich, Yermak
Yusopov, Prince Felix, 116

Z

Zaporozhi (Dnieper Cossacks), *6*, 53, *55*, 60, 89, *89*
  and the Poles, 48, 51
  and the Turks, 56, 59, 68, 69, *69*
  bandits, 78
  Michael I favours, 45-7
  prosperity, 76-7
  revolts, 41-2, 72, 74
  uniform, 104, *105*
  see also Black Sea host; Dnieper Cossacks
Zaporozhskaya Sich, 28-9, 68, 74, 89
Zarutsky, Ivan, 43, 120
Zelezhniak, 78, 88
zemstvos, 111

ACKNOWLEDGEMENTS

The illustrations for this book are reproduced with kind permission of the following picture libraries and organisations, to whom Morgan Samuel Editions are most grateful:

Archive Für Kunst und Geschichte: p.7 (top), 43 (top), 107 (left), 109 (top left), 113 (bottom right), 114 (bottom right), 124 (bottom), 130 (top), 132 (bottom); **Bridgeman Art Library**: front cover, p.26, 28, 57, 59 (top), 76, 84, 100 (top), 107 (right), 110 (bottom); **David King Collection**: p.11 (top), 120 (top), 123 (top and bottom left), 125 (top), 127 (top), 129 (top), 131 (bottom right), 133 (top and bottom); **E.T. Archive**: p.4, 10 (top and bottom), 11 (bottom), 95 (top), 113 (bottom right); **Frank Lane Picture Agency**: p.9 (top right, centre and left); **Hulton Picture Library**: p.16 (left), 21 (bottom), 24 (bottom), 25 (bottom), 27, 30 (bottom right), 42 (bottom), 43 (bottom), 68 (bottom), 79, 81 (top), 90, 98 (top right); **John Massey Stewart**: p.13 (bottom), 19 (top), 21 (top), 29 (bottom), 32 (bottom), 36, 38 (top), 44 (top), 45 (left), 59, 61 (top and bottom right), 63, 64 (top), 71, 85 (left), 87, 96, 97 (bottom left), 101 (bottom), 102 (top right), 103, 106 (top right), 108 (bottom), 111 (centre left and right), 112 (bottom), 113 (top), 114 (bottom left), 115 (top and bottom), 116 (top and bottom), 117 (top), 121, 125 (bottom right), 126 (bottom); **Jurgens, Ost und Europa Photo**: p.8.; **Magnum – Elliott Erwitt**: p.109 (centre), 136 (top) **Magnum – C.S. Perkins**: p.136 (bottom); **Magnum – Burt Glinn**: p.138 (top); **Mansell Collection**: p.16 (bottom right), 20 (bottom left), 56 (top); **Mary Evans Picture Library**: p.48, 53 (right), 66, 68 (top), 75 (left), 78 (top), 86, 88 (bottom), 120 (bottom), 122, 124 (top), 125 (bottom left), 127 (bottom), 131 (bottom left), 132 (top), 137 (bottom); **Novosti Press Agency**: back cover, p.19 (centre), 22 (top and bottom), 24 (bottom right), 25 (top), 31, 34 (top and bottom), 35, 37 (top), 39 (top), 40 (top and bottom left), 41, 42 (bottom left), 44 (bottom), 45 (right), 46, 49, 50 (top and bottom), 51, 52, 55 (right), 56 (bottom), 62 (top), 65, 69, 73, 74 (right), 80, 83, 88 (top), 93 (top right), 94 (bottom right), 97 (top right), 99 (top), 100 (top right), 102 (bottom left), 106 (bottom), 109 (top right), 118, 126 (top), 129 (bottom right), 130 (bottom), 135 (bottom), 138 (bottom); **Photoresources (C.M. Dixon)**: p.12 (bottom), 13 (centre, right and left), 14 (left and top right), 15 (top); **Prudence Cumming Associates**: p.53 (left); **School of Slavonic Studies**: p.137 (top); **S.C.R. Library**: p.6 (top and bottom), 7 (bottom, left and right), 9 (bottom), 14 (bottom right), 15 (bottom), 17 (top and bottom), 18 (top and bottom), 19 (bottom), 20 (bottom right), 23 (top and bottom), 29 (top), 30 (top), 32 (top), 37 (bottom), 38 (bottom), 39 (bottom), 41 (bottom right), 42 (top), 47 (top), 54, 55 (left), 58, 60, 61 (bottom left), 64 (bottom), 70 (top and bottom), 72, 74 (left), 77 (bottom), 78 (bottom), 81 (bottom), 83, 92 (top and bottom), 94 (bottom left), 97 (bottom right), 98 (bottom), 99 (bottom), 119, 128, 131 (top), 139 (top); **USSR Photo Library**: p.77 (top); **Osprey Publishing, London:** p.105 (top), reproduced from 'Napoleon's Enemies' by Richard Warner. **Blandford Press**, a division of **Cassell Plc.**, p.104, 105 (bottom), reproduced from 'Uniforms of the Russian Imperial Army' by Boris and John Mollo.

Editor: **Robert Saunders**

Editorial Assistant: **Nisha Jani**

Picture Researchers: **Janet Moore, Dee Robinson**

Indexer: **Jean Davies**

Designer: **Ian Sheppard**

Production: **Peter Price**

Publisher: **Nigel Perryman**

In addition, Morgan Samuel Editions would like to express their gratitude for the help of Richard Bishop, John Swannick and John Ward, without whom this publication would not have been possible.